The STRANGE CASE *of* ALGER HISS

The STRANGE CASE *of* ALGER HISS

THE EARL JOWITT

DOUBLEDAY & COMPANY, INC.
GARDEN CITY, NEW YORK, 1953

LIBRARY OF CONGRESS CATALOG CARD NUMBER 53-5605

PRINTED IN THE UNITED STATES AT
THE COUNTRY LIFE PRESS, GARDEN CITY, N.Y.

PREFACE

Some time ago, when I was still Lord Chancellor, I had sent to me the full transcript of the second trial of Alger Hiss, which resulted in his conviction for perjury.

I had heard something about the case, although I knew no more about it than any reasonably well-informed reader of the newspapers. It had struck me, from the little I did know, as being a case of unusual interest—and a closer acquaintance with the facts has confirmed this first impression. But whilst I was still in office, I had no spare time to devote to a reading of the case. Now that I have more leisure, I have read the case and analysed the evidence—and the result of my analysis is embodied in this book.

The Hiss case has already been the central theme of two books—the one, *A Generation on Trial,* by Mr. Alistair Cooke, and the other, by Messrs. Toledano and Lasky, entitled *Seeds of Treason.* More recently Mr. Chambers himself has published his book under the title *Witness,* which reveals his whole life and is an interesting study of a complex personality. In the course of this book he deals at length with the history of the trial and with the circumstances of his association with Alger Hiss.

None of these writers has, however, attempted to deal with the case from the detached point of view of a lawyer who desires merely to review the evidence which was presented in the course of the case. It occurred to me that it would be worth while to undertake such a review, and perhaps not the less so in that I am an English lawyer with a considerable experience of trials in this country. It is common enough for members of the English Bar to publish accounts of trials which have taken place in this country. It is useful that this should be done, for it is all to the good that our judicial system, as revealed by a review of a trial, should be exposed to the criticisms of the ordinary reader. It is unusual for an English lawyer to embark upon the task of presenting to his readers a review of an American case.

I had, of course, realised that there were striking differences between a trial in the courts of the United States and a trial in the English courts, but until I studied this case I had not realised how far-reaching these differences were. I recall a speech by Mr. Choate at a farewell banquet given to him in the year 1905 by the English Bench and Bar, at a time when he was about to relinquish his position as American Ambassador at the Court of St. James's. After recognising the tribute which the legal profession were thus paying to him, he used these words:

> I said a little while ago that perhaps you excel us in your tribunals in dignity and in the control which the court exercises, and ought to exercise, over the Bar. It is all illustrated by a single difference of phraseology. In America we say that the counsel try the case and that the judge hears and decides; but, if I understand your common parlance here, the judge tries the case and the counsel hear and obey.

I had never understood the full significance of that statement until I came to read the second trial of Alger Hiss. I shall call attention in the succeeding pages to the consequences which arise from the differing functions assigned in the American and in the English jurisdictions to judge and counsel.

No doubt the amount of control which the court "ought to exercise over the Bar" gives ample scope for difference of opinion. It is a far larger measure of control in England than in the U.S.A. The law is a conservative profession, and any lawyer tends to be prejudiced in favour of a system with which he is familiar; yet it is wholesome for him to study the workings of a different system. If, from time to time, I seem to criticise I sincerely hope that my criticisms will not be resented and will not be considered impertinent. I have been proud to be an honorary member of the American Bar Association for nearly twenty-five years, and I have an admiration for the distinguished members of that association whom I have been privileged to meet. No one who reads the account of the trial presided over by Judge Goddard can fail to be satisfied that he was endeavouring to the utmost of his ability to see that right was done. His direction to the jury within the very limited scope which is considered appropriate in the American courts was, if I may be allowed to say so, manifestly fair.

I have been privileged to take many distinguished American lawyers to our trials in this country, and I always invited their criticism of our methods, for there is much that we can learn from each other; perhaps, indeed, there is much that we must learn from each other if we are successfully to withstand the assault which is now being made on our common way of life. Let me admit that I have no sympathy whatever with the Communist ideology so far as I understand it. Indeed, it seems to me that the "cold war" which is now being waged between the democratic way of life and Communism is in reality a contest between a wide idealism and a narrow materialism; between the concept of man as a creature made in the image of God and the concept of man as a soulless creature destined merely to perform those tasks which are allotted to him. The due administration of justice is, I believe, the foundation on which our democratic system rests. We must take care, if we are to be true to our ideals (and we shall not win the "cold war" unless we do remain true to our ideals), that no individual becomes a scapegoat for the sins of society. It is fitting that we should cleanse the Augean stable, but in so doing we must beware of inflicting injury on any innocent occupant of the stable.

Let me conclude by saying that I have no sort of interest in this case other than that interest which I have derived from an analysis of the problem the case presents. I know none of the actors involved in this drama; I am entirely detached from any political issue involved, in so far as there may be any political issue. I have not been requested—still less commissioned—to write this book. I shall express no opinion as to whether or not Alger Hiss was guilty. I should be most reluctant to do so without having had any opportunity of seeing the witnesses or hearing them give their evidence. In any criminal case, and more especially in a case against a man who has previously enjoyed a high reputation for integrity, we demand on both sides of the Atlantic that the case against him should be established beyond any peradventure. I do not doubt that, alike under the American and the British systems of jurisprudence, many guilty men are acquitted—this is the price we must pay to reduce to a minimum the risk of an innocent man being convicted. The real problem in this case, as I see it, is whether, in view of the extraordinary nature of the evidence, the case against Alger Hiss was so established.

My endeavour in writing this book is to present the facts fairly to the reader so that he may become acquainted with the issues involved and form his own conclusions.

Jowitt

CONTENTS

	PREFACE	5
I	THE HISTORY OF THE CASE	15
II	THE ISSUES DEFINED	25
III	OF WHITTAKER CHAMBERS	41
IV	THE STORY TOLD BY WHITTAKER CHAMBERS	49
V	OF ALGER HISS	59
VI	THE STORY TOLD BY ALGER HISS	69
VII	THE CONTRAST BETWEEN THE TWO STORIES	73
VIII	OF MRS. CHAMBERS AND MRS. HISS	81
IX	OF THE SUBLETTING OF THE APARTMENT, ETC.	91
X	OF THE VISITS, TRIPS, ETC.	107
XI	OF THE SUPPOSED COMMUNIST GROUP	119

XII OF THE EARLY STATEMENTS MADE BY CHAMBERS 127

XIII OF THE HOUSE COMMITTEE ON UN-AMERICAN ACTIVITIES 139

XIV THE PROCEEDINGS BEFORE THE HOUSE COMMITTEE 151

XV THE CONFRONTATION OF ALGER HISS AND WHITTAKER CHAMBERS BEFORE THE HOUSE COMMITTEE 159

XVI THE PAYMENT OF DUES 175

XVII THE LIBEL ACTION 181

XVIII WHAT'S IN A NAME? 189

XIX AFTER THE FIRST TRIAL 195

XX OF TRIAL BY JURY 199

XXI THE EVIDENCE AT THE SECOND TRIAL 207

XXII THE FIRST ALLEGED ACT OF TREACHERY 225

XXIII OF DONALD HISS 233

XXIV OF WHITE, WADLEIGH AND OTHERS 243

XXV THE SUPPOSED CONTROVERSY BETWEEN MR. JOHN FOSTER DULLES AND ALGER HISS 251

XXVI HEDE MASSING AND HENRIKAS RABINAVICIUS 265

XXVII OF THE TYPEWRITER 271

XXVIII OF THE LIFE PRESERVER 279

XXIX THE FOUR HANDWRITTEN DOCUMENTS 283

XXX THE PHOTOGRAPHED DOCUMENTS 301

XXXI THE TYPEWRITTEN DOCUMENTS 307

XXXII THE CLOSING SPEECHES 311

XXXIII THE CHARGE OF THE COURT 325

XXXIV RETROSPECT 335

APPENDICES

I NOTES MADE BY MR. ADOLF BERLE OF HIS CONVERSATION WITH WHITTAKER CHAMBERS IN SEPTEMBER 1939 345

II MEMORANDUM OF CONVERSATION BETWEEN MR. RAY MURPHY AND WHITTAKER CHAMBERS, 20TH MARCH 1945 349

III MEMORANDUM OF CONVERSATION BETWEEN MR. RAY MURPHY AND WHITTAKER CHAMBERS, 28TH AUGUST 1946 353

IV STATEMENT TO FEDERAL BUREAU OF INVESTIGATION SIGNED BY ALGER HISS, 4TH DECEMBER 1948 357

V STATEMENT TO FEDERAL BUREAU OF INVESTIGATION SIGNED BY PRISCILLA HISS, 7TH DECEMBER 1948 365

VI THE DOCUMENT WRITTEN IN THE HANDWRITING OF HARRY DEXTER WHITE WHICH WAS CONTAINED IN THE ENVELOPE PRODUCED BY WHITTAKER CHAMBERS AT BALTIMORE ON THE 17TH NOVEMBER 1948 369

INDEX 373

The STRANGE CASE *of* ALGER HISS

Many names were misspelled in the official documents of the case. These errors have been corrected in this book.

CHAPTER I

THE HISTORY OF THE CASE

Alger Hiss was on the 21st January 1950, at the conclusion of the second trial, found guilty of perjury in denying that he had handed over secret documents to a Communist agent, Whittaker Chambers, and denying that he had seen and conversed with him in or about February and March 1938. The information which he was said to have handed over consisted in part of documents which had been typed on his own typewriter. Who typed them? If, as the prosecution asserted, they had been typed by Hiss or his wife, then I see no escape from the conclusion that Hiss was guilty. The only other possible view is that in some way or other Whittaker Chambers or his agents got access to the typewriter and manufactured a case against Hiss by typing on that typewriter documents which had been previously stolen from the State Department. If this is what happened, it is, so far as I am aware, the first case of forgery by typewriter.

These, however, were not the only documents which Hiss was said to have handed over to Chambers, for Chambers also produced four documents which were undoubtedly in the handwriting of Hiss, which he said Hiss had given him. Was it a fact that Hiss had handed over these documents to Chambers in order that he might convey them to the Communists? Or had they been written by Hiss for the legitimate purpose of enabling him to make a report to his superior in the State Department, and then been stolen from him by some Communist agent who had passed them to Chambers? Here again, if these documents had been handed to Chambers by Hiss, then Hiss was guilty; but if, on the other hand, they had been stolen from Hiss by some Communist agent and were then used by Chambers to establish a case against Hiss, Chambers was guilty of an act almost unparalleled in its wickedness. The answer given to this question may throw light on the origin of the typewritten documents.

Besides these documents in the handwriting of Hiss and those typed on his typewriter, Chambers produced photographs of other secret documents. The photographs had been taken by a Communist agent, but from whom had the agent got possession of the original documents? Chambers testified that they had been handed to him by Hiss; and, if that be true, then Hiss was guilty. But, on the other hand, if they had come from some other source in the State Department, then Chambers was guilty of building up a false case against Hiss. It is, unhappily, only too probable that in about February and March 1938 (the time when all these documents came into existence) there were Communist traitors in the State Department.

Now, if there were such traitors it is not difficult to imagine that the original documents might have been handed to Chambers by some person other than Hiss; that they might have been photographed; and that Chambers might have said, albeit untruly, that they had been given to him by Hiss. Indeed, if Chambers had been wicked enough to take part in, or arrange for, what I have described as "forgery by typewriter," it is not difficult to imagine that he would have been prepared falsely to attribute the handing over of the original documents, which were then photographed, to Hiss. For this reason I think the latter documents add little or nothing to the strength of the case against Hiss, which must, in my view, stand or fall on the handwritten and typewritten documents.

The offence of perjury can be established only if the evidence of the accusing witness be corroborated; if Chambers had said:

"I produce photographs of secret documents—the secret documents were handed to me by Alger Hiss," there could have been no conviction without some corroboration—and there was, as I see it, no such corroboration, except such as could be deduced from the documents themselves, and no such deduction could be made in the case of the documents which had been photographed. The Court held that it was otherwise in the case of the handwritten and typewritten documents, for there it decided that the fact that the documents were either written in the handwriting of Hiss or typed on his typewriter did afford corroboration of the evidence of Chambers that they had been handed to him by Hiss.

I confess that, for my own part, I find it much easier to follow the Court's reasoning in the case of the typewritten documents than in the case of those in the handwriting of Hiss. For with regard to the handwritten documents, the issue was: Had they been stolen from Hiss after having served a legitimate purpose; or had they been handed over by Hiss for an illegitimate purpose? I find a difficulty in seeing that the production of the documents themselves supports the one hypothesis rather than the other, unless it were supported by evidence that the precautions taken in the State Department in the beginning of 1938 were so effective that there was no reasonable possibility of theft, and therefore that that hypothesis could be eliminated. Unhappily, there was a mass of evidence which points in precisely the opposite direction. If the question were whether some article of jewellery or the like had been stolen by A from B, or whether it had been handed by B to A as a gift, would the production of the article itself by A afford the slightest evidence one way or the other?

In the case of the typewritten documents, once it was established that they had been typed on the Hiss typewriter, it was far easier to find corroboration in the documents themselves. It is impossible to imagine that this typing could have been done for any legitimate purpose; whoever typed them must have done so in furtherance of a wicked design, either to fabricate a case against Hiss or to supply information to a potential enemy. There was, moreover, no evidence that Chambers or his agents, in fact, ever got access to that typewriter; the most that can be said is that it is not beyond the bounds of possibility that they might have done so.

It may be considered remarkable that between spies who had developed to a fine art the technique of photographing documents the laborious method of typing them out first and then taking a photograph of the typescript should sometimes have been adopted—more especially since a photograph of a document supplies no clue as to its "provenance," whereas a typescript does. It may be considered remarkable, too, that sometimes this laborious technique was applied to relatively unimportant documents. But these considerations affect the weight to be attached to the evidence, rather than the question whether such evidence constitutes the necessary corroboration.

Such, in the broadest possible outline, were the issues involved at the trial. But to review this case and to present it in a readable form has been no easy task. Before me on my table as I write there are no fewer than five volumes containing the evidence given at the second trial alone, and some five other volumes of exhibits in the case. The second trial began on the 17th November 1949. The verdict was not pronounced until the 21st January 1950.

The history of the case, however, is much longer even than that. There had been proceedings before the House Committee of Congress, at which Chambers had accused Hiss of having had Communist associations. This led to a libel action which Hiss brought against Chambers, and in the course of that action Chambers for the first time produced secret documents which he alleged had been handed to him by Hiss. Hiss denied on oath that he had handed over any documents. A grand jury in December 1948 preferred a bill against him for perjury. The first trial began on the 31st May 1949 and lasted until the 8th July 1949. The jury disagreed and Hiss was discharged. There followed the second trial in November, as a result of which Hiss was found guilty and sentenced to five years' imprisonment.

The difficulty which I have felt in attempting to give the reader an account of the case arises in part from the mass of material to be dealt with, and I think it is obvious that this same difficulty oppressed the counsel engaged in the case.

By the time the second trial started, each side had a wealth of material and each side knew what the other side was going to say. There was no longer any possibility of surprise. There was, however, a grave danger that the real issues in the case might become overlaid under this mass of material, and I feel bound to say that I do not think counsel on either side altogether succeeded in avoiding this difficulty. Every side issue was pursued. Every point, however indirectly it bore upon the case, was probed and investigated. Whenever a witness on either side tended to depart by a hairsbreadth from the evidence he had given on one of the previous occasions, he was challenged as to what he had said before, and a mass of evidence from one of the previous investigations was then read to the jury. The rule which prevails in this country—and which I believe should have been observed in America—that such previous evidence should be made use of only to contradict the present evidence of the witness, was honoured rather in the breach than in the observance.

I have, therefore, tried to select those passages which bear upon the relevant issues, leaving on one side a mass of evidence which relates to side issues which were not, in my view, of major importance, except in so far as that evidence bears upon the credibility of any of the witnesses. In so far as it can be said to have this effect, I have tried to reproduce it.

I have said enough to show that this was a case which cannot be accounted for by differences of recollection, nor yet by those little embellishments which are so frequently employed even by witnesses who have right on their side, with the intention of lending colour and interest to an otherwise bald and unconvincing narrative. A judge comes across lying of this sort as part of his daily task; it is one of the chief reasons why it is so difficult to ascertain where the truth lies. Anyone may forget the name of the person from whom he bought a car nine or ten years before, or the price which he paid for it, or the amount for which he sold it, or the month or the year in which any of these transactions took place. The average man, unless his recollection was reinforced by some contemporary diary, could not hope to answer such questions with any approximation of accuracy.

The lying which took place in this case, on one side or the

other, was not slight or trivial—it was massive and monumental. No one could forget whether he had or had not been a member of a Communist group; nor could he forget whether he had paid his Communist dues to that group; still less could the man whose task it was over a period of time to collect those dues forget the persons from whom, or the circumstances under which, he collected them.

When Whittaker Chambers testified in the year 1948, as he did, that Alger Hiss, his wife Priscilla and his brother Donald had each of them been members of a Communist group for some period between the years 1934 and 1938, and that he (Chambers) had collected Party dues from Alger Hiss in respect of himself and his wife, and from Donald Hiss on his own behalf, he was either speaking the truth or was guilty of wilful and corrupt perjury. Similarly, when Alger, Priscilla and Donald Hiss denied these statements on oath, they were either speaking the truth or were each of them guilty of wilful and corrupt perjury.

So much is obvious, but it is by no means obvious whether the one or the other was lying. Yet, as I shall show in the succeeding pages, Donald Hiss, when he denied on oath at the trial that he had ever been a member of a Communist group, was not challenged; and if he was speaking the truth it follows that the testimony of Chambers, so far as Donald Hiss was concerned, was rudely shaken. Chambers could not have collected Communist dues from Donald Hiss if Donald Hiss had never been in any way associated with the Party.

This case has many extraordinary features, but perhaps the most striking is the change which took place in its presentation in the course of the year 1948. Up to the 17th November of that year the case which Chambers developed against Alger, Priscilla and Donald Hiss consisted of the allegation that they had been members of a Communist group, supported by the further allegation that they had paid dues to the Communist Party—which would, of course, have been the outward and visible sign of membership. It was not a case of espionage; and Chambers, indeed, testified on oath before the grand jury that he had no evidence of espionage or of the handing over of documents. On the 17th November 1948, Chambers produced the handwritten and typewritten documents, which he said had been handed to him by Alger Hiss some ten years before, in or about February or March 1938; and, so far as Alger Hiss was concerned, the case became one of espionage.

Not only was the case thus changed, but in its earlier form it seems to have been abandoned. It is a fact that at the second trial—which did not begin until November 1949—there was no word from first to last about the payment of dues. Alger Hiss, like his brother Donald, denied that he or his wife had ever at any time been a member of a Communist group, and therefore inferentially denied that he had ever paid dues—but Chambers was not asked any question about the payment of dues.

It was the bringing of the libel action and the claim for heavy damages that marks what I may describe as the watershed between the two cases. This brings me naturally to another remarkable feature of this case—namely, that Alger Hiss himself, by bringing the libel action, caused Chambers to produce the incriminating documents. It is an interesting problem of psychology to consider whether a man who had treacherously handed over secret papers typed on his own typewriter or written in his own handwriting would have sued for libel the agent to whom he had handed them because that agent called him a Communist. It would require very considerable nerve to bring such an action, even though it could be by no means pleasant for a man in the position Hiss had attained to have the assertion made that he had, even many years before, been associated with the Communists. If a man so circumstanced were to decide that he had no option but to bluff it through, would he have instructed his Counsel to press and press again for the production of the documents which would destroy him?

I know of one other case where the bringing of a libel action caused the ultimate disaster—the celebrated case of Oscar Wilde. He sued the Marquess of Queensberry on the ground that the latter had publicly asserted that he, Wilde, was "posing" in a most undesirable role. The bringing of that action was his undoing, for it was established that he was not merely "posing" but was acting in that most undesirable role. It would therefore be wrong to say that such a case had never happened before, but it can surely have happened only very seldom.

I have said enough, I hope, to indicate that this case was not merely a dry legal case outside the range and interest of the ordinary public. It was, in fact, a great human drama. Hiss had achieved an important position in the public life of his country. He was highly regarded by distinguished Americans of all parties. He had risen by sheer merit from one position to another. He had won the confidence of all those for whom he had worked.

The jury decided that he had had a black and discreditable past and that he had handed over to the Communists secret and confidential papers that had been entrusted to him. He denied that he had done any such thing. He denied it under oath. The jury found, after a most careful investigation, that in making this denial he was guilty of wilful perjury, and as a punishment for this he was sentenced to five years' imprisonment.

It would be quite improper for me to comment on this sentence. To secure the due administration of justice, we must rely on the fact that witnesses who have taken the oath to speak the truth will observe that obligation. This is, indeed, the first duty of a citizen. For such as Alger Hiss who have achieved great and distinguished positions the observance of this duty is more than ever important, and a breach of it cannot be overlooked. I do not think that there was any substance whatever in the contention, advanced both in the first and in the second trial, that because the original crime of handing over documents was statute-barred, therefore perjury committed shortly before the trial took place should have been likewise barred.

Whatever strange philosophical opinions a man may hold, it is shocking to think that whilst holding and accepting a position of confidence under the government of his own country he should abuse that confidence by making available secret documents to outsiders. There is no philosophy of which I have ever heard, or indeed which I can imagine, which can excuse such conduct. So far as such a thing can be justified, it must, I suppose, be on that most hoary and obvious fallacy that the ends justify the means. In this country—and I believe in the United States of America—it is no offence to be a Communist. It may well be, and I do not pretend to know, that Communists desire the success of Russia and its satellites above that of their own land. This is no sort of an excuse for accepting a position of trust in their own country and then abusing that trust by the basest treachery. Every organised society must be entitled to protect itself against such conduct, and for one guilty of such conduct itself or for perjury in denying that he has been guilty of such conduct, I feel not the slightest sympathy. Time may afford him a defence to the original crime; time can never wash away the baseness of his conduct. But just as we should all agree about the gravity of the accusation, so should we all agree also that this makes it the more incumbent to see that the circumstances were such as to ensure that the man accused of such a crime was likely to get a fair trial, and that the trial when it took place was, in fact, fair.

In the following pages I shall endeavour to present an impartial picture of the two chief protagonists, Alger Hiss and Whittaker Chambers. I shall try to bring under review the whole system under which this trial took place, and I can only hope that those who read this book will find the case as interesting as I myself have.

CHAPTER II

THE ISSUES DEFINED

The basis of the accusation against Alger Hiss was that he had taken documents which were the property of the Government of the United States, to which he had access by reason of his employment in Government service, and had handed them over to Whittaker Chambers, who was, by his own confession, a Communist agent. This course of dishonest dealing, which may be simply—if not quite correctly—characterised as "stealing documents," began, if Chambers is to be believed, with one incident about the end of 1935, and started again early in 1937, and thereafter continued for some fifteen or sixteen months until some time in April 1938.

In the present case there was no evidence that Hiss had "turned over" (if I may use the convenient phrase adopted throughout the trial) any documents at any time after April 1938, and the accusation that he had turned over documents on or before that date had not been made until 1948—that is, some ten years later. There is a statute of limitations which bars any proceedings after a certain time has elapsed, and in consequence no proceedings could be taken against Hiss for the alleged acts of treachery in turning over documents to unauthorised persons. Hiss was thus able to escape the direct consequences of his crime (if, indeed, he had committed this crime), but there was no statute of limitations to prevent his being prosecuted for perjury committed in 1948 (if, indeed, he did commit perjury).

The charge on which Hiss was tried, and on which he was convicted, was therefore not that he had turned over documents in 1937 and 1938, but that he had falsely denied on oath in 1948 that he had so acted. There is perhaps little distinction between a charge of handing over documents and a charge of perjury in denying that he had handed over documents, save possibly this: Alger Hiss, when on his oath in 1948, might have chosen to say: "When I was much younger than I am today, when I did not realize as fully as I do today the full implications of Soviet policy in particular and Communism in general, it is quite true that I did make documents available to a man, Whittaker Chambers, whom I knew to be a Communist agent." If he had said this, he would have been protected against any possible proceedings, for the original offence was statute-barred and, on the hypothesis that Chambers' story was true, there would have been no perjury.

Yet of course, if Hiss had admitted any such course of conduct, he would have been shunned by all right-thinking people. He would have become—at least he should have become—a social outcast. He would have admitted a systematic course of base and contemptible treachery. It is inconceivable that he would have continued to occupy the position, which he then occupied, of President of the Carnegie Endowment for International Peace. He would have been a ruined man. It is plain, therefore, that he had ample motive, notwithstanding the strict legal position, for denying the allegations made against him.

There was sitting in the year 1948 a House committee charged with the duty of investigating what were described as "un-American activities," and it was before this committee that Whittaker Chambers made his first public allegations against Alger Hiss. It is not difficult to account for the fact that the matter of these allegations had come to the attention of the House Committee, for in 1939 Chambers had sought an appointment with Mr. Adolf Berle, who then occupied the position of Assistant Secretary of State in the State Department, and at this interview he had disclosed his knowledge of Communist infiltration into the United States Government. Notes of the interview[1] which Mr. Berle made were preserved and were produced at the trial, and at some time later Mr. Berle had handed over these notes to the F.B.I. Chambers also on two subsequent occasions, namely the 20th March 1945 and the 28th August 1946, had made statements to a Mr. Ray Murphy, who was the security officer at the State Department. Mr. Murphy took notes of the information given by Chambers at these interviews, and these notes[2] were also produced at the trial.

It was therefore natural enough that the allegations Chambers had made alike in 1939 to Mr. Berle and on the occasions in 1945 and 1946 respectively when he saw Mr Murphy should have been brought to the attention of the House Committee. I shall in due course consider these statements, for it is a matter of the first importance to discover to what extent they can be reconciled with the later statements made at the trial. It is therefore not surprising that Chambers should have been called upon to testify before the House Committee, and he so testified in August 1948.

It is important in order to get a true perspective of the case to see exactly what was the nature of the allegations which Chambers made before the House Committee and to consider also what he did not say. He alleged before the House Committee that Alger Hiss, together with certain other persons, one of whom was his brother Donald Hiss, had been a member of a Communist organisation, or, to use the technical term, a member of a Communist apparatus. It could have been expected that he would have been asked to support these allegations with documentary evidence. Curiously enough, no such question was asked; indeed, when the word "espionage" was used by a questioner, Chambers asserted that though "the whole set-up was conspiratorial . . . the purpose was not primarily espionage." However, he did give the House Committee definite evidence which, if believed, proved conclusively that Alger Hiss, and for that matter his brother Donald, had been members of a Communist

[1]Appendix I.
[2]Appendices II and III.

organisation because, said Chambers, the dues which the Communists exact from all their members had actually been paid to him.

Chambers informed the House Committee that the function assigned to Hiss was not espionage but something far more important; for Hiss had the task of "messing up policy."

It is, as I have already stated, a most peculiar feature of this case that in the early stages before the House Committee the case against Alger Hiss was primarily based upon the payment of dues collected by Chambers, whereas at the trial this evidence was completely left on one side, and the case was based on the turning over of documents—which had been denied in the earlier stages.

Immediately the allegations made by Chambers before the House Committee came to the notice of Hiss, he asked permission to come before the Committee to deny them with as much publicity as they had received. This was allowed. Hiss, on oath, roundly and vigorously denied that there was a word of truth in what Chambers had said about him, and strongly asserted that he had never been a member of the Communist Party, or a fellow-traveller, still less a member of a Communist apparatus. The name of Whittaker Chambers, he said, meant nothing to him, and he had never met a man of that name.

Thereafter, the House Committee, on the 7th August 1948, heard further evidence from Chambers in executive session—that is to say, *in camera*. A few days later, on the 16th August 1948, still in executive session, they heard Hiss again. At this stage Hiss did not know what evidence had been given by Chambers on the 7th August 1948. It was then arranged that Hiss and Chambers should be confronted, and on the 17th August, in public session, after some hesitation Hiss identified Chambers as a man he had known as George Crosley. Oddly enough, Chambers was unable to remember whether he had ever used the name "George Crosley." He was not prepared to deny that he had used such a name, but neither then nor since has he ever been able to remember whether he did or did not use this name.

At the confrontation, Chambers again made his allegation that Hiss had been a member of a Communist apparatus. Hiss challenged Chambers to repeat this on a non-privileged occasion so that he might be able to bring an action for libel. To this challenge Chambers promptly responded. He repeated over the radio that Hiss had been a member of a Communist organisation, and accordingly, after an interval of about a month (explained by the fact that the counsel acting for Hiss was away on holiday), Hiss issued his writ for libel, demanding damages of $50,000—a demand which, a day or two afterwards, was increased to $75,000. This action was started in Baltimore, and by a procedure which there prevails either party has the right to submit the other and his witnesses to an examination before trial. Hiss decided to avail himself of this procedure, and both Chambers and Mrs. Chambers were thus examined.

In the course of his evidence at Baltimore, Chambers for the first time produced certain documents which he said had been handed to him between some date in January and the 15th April 1938. Four of these documents were actually written in the handwriting of Hiss himself—they were derived from confidential documents which had come before Hiss in the course of his work in the State Department. In addition to these documents, Chambers produced a series of confidential documents which had been typed on a somewhat ancient typewriter which had for many years belonged to Mrs. Hiss. This typewriter she had used from time to time to type her own letters.

I should have thought that anyone with the slightest experience of typewriters would know that in the course of time they develop peculiarities of their own. I have no expert knowledge on this point, but it stands to reason that after much use this letter will become blurred, that letter will lose its tail, the other letter will go slightly off the straight, and so on. The expert, of course, can go much farther. He can distinguish the type of a Woodstock (the typewriter in question was a Woodstock) from the type of any other make of machine, and he can even distinguish the type of one Woodstock from the type of another Woodstock. But anyone without expert knowledge can readily understand that it is possible to identify typing as having come from a particular typewriter once that machine has had sufficient wear to develop peculiarities. Now the typewriter which belonged to Mrs. Hiss had seen many years of service.

Chambers then, who had previously denied on oath that he had any documents to prove his assertion that Hiss had been a member of a Communist apparatus, on the 17th November 1948, in the course of the Baltimore libel proceedings, produced these documents written in the handwriting of Hiss and the documents typed on the typewriter which belonged to Mrs. Hiss. He asserted that Hiss had given him these documents in the early months of the year 1938—some ten or eleven years earlier. Directly these documents came to light, Hiss instructed his counsel to bring them to the notice of the proper authorities.

The discovery of these documents, the existence of which had been denied by Chambers at the beginning of the pre-trial hearings, stirred the House Committee into fresh activity. The Committee's investigators thereupon got in touch with Chambers and asked him whether he had any further documents. By arrangement, they followed Chambers to his farm, and there one evening he led them to a patch of pumpkins and, from a hollowed-out pumpkin, he produced certain developed and undeveloped microfilms. These, when enlarged, were seen to be photographs of confidential documents, whether originals or copies, which had been in the possession of the State Department.

The properly constituted authorities, who were now, with the full approval of Hiss, placed in possession of the documents written by Hiss in his own handwriting, of the typed documents (which had been typed on the Woodstock typewriter belonging to Mrs. Hiss), and of the photographs of the confidential documents, at once caused the Grand Jury to be resummoned. The Grand Jury examined the documents, heard the witnesses, but even so were unable to find a true bill—and they were unable to find a true bill because one important link in the chain was missing. They could not at that stage connect these typewritten documents with any particular typewriter, for the old Woodstock had long ago been given away. I choose my words with care—"given away," not smashed up, not utterly destroyed, but "given away"; seldom is it that a criminal "gives away" the incriminating instrument.

But the loss of the typewriter mattered not, so long as some documents which had indubitably been typed on that typewriter could be obtained; for then the idiosyncrasies of the typewriter could be examined—and the same characteristics would be revealed on the typewritten documents produced by Chambers as were found to exist on the other documents written on that typewriter. The missing link, if only such documents could be discovered, would thus have been forged. And so it proved to be. Such documents typed by Mrs. Hiss on that old Woodstock—a report about her son, a circular relating to the affairs of her old school—were discovered. There could be no doubt that these documents and the documents produced by Chambers had all been typed on that same typewriter.

So now everything was in order. The Grand Jury met again on the 15th December 1948. They had before them the evidence of Chambers that all the documents—those in the handwriting of Hiss, those typed on his typewriter, and those which had been photographed—had been handed to him by Hiss. Hiss was recalled. He was on oath. He was then asked these questions:

> Mr. Hiss, you have probably been asked this question before, but I'd like to ask the question again. At any time did you, or Mrs. Hiss in your presence, turn any documents of the State Department or of any other Government organization, or copies of any documents of the State Department or any other Government organization, over to Whittaker Chambers?
>
> *Mr. Hiss:* Never, excepting I assume the title certificate to the Ford.
>
> *Question:* In order to clarify it, would that be the only exception?
>
> *Mr. Hiss:* The only exception.
>
> *Juror:* To nobody else did you turn over any documents, to any other person?
>
> *Mr. Hiss:* And to no other unauthorized person. I certainly could have to other officials.

Question: Now, Mr. Hiss, Mr. Chambers says that he obtained typewritten copies of official State documents from you.
Mr. Hiss: I know he has.
Question: Did you ever see Mr. Chambers after you entered into the State Department?
Mr. Hiss: I do not believe I did. I cannot swear that I did not see him some time, say, in the fall of '36. And I entered the State Department September 1, 1936.
Question: Now, you say possibly in the fall of '36.
Mr. Hiss: That would be possible.
Question: Can you say definitely with reference to the winter of '36; I mean, say, December '36?
Mr. Hiss: Yes, I think I can say definitely I did not see him.
Question: Can you say definitely that you did not see him after January 1, 1937?
Mr. Hiss: Yes, I think I can definitely say that.
Question: Understanding, of course, exclusive of House hearings and exclusive of the Grand Jury.
Mr. Hiss: Oh yes.

These answers were the foundation of the indictment—an indictment which contained two counts. Hiss was accused of having committed wilful and corrupt perjury in denying that he had turned over Government documents to Chambers, and further in denying that he had seen and conversed with Chambers in or about February and March 1938.

The function of a grand jury, as it used to be in England, was not to determine the guilt or innocence of an accused person. It was for them to determine whether there was evidence of such weight and substance as to make it proper that the accused person should stand his trial. The same principle, I believe, prevails in the United States. In Mr. Murphy's opening statement I find the following passage:

> Finally, both Mr. Chambers and Mr. Hiss were subpoenaed before the Grand Jury here in this building, and they heard, the Grand Jury did, the testimony of both Mr. Chambers and the defendant, and they heard the testimony over a number of days, until finally on December 15th, 1948, Mr.

Hiss testified and, as they say in their indictment, he lied to them on that day.

By the use of the word "say" Mr. Murphy cannot have meant that the Grand Jury had "decided" that Hiss had lied to them. They had, in fact, come to no such conclusion. They had merely said that there was evidence of sufficient weight and substance to make it proper that Hiss should be put on his trial.

The substantial case against Hiss rests on the first count of the indictment, and it is of such importance to an understanding of this case that I will set it out at length.

Was it the fact that Alger Hiss had "in or about the months of February and March 1938 furnished, delivered and transmitted to Chambers copies of numerous secret, confidential and restricted documents, writing, notes and other papers, the originals of which had theretofore been removed and abstracted from the possession and custody of the Department of State?"

The second count contained the allegation that the defendant "did in fact see and converse with the said Mr. Chambers in or about the months of February and March 1938." On this, the Counsel for the defendant obtained an order for particulars in which the Prosecution were required to state "each and every date in or about the months of February and March 1938 on which the defendant conversed with Chambers . . . and the substance of the conversation." In answer to this demand, the Prosecution said they were unaware of the exact times of the conversations, but fixed them with reference to the handing over of the documents. In reply to the demand for the substance of the various conversations, the Prosecution said that whilst they had no exact knowledge, these conversations related generally to the documents themselves and other current activities.

I think these particulars were regrettably vague, but I should have drawn the conclusion that the conversations, the subject of the second count of the indictment, were conversations which took place at the time of the handing over of the documents. The judge, however, seemed to treat the matter as though the Prosecution were not so confined, and dealt with the matter on the basis, as I understand it, that the conversations to support the second count of the indictment need not have been in relation to the handing over of documents. If the jury had found Hiss not guilty on count one but guilty on count two, this might have become a matter of importance. But as they found him guilty of turning over documents, and as it follows that there must have been some conversation at the time when the documents were turned over, I think the point is academic. I should myself have treated count two as a mere corollary to count one.

Hiss was not charged with having been a member of a Communist apparatus, and whether he was or was not such a member bears, therefore, only indirectly upon the case. The most that can be said in this matter is that if he had been a member of a Communist organisation, it is inherently more probable that he would have handed over documents. Even farther removed from the critical point—namely, the turning over of documents—is the question of the extent of the association between Chambers and Hiss. When the two men came to be confronted with each other before the House Committee, Hiss expressed considerable difficulty in recognising Chambers as being the man whom he had known as George Crosley. Of course, if they had had a very close association in the past, it would have been easier for Hiss, notwithstanding the lapse of over ten years during which they admittedly had not met, to recognise Chambers. It was possible, no doubt, judging from the demeanour of the witnesses at the time of the confrontation, to come to the conclusion that Hiss was "putting on an act" in pretending not to recognise Chambers, though it is the fact that in the sixth answer which Hiss gave at the time of the confrontation he said that he thought Whittaker Chambers was the man he had known as George Crosley. But all this bears quite indirectly upon the subject matter of the charge, and in reading the evidence I cannot help feeling that this fact was rather lost sight of.

There was a mass of material relating to the association between the two men, to the trips they had taken together, to the concession whereby Hiss allowed Chambers to occupy his house, to his allowing Chambers to use his car, to the peculiar circumstances in which that car was disposed of, to a supposed loan by Hiss of $400 to Chambers, to the giving and receiving of a rug, to the knowledge which Chambers had of the furnishing and decoration of the various houses occupied by Hiss, and to the association between Mrs. Hiss and Mrs. Chambers. All these matters, which in due course, I shall relate, must be viewed in their proper perspective. They may have some bearing—and I think do have some bearing—upon the view which a jury might take as to the credibility of Hiss, Chambers and their wives. But they bear upon the subject matter of the charge quite indirectly.

In his cross-examination, Chambers was asked whether he had not been "a spy, a saboteur and a permanent enemy of the United States"; he replied, "You have omitted the keyword, which is 'potential.'" Chambers here drew a very important distinction. If evidence is given to show that a person has been a member of a Communist group, it may well be—in the light of our present knowledge—that it follows that he was, during the period of his membership, a "potential" spy; but mere evidence of group membership would not constitute any evidence that he was an actual spy. Further evidence might, of course, be adduced—and in this case it was adduced—to show that the "potential" spy (proved to be such by his membership in the group) had become an actual spy. The transition from the one state to the other—from the potential to the actual—may be a small step, or it may be a considerable step; this will depend on the nature of the group's activities. It may or may not be surprising to find that the step was taken, but the fact that it was taken must be established by evidence going beyond mere membership in a Communist group.

This particular group, according to Chambers, was not a "spy ring but one far more important and cunning." It is therefore perhaps rather surprising to find that one member—Alger Hiss—was acting in a way which seems to have been outside the normal functions of the group. It was never alleged by Chambers that any other persons whom he originally named as members had ever handed him any documents, although he admitted, under cross-examination, that this was possible.

The critical point in the case was that Chambers had finally brought himself to assert that in or about February and March

1938 Hiss had turned over to him secret documents. He produced these documents. The fact that some of them were written in the handwriting of Hiss and that others of them had been typed on the typewriter belonging to Mrs. Hiss was held to be corroborative evidence of the story Chambers told. Hiss denied that he had ever turned over any such documents. He said that the documents in his own handwriting must have been stolen from him, and he could give no explanation as to how the other documents came to have been typed on his wife's typewriter. If the jury on all these extraneous matters came to the conclusion that the evidence of Chambers was more reliable than that of Hiss, it is easy to understand how they came to prefer the evidence of Chambers on the one point that really mattered—namely, whether or not Hiss had turned over documents in or about February or March 1938.

Had the case been tried under the English system, much of the evidence would have been regarded as inadmissible. Under our system Chambers would have been called to prove the handing over of the documents, which he would have produced, and he would no doubt have been cross-examined as to his past discreditable activities as a Communist agent. Experts would have been called to deal with the documents, and the circumstances of their care and custody would have been given in evidence.

Hiss would have been called to deny that he had handed over the documents, and he would have been cross-examined about his earlier association with Chambers in particular and with Communists in general. He would have been invited to give what explanation he could of the fact that Chambers had in his possession documents which had been typed on the Hiss typewriter and documents which had been written by Hiss in his own handwriting.

Mrs. Hiss would have been called to deny that she had ever typed out secret documents; and she, too, would have been cross-examined as to credit; though the fact that she, or still more her brother, had in or about the year 1932—that is to say, some six years before the documents were alleged to have been handed over—voted for the Socialist candidate for the presidency would not have been regarded as a matter relevant to credit.

Evidence of character would then have been called.

Such, in broad outline, would have been the course of the case in England; and I would add that in general we do not allow evidence to be given to contradict the answers given by a witness on matters relating merely to credit.

The American system of evidence appears—if I may judge from this case—to work differently in practice.

Amongst other matters brought out as a matter of substantive evidence—it was actually referred to in the opening speech of Counsel for the Prosecution—was the fact that in or about the year 1935 Hiss had turned over to Chambers certain secret documents with which he had been entrusted whilst serving with the Nye Committee; and it was asserted by Chambers that these secret documents had been photographed by Chambers in a clandestine manner in the house occupied by Hiss. A careful examination of the evidence relating to these documents points, I think, strongly to the conclusion that they were not secret at all. If this conclusion be right, it seems to follow that Chambers, so far as these documents are concerned, had no justification for the case he was making against Hiss. This, to my mind, is an extremely important matter to bear in mind in considering whether Chambers was making a true case against Hiss in regard to the documents alleged to have been turned over in 1938.

Then again, Chambers asserted that Hiss had been a member of a Communist group in the year 1934 and for some years thereafter; but he also alleged the same thing about Donald Hiss, the brother of Alger Hiss. This allegation was considered at the trial, though it was not of course investigated with the thoroughness which would have been appropriate had Donald Hiss himself been a party to the proceedings, but it is, I think, clear that this accusation against Donald Hiss completely broke down. In substance, if not in form, it was abandoned.

All these things must be borne in mind in considering whether the case Chambers made against Hiss was satisfactorily established.

There are three other matters which I ought to mention in attempting to define the issues. The first is the evidence of Mrs. Massing, a witness for the Prosecution. Her evidence was that Hiss in 1935 made some remark to her tending to show that he was then working for the Communists. I cannot understand the relevance of this evidence; nor can I explain whether it was supposed to bear upon the handing over of documents in or about February or March 1938, or upon the fact that meetings took place between Chambers and Hiss at about this time. Those were the only issues; Hiss was not accused of having been a Communist; and indeed, so far as I know, membership in that Party was not a criminal offence.

The second matter to which I ought to refer relates to the evidence of one Rosen. It was alleged as part of the case for the Prosecution that in the year 1936 Hiss was determined to hand over his old car for the benefit of some poor Communist organiser, and that as a first step in this direction he transferred it to a firm of motor agents who in turn transferred it, through the unauthorised act of some servant, to the aforesaid Rosen. Accordingly, Rosen was called by the Prosecution, though it was well known to them beforehand that he would decline to answer any questions relating to the transfer. All he would say was that he had never known or even heard of Alger Hiss. But even assuming that he had answered questions about the transfer of the car, I am quite unable to understand how this would have borne upon either of the issues in the case.

Thirdly, there was evidence of a Mrs. Murray, a coloured servant who had been until the spring of 1936 in the employment of Chambers. She proved that whilst she was with Chambers Mrs. Hiss came over on two or three occasions to see Mrs. Chambers at the house which Chambers and his wife occupied at Baltimore and that once Hiss himself came over. She was the solitary witness (other than Chambers or his wife, or Hiss and his wife) who testified to ever having seen the Hisses and the Chambers together as late as 1936. She was called in rebuttal and was, in fact, the last witness to be called. Hiss and his wife had both sworn that they had never been over to the Chambers' house in Baltimore, or indeed to any other house occupied by Chambers. Her evidence, if it was correct, established that this evidence given by Hiss and Mrs. Hiss was not true.

In the English courts such evidence would not have been

admissible in that it did not bear directly upon any issue in the case, but tended merely to show the untruth of an answer as to credit. It would appear that a far greater latitude is allowed in the American courts.

The real case against Hiss rests upon the documents; it is, to my mind, upon the documents, and only upon the documents, that the necessary corroboration of the story told by Chambers is to be found. I shall in due course examine these carefully and consider the circumstances under which they were produced.

CHAPTER III

OF WHITTAKER CHAMBERS

What manner of men were these two—Whittaker Chambers and Alger Hiss, the chief actors in this tragedy or, if I may change my metaphor, the protagonists in this duel? For duel it was, and all the other witnesses were mere seconds or sword-bearers. None of their evidence weighs heavily in the scales of justice—except the documents themselves, which Mr. Thomas F. Murphy, Counsel for the Prosecution, referred to in a striking phrase as the "immutable witnesses."

Since it is natural to consider the case for the Prosecution before that of the Defence, I shall try first to give a sketch of the man Whittaker Chambers, and in the following chapter to state the story which he revealed of his dealings with Alger Hiss.

To understand the complicated character of Whittaker Chambers, it is necessary to know something of his early environment and of the circumstances which made him a Communist; and fortunately for my purpose the materials are to hand, for he has recently published a book under the title *Witness* in which he records the experiences of his childhood and early manhood. I have recently been asked by the American Bar Association to undertake a review of this book, and for my present purposes I shall draw largely on this material.

Whittaker Chambers was born in Philadelphia in 1901 but spent his early years on Long Island. His father was a staff artist on a well-known paper, and his mother had been on the stage, so that it was not unlikely that he would possess what is sometimes called "the artistic temperament." Unfortunately, his home life was far from happy, and in his early and most impressionable years he was to come in contact with quarrels between his parents. His mother had been brought up in easy circumstances and was never, I think, quite able to reconcile herself to the straitened conditions which became her lot. It was difficult for her with her two sons—for Whittaker had a younger brother—to make both ends meet.

The two boys were exceptionally intelligent and very highly strung. Their health was not satisfactory; and in particular, Whittaker's teeth appear to have been neglected, for he records how he used as a child to lie on a sofa enduring the agonies of toothache, consoling himself with studying a print called "Death the Comforter" which hung on the wall. There was no sort of religious atmosphere in the home. On one occasion Whittaker, in some rambling child's conversation, used the phrase, "When God made the world," and his mother replied with unusual severity, "The world was formed by gases cooling in space." I wish I could record that the child countered by saying, "Then who made the gases?"

When the father, who had long become "unapproachable," decided to leave home, the mother had to contrive to meet the household expenses on a small allowance from her husband. She seems to have been very nervous, and moved the children's cots to her room, keeping an axe under her bed. The young Whittaker, although his mother did not know it, used to keep a knife under his pillow, and when wakeful would get an added sense of security by feeling it to reassure himself that it was still there. We shall see presently—for the child is father of the man—that he retained in later years this propensity for carrying a knife. There was one night, he recalls, when his mother heard screams coming from outside, so she started to scream herself and told the children to scream too. What an atmosphere in which to bring up an emotional and highly strung child. The time came for Whittaker to go to his first school, and he records that in his early days there he developed a deep distrust of the human race. He formed no friendships and had the unpleasant feeling of being "out of step." He gives us a sketch of his grandfather and grandmother. He would accompany his grandfather on his drinking bouts, for Grandfather could drink a great deal and from time to time would "disgorge like an antique Roman—and be ready for more." Then long after dark the children, tired out, would each take one of Grandfather's hands and guide him home, for he was no longer quite sure of his footing. Then the father made up his mind to return home. He lived an entirely separate life, having his meals on a tray in his room, and the chill of his presence spread through the house, so that the family life festered incurably.

When the time came for Whittaker to go to high school, he found himself becoming impudent and rebellious. He forced himself to acquire the art of cursing and determined that since he was to be outcast he would be outcast up to the hilt. He would say to himself: "I am an outcast. My family is outcast. We have no friends, no social ties, no church, no organization that we claim and that claims us, no community." And generalising, as was his wont in later life, he came to the conclusion that the world had lost its soul.

He had a brief spell as a labourer, but when he was nineteen he returned home. It was arranged that he should go to Williams College, but after one or two days he decided that it was not the place for him and entered Columbia University. There he got into trouble with the authorities by writing a blasphemous play, under the pseudonym John Kelly, ridiculing the resurrection. He then left the university for a time—he was not, he says, expelled—and in 1923 went on a tour to Europe, visiting Germany and Belgium. On his return he took a part-time job with the New York Public Library and at the same time went back for a term or two to Columbia University. There came a time when some books were found to be missing from the library, and the authorities began to make investigations. They went to Whittaker Chambers' desk, where they found Communist leaflets; when they went with him to his home, they found there books which he had taken from the Columbia University Library. As a result, he was dismissed from the New York Library.

He returned home to find that Grandmother had come to live with them. She was insane and was given to picking up knives. There were scenes, too, between the grandmother, armed with scissors, and the father, who would fling himself against her door in anger. Indeed these scenes became a regular part of the family life—and what a life it must have been. About this time his brother started to drink and asked Whittaker to enter into a suicide pact. He asked in vain, but determined on a solitary suicide. Whittaker, much to his brother's regret, stopped him once; then after horrible fights between the father and the brother about women, the brother was found dead with his head in a gas oven; and Whittaker, believing himself to be too gentle for this world, thinks that he was wrong to let his brother make the journey alone.

Here, indeed, with a drunken grandfather, an insane grandmother, a suicidal brother, and disunited parents, we have all the elements of a Greek tragedy; and Whittaker Chambers, believing that the world is dying a death of the spirit, now becomes an irreconcilable Communist. In 1925 he joined the Party and took a job with the *Daily Worker*, becoming its editor in 1928. Two years later he had what is euphemistically called a "Communist marriage" with one Ida Dales—it was of course no marriage at all—and in the following year he married his present wife Esther Shemitz.

In 1932 he was sent for by one of the members of the Central Committee of the Communist Party and told he was to enter the underground section of the movement. He was particularly warned that he must absolutely separate himself from all contacts with Communists and the Communist Party and live like a respectable bourgeois. He learned that only the chief knew the identity of the workers; the workers themselves knew each other only by their underground pseudonyms, such as "Bob," "Carl" or "Don." They were absolutely forbidden to drink. He learned the art of photographing documents, although he never, he says, became really proficient at it. He used to carry a sheath knife under his clothing, for he had learned to distrust everyone—even his Communist fellow workers—with whom he came in contact.

Thus it came about that in 1934 he was sent to Washington, and there begins the story of his contact with Alger Hiss, with which I shall deal in my next chapter. He decided either in 1937 or in April 1938 to leave the Communist Party; he gave the former date up till the time when he decided to produce the documents which formed the charge against Alger Hiss; the latter date he adopted after he had produced the documents, all of which were dated in the first four months of 1938. His desire to establish a "life preserver" by retaining incriminating documents, the steps he took to hide those documents, his visit to Mr. Berle in 1939 and to the Federal Bureau of Investigation in later years belong to a different part of this story.

There is, however, one incident so revealing of the man's character that I must mention it. For many years he failed to reveal the existence of the documents which, as a Christian patriot—he had ceased to be a Communist and atheist in 1937, had joined the Episcopalians in 1940 and the Quakers in 1941—he should have felt in duty bound to turn over to the authorities. Even after being challenged in the libel suit in 1948, he swore on his solemn oath that he had no such documents; this was during the first days of the pre-trial hearings. Only at long last did he decide to produce the documents. He describes in his book the mental agony he went through before he could bring himself to produce them and the still greater agony he experienced before he could bring himself to testify about them. He felt the time had come to remove himself as the only living witness. Let the documents and the microfilm speak for themselves. So he wrote a letter to his wife, to each of his children, and finally a letter addressed simply "To All." He explained that the act he was about to commit was not suicide but self-execution, a subtle distinction which I fail to appreciate. He had bought tins of chemical which liberated a lethal gas in the presence of moisture. He poured some of the chemical into the cover of each tin and moistened it. He went to bed, taking with him pictures of his children, and lay down with his head inside some receptacle which he had rigged up to concentrate the fumes, with a damp towel draped across the front—and fell asleep almost at once because he was very tired. What happened? When the fumes began to take effect, his body, although he was asleep, involuntarily moved away from them; the towel fell from the front of the receptacle; the fumes poured out and the air came in. If only he had read the instructions on the tin more carefully, he would have avoided any chance of recovery.

I began this chapter with the question: What manner of man was Whittaker Chambers? It is not difficult to judge. He was a man of great intelligence, of great enthusiasms, who was guided far more by his emotional than by his intellectual qualities. At the trial eminent doctors were called and testified that in their view he possessed a "psychopathic personality." I am in no way qualified to express any such opinion—and, indeed, I have no clear conception as to what is meant by a "psychopathic personality"—but if these doctors had had available to them the information contained in the book *Witness*, which had not then been published, it is clear that they would have had far more material on which to base a conclusion. Anyone who can attempt suicide in the way which is described in *Witness* must be quite out of the run of ordinary mortals.

Having read his book, and having studied his evidence both before the House Committee and at the second trial, I think it unlikely that a jury would think it safe to place reliance on any statement made by Whittaker Chambers unless it was corroborated. Anybody may be excused for giving a story a "new hat and stick," if I may borrow the phrase from Sir Walter Scott; but with Chambers the desire to embroider and embellish is so transcendent that I do not believe he knows when he is leaving the straight and narrow path of truth.

His judgment on public affairs seems to me to be equally unreliable. Unconsciously he dramatises all the ordinary events of life. Having experienced at first hand the evils of Communism, he now sees himself clad in shining armour, engaged in deadly combat with that evil. He, by the grace of God, has been appointed the champion to win over the soul of the American people. Those who are not for him, he thinks, are not merely against him but are against the cause for which he stands; and that cause is the maintenance of the American way of life as he interprets it. He is confident that he is right and that those who differ from him are wrong. There must be no deviation from the path he lays down. With the enthusiasm of the convert he hates Communism and Communists with a passionate intensity, and he finds Liberals, Socialists, New Dealers, and all such people differing from Communists only in this—that they, unlike the Communists, do not realise the destination towards which they are travelling.

I can well understand that Chambers, if my diagnosis is correct, would bring himself to believe that a man holding views or sympathies which inclined to the Left—no matter how sincere or how honest that man might be—was no better than a Communist. If Hiss did hold such views—and I should think it not improbable, for his wife admitted that she had once voted for the Socialist presidential candidate—I can well imagine that Chambers would be sincere in putting him into the category of a Communist; and if he was put into that category, then he would seem to Chambers to be one of those enemies of society against whom the American people must be protected.

I do not know whether a man holding, or having held, Communist views might regard himself as justified in taking steps to destroy such an enemy by means which would never occur to those cradled in the ideals of Western democracy. I do not doubt the passionate sincerity of Chambers to protect the free world against the perils of Communism, of which by his experience he had become so well aware. I distrust his judgment—and his evidence—just because it is so passionate. There may be much good in Whittaker Chambers, though I wish he could come to cultivate the virtue of tolerance. It is natural, and indeed inevitable, that there should be little evidence of that inherent good during his days as an irreconcilable Communist. But I cannot find anything to his credit, either, during the transition period; and, for my own part, I find it easier to excuse unworthy and discreditable transactions from a man who has accepted as the basis of his life atheistic Communism than from a man who has come to believe in a higher control. But this at least should be said: after leaving the Communist Party and after going through hard times, he was fortunate enough to become employed by the well-known periodical *Time*, and there his natural abilities found full scope. He gave himself to his work with unflagging energy. He won, and he deserved to win, the confidence of his employers. He rose to the position of senior editor and, at the time the Hiss case began, was enjoying a salary of $30,000 a year; and those who were concerned with the Prosecution could not unnaturally point out that a man in such an important position, enjoying such a handsome salary, was unlikely to surrender that position to start a campaign founded on a basis of conscious untruth. I should add, too, that his family life seems to have been ideal. He was devoted to his wife and as attached to his two children as they were to him. Yet there were times when his output of energy proved too much for his frail constitution, and he had at least one bad breakdown.

The doctors based their conclusions in part upon the fact that he had hidden the rolls of microfilm in a pumpkin. I think that this fact corroborates the view which I have expressed, that he loved drama, he loved sensationalism, he found himself at his best when basking in the full sunlight of publicity. The contribution his brilliant intelligence could have made to society in these difficult days had been frustrated by his acceptance of a false ideology. He was determined to make up for his past failure by his present activities. Such, then, as I see it, was the complex character of this most remarkable personality.

CHAPTER IV

THE STORY TOLD BY WHITTAKER CHAMBERS

Whittaker Chambers joined the Communist Party in 1925. He had originally testified that he joined the Party in 1924, but in the course of cross-examination a letter was produced which he himself had written, which clearly fixed the date of his joining as February 1925. His brother committed suicide in September 1926. This event had a profound effect on him, an almost paralysing effect; and thereafter he says he became a fanatical Communist. He described in graphic language what that involves. He said that no Communist recognises the sanctity of an oath; every Communist is dedicated to the wiping out of all religion and to the destruction, or overthrowing, of the government in every non-Communist country by any and every means; atheism and disloyalty are matters of principle.

It is not surprising to learn that Chambers, so long as he remained a fanatical Communist, was engaged in all sorts of discreditable activities. Much time, for example, was occupied in proving that he fraudulently obtained a passport in the name of Breen. It appeared that a child called Breen had died in early infancy and that the Communist organisation obtained for Chambers a passport in the name of Breen by falsely pretending that the birth certificate of the dead child related to Chambers. Nor is it surprising to find that he was passing under many aliases—Breen, Cantwell, Dwyer and perhaps Crosley—and that he was receiving secret papers from at least one person in the employment of the Federal Government, which he knew were being treacherously and dishonestly handed over. Chambers himself admitted that in his Communist days he was bound by no scruples and by no morality. He was, in short, an enemy of society.

The story which Chambers told at the second trial can be simply stated. In May or June 1934 he said that he came to Washington as a Communist functionary in the "underground." There he met Harold Ware, who was killed in a road accident in 1935. Chambers had known Ware in New York—and had known him as a fellow Communist. Ware was the organiser of a large Communist organisation in Washington, D.C., at the time when Chambers first arrived. It was, said Chambers, through Ware that he first came to meet Alger Hiss.

The meeting took place in or about June or July 1934 at a restaurant in downtown Washington. There were present four persons: one J. Peters, who was head of the entire "underground" of the American Communist Party, Harold Ware, Alger Hiss and Whittaker Chambers himself. Chambers, who was then using the name "Carl"—the use of a single name such as this was, he said, common amongst Communist functionaries—was introduced to Hiss by Peters and Ware as "Carl." The substance of the conversation which then took place was that Hiss was to be disconnected from Ware's apparatus and was to become instead a member of an organisation which Chambers was to form. If I may anticipate for a moment, it will be found that when giving evidence before the House Committee Chambers put the date of this "disconnection" as about 1936.

About two weeks later Chambers, as Carl, called by appointment on Hiss at his apartment in 28th Street in Washington. Hiss lived in this house from the 9th June 1934 till the 19th April 1935. Chambers then met both Hiss and his wife. He was unable to recall any particular conversation which took place at that meeting. He was, he said, introducing himself to two strange people.

Some time afterwards—Chambers was unable to fix the date—he called again at the 28th Street apartment. Hiss then said that he had an opportunity of using his position in the Nye investigation to obtain confidential documents from the State Department and asked Chambers whether he would like him to bring them out. Chambers—he was still Carl—replied that he must consult J. Peters; and shortly afterwards, when he had asked Peters, he told Hiss that he would like him to bring out the documents. Thereafter Chambers received the documents and photographed them at the house in P Street, which the Hisses occupied from April 1935 till June 1936. These papers, Chambers said, dealt with "some phase of munitions traffic," and I shall consider them in a subsequent chapter, called "The First Act of Treachery."

The next incident which Chambers related explained how it came about that he occupied the Hisses' 28th Street apartment after they had moved to P Street. Chambers alleged that in the course of conversation Hiss suggested that "since he had leased a furnished house in P Street I might move into his 28th Street apartment, which had furniture left in it, and stay there for the balance of the lease on the 28th Street apartment—a matter of two or three months." Chambers said that it was then agreed that there was to be no rent. He said that when the time came for them to move in, Hiss drove over to Baltimore from Washington in his Ford roadster, and loaded into it the baby's collapsible bathtub, high chair and some of the other belongings. Chambers, his wife and baby stayed in the 28th Street apartment for some two or three months. They then moved to Professor Schapiro's house in 4th Street, New York, making the journey there by train; but Mrs. Hiss, said Chambers, drove up with the baby's things. They were not comfortable in this house, and Chambers said that Hiss brought to their notice an advertisement of a house at Long Eddy on the Delaware River. The Hisses, he said, drove him there one Sunday in their car, but the place was found to be quite unsuitable.

From the 4th Street house Chambers and his wife and the baby, together with his friend Maxim Lieber, a fellow Communist, moved to a place called Smithton, about six miles south of Frenchtown, New Jersey. They hired a cottage from a Mr. Boucot, who was himself living at Smithton. They were there for two or three months. Chambers said that he and his wife and child then went to stay with the Hisses for several days in their P Street house. During this visit Chambers stated that he had a conversation with Hiss about Mrs. Chambers and the child staying with the Hisses if Chambers went to England to work in the Soviet apparatus. There had been a proposal, said Chambers, that he should go to England and establish himself there as Maxim Lieber's representative; he was to have a religious cover, that is, attend a church so as to conceal his real activities. It was for the purpose of this visit, so Chambers said, that he had obtained the passport in the name of Breen on the 28th May 1935; he admitted that he had not told Hiss about the passport. As it happened, the trip to England never materialised.

In August 1935 Hiss joined the Department of Justice, and Chambers testified that, before joining, Hiss asked for the views of the Communist Party; Chambers told him that the Party wished him to enter that Department. Hiss was there for only about a year, when he had the opportunity of transferring to the State Department. He entered the State Department on the 1st September 1936, having, so Chambers said, again asked for the Party's views.

In the fall of 1936 Chambers said that he talked to Hiss about a Colonel Bykov, a Russian underground worker who was passing under the name of Peter. I shall, however, refer to him as Bykov, to avoid confusion with J. Peters, the head of the American Communists. At Bykov's request a meeting was arranged which took place during January 1937 in New York. The date, and it is a matter of importance, was fixed in Chambers' mind for this reason: just before the meeting Chambers said he gave Hiss a rug on the instructions of Bykov—"as a gift in recognition of the work of the American Communists." Chambers was, as I shall show later, firmly anchored to early January 1937 as the date of this gift.

This alleged meeting in New York in January 1937 between Bykov, Hiss and Chambers is one of the turning points in the case, for Hiss said that such a meeting never took place. Whereas, according to Chambers, it was at once the prelude and the explanation of the second act of treachery. Bykov, who spoke in German which was interpreted by Chambers, told Hiss that the Soviet Union was acutely endangered by the rise of the Fascist powers and that he could greatly help if he would procure documents from the State Department, especially those relating to the Far East, Germany and Italy. Hiss, said Chambers, agreed apparently without a moment's hesitation. Bykov then asked him if Donald Hiss could also procure documents (Donald Hiss had joined the Labour Department in June 1936 and did not enter the State Department until February 1938). Alger Hiss replied to this that he did not know whether his brother Donald was "yet sufficiently developed for such work"; to which Bykov answered, "Perhaps you can persuade him."

As a result of this meeting, Chambers said that he used to call at the Hisses' house between 4:30 and 6 P.M. once a week or once every ten days and receive whatever documents Hiss had managed to bring out from the State Department. Chambers took these to Baltimore with a photographer called Felix Inslerman (he generally but not always accompanied Felix on his journey); then either Chambers or Felix would bring the documents back at about one o'clock that night, and Chambers would return them to Hiss at his house. Chambers thought that Hiss had given him a key to the P Street house, which Hiss occupied until June 1936, but he could not remember whether he had a key to the Hisses' house in 30th Street (July 1936 to December 1937) or to their house in Volta Place (December 1937 to October 1943). He said he either had a key or rang the bell, and the door was opened by Alger or Priscilla Hiss, and he would then return the documents. When he called back, some time after midnight, he would frequently have a chat lasting about half an hour, but he could not remember whether Hiss and his wife would still be up or whether one or the other of them had usually gone to bed. Pressed further about the key, he admitted that he had found no key in his possession; he was sure he did not have one to the Volta Place house and was not sure whether that house had a doorbell or merely a knocker.

This arrangement continued, so Chambers said, until about the middle of 1937, when he had a further conversation with Hiss. Chambers then told him that "we wish to have the papers brought out every night or approximately every night, and some of them typed as nearly verbatim as possible and some of them paraphrased." To this Hiss agreed. Chambers said that there was some discussion as to who should do the necessary typing, but that it was arranged that Mrs. Hiss should do it, for she said that she had always been restless in "underground" work and sought some activity; this typing would give her just the opportunity she needed, and she would therefore be the typist. This interview between Chambers and Hiss may be regarded as the prelude to the third act of treachery.

Under the new regime Chambers still followed his old practice: that is, the documents were taken to Baltimore either by himself or by Felix and there photographed; the originals were returned by Chambers that same night; and the typed documents, after they had been photographed, were burnt. The photographs were then handed by Chambers to Colonel Bykov. Chambers said that from time to time Hiss used to give him small handwritten notes about documents which had passed under his eyes quickly, which he thought important but which for some reason or other he was unable to bring out. When this happened, the handwritten notes were sometimes given by Chambers to Bykov as they were, or sometimes photographed, in which case the photographs were handed over.

This routine continued until Chambers made up his mind to break with the Party. He had been thinking of this, so he said, since the early fall of 1937 and had talked it over with his wife; but there were various preparations he felt he must make. His first step was to join the "National Research Project," an agency run by the Government of the United States. George Silverman and Irving Kaplan helped him to get this job. He filled in the regular form, giving all details about himself and his previous work and employers, and all was accomplished very quickly. His application form was dated the 18th October 1937, and on his appointment he took an oath to support and defend the Constitution of the United States against all enemies, foreign and domestic. He was asked in his cross-examination at the second trial how he could square the taking of this oath with his position as a Communist, since he had said that all Communists were traitors. He replied that at this time he was a deserter from the Communist Party—an entirely inadequate answer, since by his own admission he continued to collect and hand over secret documents between the 18th October 1937 and the 15th April 1938. Most of the information which he gave to obtain his position with the Government was false, although, as he said in his evidence, he had by that time come to believe in God. It is obvious that this belief did not prevent him from telling lies to get his position or from continuing to hand over documents.

His second preparation before leaving the Party was to buy a car; and in order to do this he alleged that he borrowed in November 1937 the sum of $400 from Alger Hiss, on the pretext that he needed a car to help him in his work for the Communists, whereas in reality he wanted it to enable him to break with the Party. I shall deal with this matter further in Chapter IX.

There was a meeting, said Chambers, between his family and the Hisses at about Christmas 1937. Alger and Priscilla Hiss came over to the house in Mount Royal Terrace, Baltimore, where Chambers and his wife were then living. Here again there was controversy, for Hiss said that he had never visited Chambers in Baltimore, and that long before Christmas 1937 George Crosley had completely passed out of his life—the reader must remember that Hiss said he never knew Chambers under any other name.

Finally, on the 15th April 1938, his preparations being satisfactorily completed, Chambers broke with the Communist Party; and this he did by failing to keep his next appointment with Bykov—and of course he no longer called on Hiss to collect documents. Chambers moved from his house in Mount Royal Terrace to one in the Old Court Road, Baltimore. He earned a little money by getting translating work, but for some time was in great financial difficulties.

Chambers, however, retained some of the documents which he said he received from Hiss—not everything was handed over to Bykov—and these were the documents which were produced at the trial. In his book *Witness*, Chambers says that his last preparation before leaving the Party was to keep these documents, which he describes as his "life preserver." He put those which he had received from Hiss, together with some others in the handwriting of Mr. Harry Dexter White, who was in a high position in the United States Treasury, into an envelope, which he deposited in about May or June of 1938 with his wife's nephew in New York. There they remained safely hidden away until Chambers claimed them in 1948.

At Christmas time 1938, Chambers said, he went round to see Hiss at the house in Volta Place where he was then living. He rang the bell and a coloured servant answered the door and told him that both Mr. and Mrs. Hiss were out. Chambers said that he waited on the sidewalk, and almost immediately Mrs. Hiss drove up in her car. He went into the house with her, and Hiss came in about half an hour later. Chambers said that he was afraid that he might be assassinated by Hiss or his confederates, but he soon got over his fear and was asked to stay to supper. He stayed in all for about two hours. As he was leaving, Hiss asked him what kind of a Christmas he was going to have; and on Chambers saying that he feared it would be rather a poor one, Hiss gave him a child's rolling pin for his daughter. According to Chambers, this was the last occasion on which he ever met Hiss until they were confronted with each other before the House Committee.

In September 1939, just after the Hitler-Stalin pact for the division of Poland, Chambers went round with his friend Mr. Isaac Don Levine to see Mr. Adolf Berle, who was Assistant Secretary of State in charge of security. He made a statement to Mr. Berle about Communist infiltration into the United States Government. Mr. Berle's notes of this conversation were produced at the trial.[1] In 1940 Chambers was baptised into the Episcopal Church and in the following year became a Quaker. It is clear, therefore, that by this date he knew and appreciated the sanctity of an oath. In 1945 Mr. Ray Murphy, a security

[1]Appendix I.

officer in the State Department, visited Chambers at his farm in Maryland, and Chambers reported to him his knowledge of Communist activities. Mr. Ray Murphy made notes of this conversation, and these notes,[2] together with similar notes made of a later meeting,[3] were also produced at the trial. There followed the proceedings before the House Committee at which Chambers testified on oath on the 3rd August 1948 and on several subsequent occasions. He also gave evidence before a grand jury.

It is admitted—and it is one of the most remarkable facts in a remarkable case—that Chambers never revealed either to Mr. Berle or to Mr. Ray Murphy, or to the House Committee or (until November 1948) to the Grand Jury, anything suggesting espionage or the stealing of papers. Not only did he not reveal it: he swore positively that he had no knowledge of any such thing. I will content myself with this reference to the proceedings of the Grand Jury, which took place on the 14th October 1948:

> *Juror:* Could you give me one name of anybody who, in your opinion, was positively guilty of espionage against the United States?
>
> *Mr. Chambers:* Let me think for a moment and I will try to answer that. I don't think so, but I would like to have the opportunity to answer you tomorrow more definitely. Let me think it over, overnight.

And—having thought it over overnight—Chambers came back on the 15th October 1948 and gave this considered answer:

> *Mr. Chambers:* I assume that espionage means in this case the turning over of secret or confidential documents.
>
> *Juror:* Or information—oral information.
>
> *Mr. Chambers:* Or oral information. I do not believe I do know such a name.

It was not until Hiss had launched his libel action that Chambers was submitted to a lengthy and elaborate cross-examination in what is called pre-trial proceedings. He was pressed

[2]Appendix II.

[3]Appendix III.

and pressed again about the documents. He finally decided to produce them, and on the 17th November 1948, in the course of this examination, he produced those documents in the handwriting of Hiss and those which had been typed on the typewriter of Hiss, which formed the basis of the charge. He did not, however, even at this stage, produce the photographs of documents which he later said Hiss had also given him. These latter documents, the rolls of microfilm which he had hidden in a pumpkin on his farm, he handed over to the representatives of the House Committee who came there to fetch them. In his book *Witness*, Chambers reveals the mental agony which he went through in making up his mind as to whether he should or should not produce these documents. The extent of this agony can be measured by the fact that he contemplated suicide before deciding to produce the documents and actively took steps to end his life at some time during the proceedings of the Grand Jury.

CHAPTER V

OF ALGER HISS

It is easy enough for me to sketch the career of Alger Hiss, but the materials which would enable me to attempt a sketch of his character are not to hand—all I have is the impression which has been formed in my mind by reading in cold print the evidence which he gave both before the House Committee and at the second trial. Never having had the opportunity of seeing him or of judging for myself from his demeanour what manner of man he is, my impressions—for what they are worth, if indeed they are worth anything—must be purely tentative.

Alger Hiss was born in November 1904 at Baltimore. He was educated at the grammar school and high school there, from whence he went for a couple of terms to a prep school at Duxbury. In the fall of 1922 he entered Johns Hopkins University in Baltimore. When he graduated in 1926, his career had been successful; he had been elected to Phi Beta Kappa, an honour which will convey more to an American than to an English reader. He then entered the Harvard Law School, from which he graduated in 1929, having for his last two years been on the *Harvard Law Review*.

In October 1929 he entered the service of Mr. Justice Holmes as law clerk or secretary. Here was an opportunity which any young lawyer would have grasped at eagerly; for amongst lawyers —and I should imagine amongst a much wider circle—on both sides of the Atlantic, the name of Holmes was one to conjure with. He was certainly one of the greatest figures who ever graced the Supreme Court of the United States. The fact that Holmes selected Hiss to serve him is in itself eloquent of the standing which Hiss occupied and of the reputation he had already achieved; for this much is obvious, that Holmes could have had his pick, and in picking would almost certainly have asked the advice of the Harvard authorities—and he chose Hiss. Hiss remained with Holmes for a year; and it seems clear that he left with the friendship and good will of that most distinguished of judges, for when Holmes died some five years later he bequeathed to Hiss a beautiful Queen Anne mirror.

In December 1929, while he was still with Mr. Justice Holmes, Hiss married. His wife Priscilla, whose maiden name was Fansler, had been married before to one Thayer Hobson, who had divorced her. She had a son, Timmy Hobson, who had been born in 1926 and was therefore some three years old at the time of his mother's second marriage. I should judge Priscilla Hiss to have been a woman of strong character who was likely to exercise a considerable influence—for better or worse—on her husband. She came of Quaker stock, and in her conversation at home used sometimes to reveal her origin by using the "plain speech"—that is, using the pronouns "thou" and "thee." It seems clear that she was highly intelligent and that in the early days of their marriage she developed Left-wing sympathies; for during the period of acute unemployment in the winter of 1931–32 she worked at a feeding station in New York which was being run under the auspices of the Socialist Party, and in the presidential election of 1932 she voted for Norman Thomas, the Socialist candidate.

On leaving Mr. Justice Holmes in October 1930, Alger Hiss joined a well-known law firm in Boston, which he left only to join another equally well-known firm in New York. He had the opportunity, had he been so minded, of returning to the latter firm when he decided some fifteen years later to leave the

Government service, so that it seems clear that he must have made a favourable impression on its partners. During this time in New York he took some part, at the instance of a Mr. Polier, in the activities of a body known as the International Juridical Association, which seems to have had some twenty to twenty-five associate members. This was referred to at the trial, though there was little, if any, evidence to show that the association was an undesirable body.

It was in 1933 that Alger Hiss decided to enter the Government service, and in May he joined the Agricultural Adjustment Administration, commonly known as the "Triple A." His immediate superior was Mr. Jerome Frank, later to become Judge Frank, who was General Counsel. Mr. Frank's other assistant counsel was one Lee Pressman, whom Hiss had known some five years earlier on the *Harvard Law Review*. In July or August of the same year a man named Nathan Witt also joined the Department. Witt had gone to the Harvard Law School in 1929, just after Hiss left it; he was a contemporary there with Donald Hiss, the younger brother of Alger. He had been born Wittowsky, but his father had changed the family name whilst Nathan was still an infant. Witt appears to have recommended to the authorities of the Triple A an old school friend of his, one Charles Krivitsky, who in 1935 legally changed his name to Kramer. Kramer joined the Consumers' Council of the Department late in 1933. John Abt, a lawyer who had graduated from the University of Chicago, also joined the Triple A some time in the same year—that is, in 1933.

The names of these four, Pressman, Witt, Kramer and Abt, are of some importance in the history of the Hiss case.

The duties which Hiss was called upon to perform whilst in the A.A.A. brought him in close touch with the Senate Agricultural Committee. Two of the senators on that Committee also served on another committee, commonly known as the Nye Committee from the name of its Chairman, Gerald P. Nye, which had been set up to investigate the munitions traffic. At their request Hiss, on the 30th July 1934, became legal assistant to the Nye Committee. His duties were to give opinions on legal questions and to deal with certain other topics, such as aviation. His services were, however, only lent in the first instance. He continued to be paid by the A.A.A. until April 1935, when he resigned from that Department and went on the pay roll of the Nye Committee. He had by that time long ceased to do any work for the Triple A.

It was at about the time when he joined the Nye Committee that Hiss first met the man who is now known as Whittaker Chambers but who was then—no doubt for good reasons—passing under a different name. Hiss remembered him as George Crosley, a pseudonym which Chambers at the trial was prepared neither to own nor to disown; it was possible, he said, but he was unable to remember whether he had used this name—a lapse of memory which I find hard to believe. The first allegation that Hiss had turned over secret documents to the man—be he called "Crosley," "Carl" or "Chambers"—relates to this period of service with the Nye Committee.

Hiss stayed with the Nye Committee until in August 1935 he entered the Department of Justice, where he worked in the office of the Solicitor General, Mr. Stanley Reed, now a member of the United States Supreme Court. The following spring he was detailed by Mr. Reed to work on the Trade Agreements Act, which was then before the courts, an assignment which brought him in touch with Mr. Sayre, who was in charge of a section of the State Department, and with Mr. Sayre's assistant, Mr. Dickey. It so happened that the latter was anxious to return to the private practice of the law, and either he or Mr. Sayre pressed the Solicitor General to agree to transfer Hiss to the State Department. Mr. Sayre obtained the approval of the Secretary of State, Mr. Hull, to the proposed transfer, after submitting full details of the career of Hiss, and accordingly in September 1936 Hiss entered the Department of State as assistant to Mr. Sayre, a post he occupied until June or July 1939, when Mr. Sayre was appointed High Commissioner to the Philippines. Mr. Sayre formed a high opinion of Hiss and came to rely on him more and more; at the trial he referred to him as "my right-hand man."

It is important to remember that throughout the years 1937 and 1938 Hiss was assistant to Mr. Sayre, whose general responsibility in the State Department covered the section known as Trade Agreements. Whittaker Chambers alleged that throughout the year 1937 and during the first four months of 1938 Hiss was regularly turning over secret documents to him, so that the Communists might be kept in touch with the activities of the State Department. I have dealt with this in the story of Chambers.

For the moment I shall continue to trace the career of Alger Hiss. On the departure of Mr. Sayre for the Philippines, Mr. Hornbeck, the Adviser on Political Relations, asked Hiss to join his staff as his assistant. There he remained until in 1944 he was asked to go into the newly created Office of Special Political Affairs. From August to October of 1944 he was secretary to the American delegation to the Dumbarton Oaks Conference, where he was in charge of the organisation arrangements—a post for which he was specially chosen by Mr. Stettinius.

Early in 1945 he was appointed Director of the Office of Special Political Affairs; he was selected to accompany President Roosevelt to Yalta to the conference which took place in February 1945—a conference from which we all hoped so much and from which the nations of the West obtained so little. At the San Francisco Conference, where the Charter of the United Nations was signed on the 26th June 1945, he was in charge of all the complicated security arrangements. On the conclusion of the conference, it was Hiss who was appointed by Mr. Stettinius, the Secretary of State, to take the signed copy of the Charter to President Truman in Washington. Later in the year, in December 1945, we find him taking ship to London as principal adviser to the United States delegation to the first meeting of the United Nations Assembly. Mr. John Foster Dulles, who was one of the American delegates, was a passenger on that same ship, and there was some conversation, the precise details of which were in dispute, concerning a possible position which Hiss might occupy if and when he determined to leave the Government service.

After discussing the matter fully with his superiors in the State Department, Hiss came to the conclusion that he could leave the service of the Government, and in December 1946 he was elected President of the Carnegie Endowment for International Peace—a position which he assumed in February 1947. The post carried a salary of $20,000 a year.

Such, then, was the career of Alger Hiss in the public service of his country. It had started in May 1933; it ended in February 1947. In less than fourteen years he had risen from a humble position in the A.A.A. to a position which made it not unlikely that he would incur the envy of his less fortunate associates.

Perhaps on receiving his appointment as President of the Carnegie Endowment he stopped for a moment to look back on his past career. Of course, if he had consciously had Communistic associations, still more if he had handed over secret documents, he had much to fear; but assuming he was entirely innocent, he might have realised that there was a cloud in the sky—even if the cloud was no bigger than a man's hand. For in March 1946 (just after Hiss had returned from the meeting of the United Nations in London) Secretary of State Byrnes had sent for him. He warned him that several members of Congress were threatening to make speeches on the floor of the House calling him (Hiss) a Communist. Hiss assured his Secretary of State that there was no possible basis for such an allegation; and Mr. Byrnes then advised him to go to the Federal Bureau of Investigation, commonly known as the F.B.I., and submit himself for interrogation, because, said Mr. Byrnes, all the reports seemed to stem from the F.B.I. So Hiss in that same month contacted the F.B.I., and was referred to Mr. Ladd, a senior official, and he had been interrogated by Mr. Ladd. He had answered all Mr. Ladd's questions about Pressman and the International Juridical Association, about Mr. Polier and about much else, but he was not then asked about a Mr. Whittaker Chambers—and, of course, if he had been asked, the name would have meant nothing to him, as George Crosley, his friend of ten years ago, had never used such a name. But Hiss, as he explained at the trial, thought that it had all blown over, for down to the day he had received his appointment as President of the Carnegie Endowment he had heard no more about it. He had taken the precaution of getting Mr. Acheson specifically to check with Secretary of State Byrnes whether he would be well advised to accept the presidency of the Carnegie Endowment, for he did not want to appear to resign from the State Department under fire. Mr. Acheson had reassured him about Mr. Byrnes's views, and Mr. Byrnes had communicated with him directly; and it was after all these things had happened that he had been elected President.

But it soon became apparent that the cloud in the sky, which might perhaps have been observed in March 1946, was only the first of many other clouds. Early in 1947 Mr. John Foster Dulles told Hiss that he had had a communication to the effect that Hiss was a Communist. I deal with this and other communications to the same effect when I consider the evidence of Mr. Dulles.

In May or June 1947 two representatives of the F.B.I. came round to the office of the Carnegie Endowment and asked Hiss about his previous association with a number of persons they then named; and one of the people named was Whittaker Chambers—a name which conveyed nothing to Hiss. Then again, at a cocktail party early in 1948, there had been a lady who said that she had heard that Hiss and his brother were Communists, and that she had got it from a Mr. Chambers, a man on *Time*. Thereupon a Mr. Miller—a friend of Hiss—tackled her about this and, as a result, she had called up Mr. Miller and told him that she had gone back to Chambers and found out that it was "just talk." Still Hiss did not take the trouble to investigate who Mr. Chambers—"the man on *Time*"—might be.

In March 1948 Hiss was again interviewed by the F.B.I. The name of Chambers came up, together with that of Post and Sayre (the latter name becomes significant in view of the later evidence of a Mr. Cowley), and of course the names of Pressman, Witt, Abt and Kramer were mentioned again. In addition, there was mentioned the name of an old friend of Alger Hiss called Collins.

That same month of March 1948 Hiss appeared before the Grand Jury, and the same day that he so appeared he went again to see Mr. Dulles, who had received further communications.

The storm clouds were gathering, and on the 3rd August 1948, the day on which Chambers first testified before the House Committee, the storm broke. I have dealt shortly, but I hope accurately, with the career of Alger Hiss; perhaps I have said enough to indicate the nature of the reputation he bore. I shall not hereafter trouble the reader with the mass of evidence which was called at the trial as to the high reputation he had attained alike for intelligence, industry and integrity. I shall content myself with the reflection that it is manifest that those concerned with his election to the presidency of the Carnegie Endowment would have made every enquiry before selecting a candidate to such an important post; those concerned included men of the calibre of Mr. John W. Davis, one-time Ambassador to the Court of St. James, Mr. John Foster Dulles and others of great distinction in American life. They would have failed in their duty if they had not taken every step open to them to make sure that they selected the best available candidate—and they were not the sort of men likely to fail in their duty.

If the career in the public service were not testimony enough, the election to this post would satisfy anyone as to the honourable reputation Hiss had won. It was eminently right and proper that at the trial evidence should be called to establish this reputation, though I confess I think it was established with an unnecessary expenditure of time, for in reality, in a case such as this, the facts speak for themselves. Mr. Murphy, in his closing speech to the jury, was inclined, so it seems to me, to make light of the evidence of character. This is how he dealt with it:

> I ask you, ladies and gentlemen, what kind of reputation did a good spy have? Of course it must be good. The fox barks not when he goes to steal the lamb. It has to be good. But we are here on a search for truth. We are not concerned with reputations. Poppycock.

Of course the evidence of character does not prove that the accused did not commit the crime, but it does go to show that he belongs to a category of people who are not likely to commit dishonourable or discreditable acts. It would be, to my mind, quite wrong if the fact that a man had won a high reputation for integrity were to count for nothing in his day of trial. Is it to be seriously suggested that the burden of proof should be precisely the same in the case of a man of proved integrity as it would be in the case of an unmitigated rascal?

The object of calling evidence to show that a witness possesses a high reputation for integrity is, so it seems to me, nothing less and nothing more than this: that in judging whether such a man has committed a mean and dishonourable action we should be especially careful to see that the act attributed to him is proved beyond a peradventure. The question for the jury in the trial of Alger Hiss must have been whether the particularly mean and particularly dishonourable course of conduct which was alleged against him was so proved. It is, I think, self-evident from a consideration of his career that he must have possessed many sterling qualities. There is no man who has not got his weaknesses, and Hiss could be no exception to this rule. Nor is it good for any of us to have an unbroken series of successes. It is the setbacks and difficulties which help to form and strengthen character; and it is difficult to see in this career any setbacks or any difficulties, at least down to the time of his appointment as President of the Carnegie Endowment.

On reading the evidence, I get the impression of a man somewhat conceited, too conscious that he had met on intimate terms the most distinguished of his countrymen, not over-ready to be forthcoming with his less distinguished compatriots, and in short not suffering fools gladly and not being a "good mixer." I get the impression, too, of a man so immersed in his official life that he took little or no trouble about the affairs of his private life. I do not, however, from reading and rereading his evidence, get the impression of dishonesty; indeed, if he had been dishonest, I find myself wondering why he did not supply the answers which must have been—to such an intelligent man—an obvious way out of the difficulties which arose in his cross-examination.

I should be the first to admit that impressions from reading the evidence are but a poor substitute for seeing and knowing the man. One who did both see and know him—no less a person than Whittaker Chambers himself—described him as being "a man of great simplicity and great gentleness and sweetness of character," and again he described him as having "a charming personality, absolutely sincere in his convictions and motivated by the idea that he was on the right track."

CHAPTER VI

THE STORY TOLD BY HISS

Having set out the main facts of the career of Hiss and the impressions I have formed of his character, let me now give a broad outline of the story he told of how he came to meet a man calling himself George Crosley, who proved to be the same individual as the Whittaker Chambers of the trial.

Hiss said that it was at the end of December 1934 or early in January 1935, at a time when he was working for the Nye Committee, that Chambers came to the room he was occupying in the Senate Office Building. Hiss had no regular office and used whatever room happened to be vacant. Chambers introduced himself as George Crosley, a free-lance writer, who was contemplating writing a series of articles on the munitions investigation. It was one of the duties of Hiss to see representatives of the press who called to make enquiries, generally at the conclusion of a particular hearing. They would come round to his room after the hearing to ask for more detailed information. The Committee were anxious to get wide publicity for their proceedings and knew that Hiss was seeing press representatives.

Hiss said that the first time he saw George Crosley they talked for about twenty minutes. Hiss suggested he might like to look through some of the exhibits, and he did so. They met a second time some ten or fourteen days afterwards. Crosley read through a copy of the exhibits and made notes on them. About a fortnight later Crosley telephoned to Hiss and said that he wanted to see him, and it was arranged that they should lunch together. This lunch took place at the States Restaurant, where Hiss frequently lunched. The work of the Nye Committee was discussed.

They lunched together again about a fortnight later. Crosley said that he was planning to come to Washington for a couple of months in order to finish his articles, which he hoped to have published, and said that he was planning to bring his wife and child with him. It so happened that at that time Hiss was about to move out of his apartment on 28th Street, Washington, into a house, No. 2905 P Street, Georgetown, Washington. His lease of the 28th Street apartment had still about two months to run (it expired on the 1st July 1935), but he had not thought it at all possible to sublet the apartment for such a short time at that time of the year and had not made any effort to do so; indeed, he had instructed the Potomac Electric Light Company to disconnect their service as on the 1st May 1935. He told Crosley, therefore, that he expected to have the apartment on his hands for about a couple of months and that he would be very glad to let him have it at cost.

Hiss and his wife moved to the P Street house on the 19th April 1935, and shortly before they moved out Crosley came to look at the 28th Street apartment to see if he liked it. Hiss did not recall Mrs. Crosley coming but said that she might have done so. He remembered introducing Crosley as his sub-tenant to Mrs. Jeffries, the resident manager of the apartments, so as to ensure that he could obtain permission to leave his baby carriage in the front hall; he said he remembered that some arrangement to that effect was made after he had introduced Mr. Crosley to Mrs. Jeffries. He left behind him in the 28th Street apartment all the large pieces of furniture and, in fact, nearly all the furniture, except possibly Timmy's bed, as the new house he was going to on P Street was a furnished house. As a result of the arrangement with Crosley, Hiss said that he must have changed his instructions to the Potomac Electric Light Company, but he could not recall the circumstances.

The next time Hiss met Crosley was, he said, the very day Crosley was going to move into the 28th Street apartment. As Hiss recalled it, Crosley said that he and his wife and child had arrived but that their furnishings were delayed and they were not ready to start housekeeping. Hiss said that Crosley gave an explanation that the van bringing these things had been delayed, so Hiss offered to put them up overnight on the third floor of the P Street house until the van came. They stayed at least two nights—it might have been three—and Hiss recalled that he was told that the van did not arrive the next day.

Hiss remembered letting Crosley have the use of his car once or twice whilst he was occupying the 28th Street apartment, and remembered that at that time Crosley spoke to him about wanting a car. I do not propose at this stage to deal with the complicated stories of transactions about this car, as I shall examine these in a later chapter. Suffice it at the present time to say that Hiss asserted that he had allowed Crosley to use his old car and had subsequently, in 1936, given it to him.

Crosley never, in fact, paid any rent, and Hiss did not write to him demanding rent. Hiss had never proposed to charge him anything for the use of the furniture which he left behind, and Hiss continued to pay for the utilities, gas and electricity; nor did Hiss ask him to pay for the telephone. Crosley said several times that he expected to pay the rent as soon as he had sold his articles, but, in fact, he never succeeded in selling his articles and never paid anything.

Crosley came to the P Street house in the spring of 1936, when he gave Hiss a rug. Hiss unrolled the rug and thanked him for it. The rug was used in the P Street house, which Hiss finally left on the 15th June 1936, so that it must have been given to Hiss before that date. Crosley told Hiss that it had been given to him by some patron and that he, in turn, was making a gift of it to Hiss.

The next time Hiss saw Crosley after this was when Crosley came to pick up the Ford finally, and this was in about May or June 1936, whilst Hiss was still living at P Street. On the occasion of the last meeting with Hiss, Crosley requested another small loan. He had borrowed several small sums from Hiss during the period of their acquaintance. Hiss told him then that he did not think he was ever going to get his money back, and said that he thought they had better discontinue seeing each other. Hiss never saw him again after that until they met before the House Committee in 1948. Hiss said that he supposed he had seen Crosley ten or eleven times in all. They had established some kind of personal relationship.

Hiss said that it was entirely untrue to say that he was asked to produce any secret documents, or offered to do so, or that he did in fact do so. All the documents which he had while he was with the Nye Committee were supplied by the State Department and were available for publication. He said it was wholly untrue that when he transferred to the State Department in September 1936 he had ever handed over to Crosley any documents. Hiss used frequently to lunch with Mr. Sayre and sometimes took with him memoranda relating to documents he wanted to discuss with Mr. Sayre. Hiss admitted that four of the documents were in fact in his handwriting and was quite unable to account for the fact that the typewritten documents had been typed on his typewriter. Hiss said that he had had that typewriter for many years. It had been given to Mrs. Hiss by her father when he retired from business, and that must have been in the early thirties. Hiss could not remember how he disposed of the typewriter. Finally Hiss denied most categorically that he had ever been a Communist or a fellow-traveller.

Such, then, was the story told by Hiss of his association with George Crosley. There is, however, one further fact about the attitude of Hiss after the outbreak of the Second World War which is of some importance. In September 1939, at a time when there was an agreement between Russia and the Nazis, Hiss prepared a memorandum in the State Department maintaining the view that the U.S.A. were entitled, without violating international law, to aid the Western allies. This was in answer to the contrary view which had been expressed in the New York *Times* by Professors Hyde and Jessup. This memorandum was dated the 26th September 1939 and was sent through Mr. Hornbeck to the Secretary of State for his attention.

CHAPTER VII

THE CONTRAST BETWEEN THE TWO STORIES

Let me now try to state the outstanding points of conflict which emerge from a consideration of the rival stories of Hiss and Chambers. They are, I think, five in number, as follows:

(1) The original introduction when Chambers first met Hiss.
(2) The occasion when Hiss volunteered to turn over secret documents belonging to the Nye Committee.
(3) The meeting in January 1937 when Chambers introduced Hiss to Bykov, at which Hiss, being asked by Bykov to turn over secret documents from the State Department, consented to do so.
(4) The meeting in the middle of 1937 between Chambers and Hiss and Mrs. Hiss, at which Chambers asked Hiss to arrange for the typing out of secret documents and at which Mrs. Hiss agreed to do the typing.
(5) The meeting at Christmas 1938 when Chambers asked Hiss to break with the Communist Party.

The evidence which Hiss gave differed fundamentally from that of Chambers in regard to point (1); and with regard to points (2), (3), (4) and (5) Hiss said that they were all pure inventions. I propose to consider the points in order.

The first point relates to the manner and circumstances of their introduction to each other. Was it made at a meeting between Peters, Ware, Chambers and Hiss? Was Hiss at that time such a disciplined Communist that he could be ordered to move from one apparatus (that under the control of Ware) to another apparatus (that to be under the control of Chambers)? Was Chambers introduced simply as Carl—which would be appropriate, it would appear, amongst Communists? Or was it the fact that Chambers had introduced himself to Hiss as George Crosley, a free-lance journalist who was interested in the affairs of the Nye Committee?

If we could give a certain answer to these questions, we should have gone a long way towards solving the problems in this case; but Ware was killed in a road accident in 1935 and Peters was not called at the trial, and if he had been—judging from his behaviour before the House Committee—he would have declined to testify. So it remains, and must remain, a conflict between the evidence of Chambers and that of Hiss; and to the solution of that conflict I can only offer these considerations.

First, that there is strong reason to believe—in spite of the fact that Chambers said he could not remember—that Chambers, during his association with Hiss, did in fact pass himself off as George Crosley and not merely as Carl. I set out the reasons which lead me to that conclusion in Chapter XVIII, entitled "What's in a Name?"

Secondly, there is the fact that when he was before the House Committee Chambers said that Hiss was not in fact transferred to his apparatus until 1936, and if that be right, it is unlikely that the order for his transfer would have been made in June 1934. I quote the following passage from the House Committee Hearings:

> *Mr. Chambers:* After I had been in Washington a while it was very clear that some of the members of these groups were going places in the Government.
> *Mr. Hébert:* What year is this?
> *Mr. Chambers:* I should think about 1936. One of them

clearly was Alger Hiss, and it was believed that Henry Collins also might go farther. Another was Lee Pressman. So it was decided by Peters, or by Peters in conference with people whom I don't know, that we would take these people out of that apparatus and separate them from it physically—that is, they would have no further intercourse with the people there —but they would be connected still with that apparatus and with Peters through me.

It will be observed that according to this statement of Chambers he had been in Washington "a while" when Hiss was transferred to his apparatus; it is entirely inconsistent with his later evidence at the trial that Hiss was told he was to be transferred the first time he and Chambers met, just after the latter came to Washington, when Peters and Ware were present.

Thirdly, there is the broad question of whether Alger Hiss was a member of the Communist Party in 1934. Chambers, of course, knew that all Communist members must pay dues, and when before the House Committee he asserted that both Alger Hiss and his brother Donald had paid their dues—which he (Chambers) had in fact collected. At the trial no attempt was made to prove the payment of dues; and it is clear that any such case—at least against Donald Hiss—would completely have broken down. I shall deal with this in greater detail in Chapter XXIII, "Of Donald Hiss."

The second main point of controversy which arises in the rival stories is that relating to the Nye Committee documents. Did Hiss volunteer—for if Chambers was telling the truth no persuasion was needed—to deliver to Chambers "secret documents" relating to this committee? I set out the entire evidence on this topic in Chapter XXII, entitled "The First Alleged Act of Treachery."

I think that there are strong grounds for concluding that the documents delivered to Chambers were not secret at all, but were just those documents which would have been delivered to any journalist who was sufficiently interested to ask for them; and if this is so, all the elaborate story of photographing these documents in the Hisses' house on P Street falls to the ground.

The third point of controversy relates to the occasion in

January 1937 when Chambers took Hiss to meet Colonel Bykov; and Bykov, speaking in German which was interpreted by Chambers, asked Hiss to turn over documents which were undoubtedly secret. Hiss, said Chambers, without a moment's hesitation consented to do so. Colonel Bykov was not called at the trial. This mysterious person had no doubt gone back to Russia. I call him mysterious because Chambers said he had two arms, and Wadleigh—a man to whom the reader will presently be introduced, who did deliver secret documents from the State Department to Chambers—said he had only one arm.

Hiss said he had never met Bykov and had never even heard of him, so again we have a straight conflict between the evidence of Chambers and that of Hiss.

The date "January 1937" which Chambers assigned to this meeting is significant, for according to Chambers it took place just after Chambers, on the instructions of Bykov, had presented a rug to Hiss, which was obviously intended as a "sweetener." Chambers was tied to early January 1937, as we shall see when we come to consider the whole question of the gift of the rug, though there are grounds for thinking that it may have been given some time earlier.

Chambers, in his evidence in Baltimore on the 17th November 1948, which was recalled to him at the trial, had given this evidence:

> Some time in 1937, I think about the middle of the year, J. Peters introduced me to a Russian who identified himself under the pseudonym Peter, I presume for the purposes of confusion between his name and J. Peters. I subsequently learned from Mr. Krivitsky that the Russian Peter was one Colonel Bykov.

He had continued on the same occasion:

> I should think in August or the early fall of 1937 I arranged a meeting between Alger Hiss and Colonel Bykov. For that purpose Mr. Hiss came to New York, where I met him.

It is self-evident that Chambers could not have introduced Hiss to Bykov before he (Chambers) had himself met Bykov, and that was "about the middle of the year 1937"; and, indeed, Chambers himself put the date of the meeting as "August 1937." But the acceptance of any such date completely destroys the chronology of Chambers, according to which Hiss delivered secret documents for about six months, and thereafter came the request to go one better and get the documents typed out; and the origin of the delivering of secret documents was the meeting with Bykov.

The fourth point of controversy was the meeting "in the middle of 1937" when, according to Chambers, it was arranged that the documents which Hiss had brought out on the nights when Chambers did not call should be typed out. This rests, and must rest, upon the evidence of Chambers on the one side and that of the Hisses on the other. If it be the fact that Mrs. Hiss was so anxious to undertake this work, she must indeed have been an enthusiastic Communist. I find it strange in this connection that Chambers, in his statement to Mr. Berle in 1939, should have described Alger and Donald Hiss as Communists but Mrs. Alger Hiss as a mere Socialist. It is strange, too, that the promise to undertake this work should have been given without time for consideration; for, after all, it was a dangerous game, and incidentally no one knew its dangers better than Chambers. Would it not have been possible for the Communists to arrange to have the documents photographed in Washington? We read in *Witness* that the Communists had established a permanent photographic workshop in Washington as well as the one in Baltimore. Was the laborious work of typing them out really necessary?

The fifth point of controversy relates to the meeting between Chambers, Hiss and Mrs. Hiss when Chambers asked Hiss to break with the Party. We should go far towards solving the problem this case presents if we knew for certain on whose side the truth lay in this matter.

Chambers did not mention this visit to Mr. Berle in 1939, although he could quite well have done so without revealing the existence of documents. In his conversation with Mr. Ray Murphy on the 20th March 1945, the matter is mentioned (after a reference to Ware, Pressman and Hiss set out "in the order of their importance") as follows:

The informant dealt with these people from 1934 to 1937, when he broke with the Party and attempted to persuade various of these contacts to break also. He remembers various conversations with Alger Hiss in the early part of 1938 during which Hiss was adamant against the plan of breaking with the Party.

In his later conversation with Mr. Ray Murphy on the 28th August 1946, I find the following passage:

> My informant asked Alger Hiss personally to break with the Party in early 1938, but Hiss refused with tears in his eyes and said he would remain loyal to the Party.

In both these conversations it will be noticed that Chambers dated this interview with Hiss "early 1938."

Before the House Committee Chambers was asked, "When you left the Communist Party in 1937, did you approach any of these seven to break with you?" Chambers answered as follows:

> The only one I approached was Alger Hiss. I went to the Hiss home one evening at what I considered considerable risk to myself and found Mrs. Hiss at home. Mrs. Alger Hiss is also a member of the Communist Party. She attempted while I was there to make a call which I can only presume was to other Communists, but I quickly went to the telephone and she hung up, and Mr. Hiss came in shortly afterward, and we talked and I tried to break him away from the Party. As a matter of fact, he cried when we separated; when I left him, but he absolutely refused to break.

Chambers did not explain these conflicting stories. The rolling-pin incident fixes the interview at Christmas time. How, then, did he come to say it was "early in 1938"? His evidence to the House Committee had no date assigned to it, though it was given in answer to a question beginning, "When you left the Communist Party in 1937." It seems odd that he should have feared assassination from such a "gentle character" as he described Hiss to be; and I wish he had been asked at the trial to enlarge on the telephone incident which he had related to the House Committee.

If Hiss had, in fact, been delivering documents in the first few months of 1938, he would surely have asked for some reassurance about these documents; for it was vital to him that their existence should never be discovered; and he must by now have realised to his horror that he had given these incriminating documents to Chambers only just before the latter had broken.

The strength of the case against Hiss did not, I feel sure, rest primarily on the evidence of Chambers. I have said enough to show that any jury would have been most unlikely to place reliance on testimony given by Chambers, save where it was corroborated—and, indeed, the law requires such corroboration. The strength of the case against Hiss rests primarily on the documents, and to a far lesser extent on the evidence of the association between Hiss and Chambers, which is supported by the transactions of the cars and the rug. I shall deal with these matters in Chapters IX and X.

I have considered in this chapter what, in my opinion, are the major points of conflict in the two stories. It is of course true that there were a large number of minor points on which acute controversy arose. Among these was the date of the visit which the Chambers family paid to the Hisses in their P Street house. The Hisses said that this visit took place immediately before the Chambers moved into the 28th Street apartment, whereas the Chambers maintained that it happened after they had had a holiday lasting some two months at Smithton, and therefore not until the fall of that year, 1935.

There were also minor controversies about other visits which the two families paid to each other, in particular whether or not Mrs. Hiss stayed with the Chambers at Smithton. I shall try to deal with these points in my succeeding chapters.

CHAPTER VIII

OF MRS. CHAMBERS AND MRS. HISS

It has happened in the past in the history of the law that a wife, loyally determined to support her husband, has wandered from the narrow path of absolute truth. It may be the fact—I strongly suspect it is—that both these ladies, in the cause of that loyal support, occasionally so wandered. I must give a short sketch of the two wives and deal with their evidence in so far as it is not already covered under particular topics.

First of Mrs. Chambers. In her early days she had worked with the Young People's Socialist League and was chosen by them to go to the Rand School. She then joined a Communist Front organisation and became secretary to a union for garment workers. There was a strike, and she went over to "stir up trouble." There she met her husband, who was engaged in the like pursuit. She had never been, so she said, a member of the Communist Party, but she had been in sympathy with its views and had been a convinced atheist. Chambers, in his book, describes her at that time as relentlessly dedicated to the revolution, and adds that her lack of practical experience was equalled only by her lack of humour and her implacable ferocity.

Chambers in *Witness* describes the manner of their courtship; and, like most other things in his story, it was certainly not lacking in drama. When he called at her house one evening, his future wife, then Miss Shemitz, refused to open the door. He beat on it with his fists, but she replied, "Go away. The Party says I cannot see you. We can never meet again." (This was a hard ruling from the Party, of which, be it remembered, she was not a member.)

But the young man was angry. His blood was up. In the early dawn he went back to her house and discovered that opposite her bedroom window, high up above a flagged court, was a landing; and swinging himself from the rail of that landing, he reached her window ledge and, pushing up the window, climbed in. He states with becoming modesty that no ordinary man could have accomplished such a gymnastic feat.

Sitting beside her bed, he explained that she must make a choice. This, said he, was not any question concerning politics. It was for her, nevertheless, a choice between life and death. So she chose life. They were married in 1931, and in the words of the fairy story (a quotation from such a source seems not inappropriate) "they lived happily ever after." This is not surprising, for she appears to have had one simple guiding principle: her husband was a great and good man and whatever he did was right. When he was an irreconcilable Communist, he was right; when he became a fanatical anti-Communist, he was still right. As to the varying names they employed—Breen or Dwyer or Cantwell—Mr. Murphy, as was his wont, summed it up wittily in the following question: "If he told you that, starting tomorrow, we are going to Ypsilanti and your name was Hogan?" To which Mrs. Chambers replied: "We would go to Ypsilanti and we would be Hogans." It is perhaps hardly necessary after this to say that she corroborated her husband's testimony about visits—but about documents she knew nothing.

Once during the six or eight weeks when they were living at the Hisses' 28th Street apartment Mrs. Hiss came to lunch with Mrs. Chambers. (It was the occasion when the maid Julia Rankin was present, to which I shall refer later in dealing with the problem of the name.) It is noticeable that it was not apparently suggested that Alger Hiss ever went round to visit the

Chambers during the time they spent in his apartment; and this was the only visit which Mrs. Hiss was said to have paid. Mrs. Chambers spoke of visits which she said the Hisses had paid to her various houses in Baltimore, and of the visits she and Chambers had paid to the houses which the Hisses occupied in Washington.

Two of these latter visits call for notice, because they were said to have been made to the house in Volta Place. The Hisses did not get possession of this house until the end of December 1937; and if, therefore, the Chambers did visit them there, it would follow that the acquaintanceship had not by that time finally come to an end. Mrs. Chambers said that she and her husband attended a housewarming party with the Hisses just after they had moved in; and she remembered a later visit at which Alger Hiss was present in evening dress with a swallow-tail coat, though she could not remember why he was wearing formal clothes. She mentioned this incident for the first time at the second trial; she had, she said, forgotten all about it at the first trial. She recalled, too, a visit the Hisses paid to herself and Chambers in Baltimore at about the same time. It was the Hisses' wedding anniversary, and they brought some drink with them which she said made her sick.

She spoke of the various drives they had taken together. One was to see the autumn colouring, and others were to Haines Point, Mount Vernon, and Normandie Farms. Generally, she testified to a frequent association between herself and Mrs. Hiss, and less frequently with Alger Hiss. But her evidence at the second trial differed considerably from what she had said at Baltimore, and she was quite uncertain about dates and places.

She was asked about the loan of $400 in November 1937 which enabled her to buy the car. She admitted that she had said in her Baltimore examination that she thought this had come from Mrs. Chambers, her mother-in-law, but said simply that the money had been handed to her by her husband.

Mrs. Chambers also described a conversation in the house the Chambers had occupied in Eutaw Place, Baltimore, from about September 1935 to April 1936. Priscilla Hiss, she said, wanted to take a course in nursing at the Mercy Hospital in Baltimore and discussed the project with the Chambers and Alger Hiss. She dealt with the occasion about which her maid Edith Murray later testified—a matter of some importance—because Edith Murray was the one witness, other than the Chambers, who ever saw the Hisses and the Chambers together. Mrs. Chambers said that the reason for this visit was that Mrs. Hiss came to look after the baby while she (Mrs. Chambers) went for pre-natal care before the birth of her second child. She felt sure, she said, that Mrs. Hiss stayed the night, though she admitted she had previously testified that Mrs. Hiss had gone back to Washington the same day.

She described the events of their life after Chambers had left the Communist Party, and spoke particularly of the precautions they took against assassination.

She used to sleep with an axe under her bed, and so history repeated itself, for this somewhat unusual precaution was exactly that which her mother-in-law, Mrs. Chambers, had taken when Whittaker was a small boy.

I do not think it necessary to deal at greater length with Mrs. Chambers' evidence, which in all accounts for some 120 pages of transcript—this seems to me to be an overgenerous allowance.

Priscilla Hiss was born in 1903 and was therefore a year older than her husband. Her father, whose name was Fansler, had been in the insurance business. He was a Quaker, and his children were all brought up as members of that community. She had several brothers, one of whom, Thomas Fansler, was a witness in the case. She was educated at St. David's, Pennsylvania, and later at Bryn Mawr. Much later in her life, during the year 1936–37, she became President of the Bryn Mawr Alumnae Association of Washington, D.C.; and the report of her year's presidency, which she had typed on the old typewriter which had been given her by her father, was one of the documents used to establish the identity of the typewriter.

At Bryn Mawr she studied English literature and philosophy, and then, winning a scholarship to Yale, she did a year's further work there in English literature. She then took a job on the magazine *Time*, being placed in charge of the office staff and acting as assistant to the editor. Afterwards she went to Columbia University, where she obtained an M.A. degree.

In the meantime, she married one Thayer Hobson, and in September 1926 her son Timmy Hobson, the only child of that marriage, was born. She was divorced in January 1929 by her husband Hobson, but was allowed to retain the custody of the child, who was at that time under three years old. Thayer Hobson contributed for many years towards his education and maintenance. In December 1929 she married Alger Hiss, who was then serving as law clerk to Mr. Justice Holmes. They had no honeymoon. By 1933 they had become established in Washington, D.C.; and there they remained—though they frequently changed houses—until 1947.

Throughout her married life Mrs. Hiss continued from time to time to be engaged in outside occupations. She had some job with the Wickersham Commission; she worked in the Library of Congress; she wrote a book, in collaboration with her sister-in-law, Mrs. Thomas Fansler, dealing with research in fine arts; and she used to teach in various schools, including the Bryn Mawr summer school. I think the fact that she became President of the Bryn Mawr Alumnae Club and went back to teach there shows that she was highly thought of by the authorities of that establishment. She was obviously very highly educated and, I should judge, a very intelligent woman. As to her ability to use a typewriter, there was some discussion. There was no doubt that whilst at Columbia she had passed a test in typing, but she was by no means an expert; for example, she said that she could not type without looking at the keys and did not use all her fingers. But she admitted that she knew how to type and that she did in fact use a typewriter.

In the early days of her married life to Hiss—before he entered the Government service—she admitted that she had contributed, in the winter of 1931–32, towards the expenses of a feeding station run by the Socialist Party in New York to help the unemployed, and she admitted that at that time she had attended Socialist meetings in New York. She was asked about the way she had voted at the presidential elections, and she said that in 1932 she had voted for Norman Thomas, the Socialist candidate. She was cross-examined about this and said that she was not a registered member of the Socialist Party and could not account for the fact that she was so registered by the Board of Elections.

She was asked in cross-examination whether her brother Thomas Fansler was registered as a Socialist, and replied that she did not know; a document was then produced in his handwriting, which she identified, which showed that in 1932 he had been a member.

I think this cross-examination was unduly wide. The issue in the case was whether Hiss, "in or about February or March 1938," handed over secret papers to Chambers. Here we have a witness—not Hiss himself but his wife—being asked questions about the way she voted at a time long before she or her husband ever met Chambers; and then we find her being asked how her brother voted at that time. Finally we find evidence being called in rebuttal to prove that she was registered as a member of the Socialist Party, thereby providing material on which the jury might well have come to the conclusion that when she said she was not a registered member of the party in the year 1931–32 she was not speaking the truth. Any counsel who attempted to adduce any of this evidence in England would receive short shrift from the judge.

The evidence, which was admitted without objection, certainly shows that in those early years she had sympathy with the Socialist Party; and as it was in the early days of her married life, it is not unreasonable to assume that her husband shared her views. It may well be the fact that both she and Alger Hiss retained those sympathies during his later period of Government service, and if so, it would not be surprising if, in the course of conversation, Chambers had guessed broadly where their sympathies lay. To a man like Chambers, who admits that he saw no substantial difference between Liberals, Socialists, and New Dealers on the one hand and Communists on the other, this may have been proof "as strong as Holy Writ" that Hiss was a Communist.

I must, however, return to Mrs. Hiss. A letter was produced, which she admitted she had written to the Mercy Hospital with regard to taking a course in nursing. It will be remembered that Mrs. Chambers had spoken of a conversation about this topic, which she said took place at the house in Eutaw Place, Baltimore, which she and her husband occupied between September 1935 and April 1936. Mrs. Hiss's letter was dated May 1937, and she said she did not know how Mrs. Chambers knew anything about the idea. She could not remember having met her since about 1935.

For the rest, Mrs. Hiss supported her husband's evidence. She denied ever having visited the Boucot cottage. She denied the alleged trip to Peterborough in August 1937 to see *She Stoops to Conquer*, and said that she was with the children at the time at their holiday camp. She stated that she had known the Chambers as "Mr. and Mrs. George Crosley." She said that she had never visited any house which they occupied. She could not recall ever having seen Mrs. Chambers after their visit to the P Street house; although she said she had met Chambers four or five times during the winter and spring of 1935–36.

She remembered the incident in the spring of 1936 when Crosley came round with the rug—that was when they were still living in the house on P Street—and she remembered putting it in Timmy's playroom there. They left that house in June 1936. She was not challenged about the rug in cross-examination. She recalled her impression of Crosley—a short, somewhat round person who laughed a great deal. She described the circumstances of the withdrawal of the $400 in November 1937, and mentioned some of the articles she had bought in anticipation of the move to Volta Place. There can be no doubt that this house was a good deal larger than the houses the Hisses had previously occupied.

She was cross-examined with regard to inaccuracies in previous statements she had made. She had said that she thought her former coloured servant, Clidi Catlett, was dead, and that she thought she had given the typewriter away to the Salvation Army. It was fortunate for her that Clidi Catlett was still alive, for she gave evidence for the Defence—and I cannot conceive any possible reason for deliberately stating that she was dead, unless Mrs. Hiss believed this to be the fact. As to the typewriter, Mrs. Hiss explained that she had got confused between two typewriters. It was the fact that one had been given to the Salvation Army. Anyone trying to recount the events of ten or twelve years ago might fall into these sorts of errors.

Such, then, was the evidence of the wives of the two protagonists. But before I finally leave this part of the case I must deal with one other topic upon which a great deal of time was expended. Both Chambers and Mrs. Chambers were asked to describe the various houses at which the Hisses had lived in Washington. After leaving the P Street house, at which it will be remembered that the Chambers spent two or three days, the Hisses moved to a house on 30th Street, where they undoubtedly lived from July 1936 to December 1937. They then moved to a house in Volta Place. If either Chambers or his wife could describe the 30th Street house or the house in Volta Place, it was reasonable to infer that they had paid a visit to the house they so described; equally, their evidence about having visited a house would have been badly shaken if they had been quite unable to describe it. Both Chambers and his wife described these two houses, and both Hiss and his wife said that their descriptions were quite inaccurate.

It seems to me that there is no inherent improbability in either Chambers or his wife having been in the house at 30th Street, though it is the fact that the Hisses remembered no such visit. Their recollection may have been at fault, as was the recollection of Chambers: for Chambers had previously stated that he spent a night at the 30th Street house, but on finding out that there were only two bedrooms in that house, one of which was occupied by the Hisses and the other by Timmy Hobson, Chambers realised that he must have made a mistake and withdrew his earlier statement. It is certain, moreover, that in July 1936, the month in which the Hisses moved into the 30th Street house, there was still some association between Hiss and Chambers. It will be found, for example, that in this very month Hiss finally transferred his ownership of the Ford car. But the Chambers could not have visited the Hisses at the Volta Place house—to which they moved in December 1937—if, as Hiss asserted, his association with Chambers had stopped long before that date.

The story which Chambers told involved his having gone round to the house in Volta Place on many occasions to collect the incriminating documents during the first three months of 1938. In order to sustain such a story—whether it was true, or still more if it was false—he must have prepared himself to describe what this house looked like. And if it was the fact that he was prepared to tell an untrue story about calling round to collect documents, he would surely not have scrupled to describe the house if he could get the material together on which to do so. I cannot believe that he would have had much difficulty in getting this material had he wanted to do so. A call at the house under some pretext or other when the Hisses were not at home—or a few questions addressed to Clidi Catlett—might have yielded him some information. Moreover, he worked with the Federal Bureau of Investigation day in and day out for some three months, and with them interviewed Clidi Catlett; he admitted that he asked her questions about the interior of the house. The F.B.I. had themselves called on at least one friend of the Hisses and had questioned her about the houses. They had interviewed the builder who had done work on the Volta Place house, and had actually obtained plans.

I cannot say whether the descriptions which Chambers and his wife gave of either the 30th Street house or of the house in Volta Place were tolerably accurate. I know that I myself should find it quite impossible to describe a house which I had visited on a few occasions some ten years before. It seems to me, in any case, that descriptions of these houses cannot make much difference in solving the problems of the case.

CHAPTER IX

OF THE SUBLETTING OF HISS'S APARTMENT TO CHAMBERS, OF THE GIVING AND RECEIPT OF THE RUG, OF THE ALLEGED LOAN OF $400, AND OF THE HISTORY OF THE AUTOMOBILES

The events which I have indicated in the heading of this chapter occupied the larger part of the proceedings at the trial. None of them, of course, directly bears on the question whether Hiss did, in or about February and March 1938, turn over secret documents to Chambers. At the same time they had an indirect bearing on the case, for they might throw light on the credibility of Chambers and Hiss respectively. Moreover, they might have led the jury to suppose that the association between Chambers and Hiss was far more intimate and continued over a longer time than Hiss was prepared to admit.

If the jury thought that such association was really intimate over a long period of time, they might have drawn the inference that Hiss must have known that Chambers was a Communist agent, and therefore that Hiss was a Communist sympathiser. This conclusion in its turn might have led them to suppose that the story of Hiss handing over documents was less incredible than it would otherwise appear.

The heading of this chapter, therefore, indicates matters

which the jury were entitled to bear in mind in deciding whether to accept or reject the positive evidence that Hiss had turned over documents. Of course the facts with which I am dealing in this chapter must not be considered in isolation. An act of kindness which would be readily performed by one type of character would be almost inexplicable in the case of a man of a different character, and Hiss—according to Chambers—was a kind man.

In about April 1935, after Chambers had been some months in Washington, Hiss was on the point of moving into a furnished house on P Street, which would leave the 28th Street apartment empty on his hands. Hiss asserted—and I should imagine with good reason—that it was so unlikely that he could sublet his 28th Street apartment for some two months at that time of the year that he had made no effort to do so, and indeed his instructions to have his electric light disconnected as from the 1st May 1935 demonstrate that he did not anticipate letting his apartment. These instructions, in view of what happened, must have been countermanded shortly afterwards, though the date of the countermand is not precisely fixed. The supply was finally cut off on the 29th June 1935. That Hiss allowed Chambers, whom Hiss said he knew, to occupy his apartment on 28th Street is an undoubted fact, and it is certain that Chambers was in residence at that apartment with his wife and child for some weeks during the continuance of the Hisses' lease. Chambers, in his book *Witness*, deals with this matter. He says there was no question of his renting or leasing the apartment, and "if I offered to pay rent for it, as I must certainly have done," Hiss refused to accept any money. It would appear that after reflection Chambers is not able to remember whether he did or did not offer to pay rent; at any rate, it seems clear that Hiss had nothing to lose by letting Chambers occupy his apartment, save possibly the added cost of the utilities. If Hiss's story is true, he had something to gain, for if Chambers had sold his articles he might have been in a position to reimburse the cost of the apartment.

There was sharp controversy as to the terms upon which Chambers was let into occupation. It was obviously an arrangement of a most informal character, and Hiss said that he let the premises to Chambers on the understanding that Chambers would pay the basic rent. Nothing was said about the utilities. Hiss left the bulk of the furniture behind him, and as he was moving into a house which was already partly furnished, it is obvious that he might have been glad of the opportunity of, in effect, storing part of his furniture for a short time. It was alleged by Hiss that when the time came for Chambers to move into the 28th Street apartment there was some hitch, as a result of which Chambers, his wife and child stayed with Hiss at his P Street house for two or three days. Indeed, it was admitted that Chambers and his family had stayed for some short time with the Hiss family at their P Street house, though there was controversy as to the precise date at which this happened.

This fact, that at some time or other Chambers and his family stayed with Hiss and his family, is amply sufficient to account for the fact that Chambers had acquired considerable knowledge of the intimate details of the Hiss family life. He would naturally get to know, for example, that she addressed him as "Hilly" and that he called her "Pros." Chambers must have seen that Hiss was interested in bird life and that his hobby was bird-watching, for the Hiss house was in part decorated with pictures of rare birds. He would almost certainly have heard that Hiss had been fortunate enough to see a rare and beautiful bird known as a prothonotary warbler. He would have discovered about the spaniel. I am amazed to observe that the fact that Chambers had this knowledge and was able to recall it was in some way regarded as a proof of his story. Once it was admitted, and everyone did admit it, that there had been this visit (the only matter in controversy was the precise date of the visit), all these things are easily accounted for and lose any significance as supporting one story against the other.

It must have been obvious to Hiss at this time that Chambers was passing through a difficult financial time. This is not at all an uncommon experience for journalists, whether free-lance or attached to a paper. It must equally have been obvious that Chambers was a very intelligent man, and there must have been a good prospect that any articles which he wrote would sooner or later find an appreciative public. Hiss said that Chambers contemplated a series of articles dealing with the activities of the Nye Committee, who were incidentally very anxious to get all the publicity they could. If in due course the articles had been produced, there was obviously a very fair chance that Chambers would have been in a financial position to honour his obligations. In fact, the articles never were written and the rent never was paid. According to Hiss, Chambers was always hoping that the articles would appear, and Hiss admits that he did not dun Chambers for the rent—and, indeed, it would have done precious little good if he had.

At some later date, however, the precise date being a matter of controversy, Chambers did undoubtedly give Hiss a rug, the value of which was about $200. Hiss regarded this, as he said in evidence, as being the equivalent of a part payment, and if it can be so regarded there can be no doubt that Chambers had made a substantial return for the accommodation with which Hiss had provided him.

Not only did Hiss provide Chambers with this accommodation, but there were also certain transactions between them about an automobile which gave rise to sharp controversy. I had better set out here an extract from the evidence which Hiss gave before the House Committee. He was asked the following questions:

Mr. Stripling: What kind of automobile did Chambers have?
Mr. Hiss: No kind of automobile. I sold him an automobile. I had an old Ford that I threw in with the apartment and had been trying to trade it in and get rid of it. I had an old, old Ford we had kept for sentimental reasons. We got it just before we were married in 1929.
Mr. Stripling: Was it a Model A or Model T?
Mr. Hiss: Early A model with a trunk on the back, a slightly collegiate model.
Mr. Stripling: What color?
Mr. Hiss: Dark blue. It wasn't very fancy, but it had a sassy little trunk on the back.
Mr. Nixon: You sold that car?
Mr. Hiss: I threw it in. He wanted a way to get around, and I said, "Fine, I want to get rid of it. I have another car and we kept it for sentimental reasons, not worth a damn." I let him have it along with the rent.

There is no doubt that the recollection of Hiss was in some respects wrong. For he did, in fact, not purchase another car until the month of September 1935, when he bought a Plymouth sedan. He could not, therefore, have said in conversation before Chambers moved into 28th Street—and he did not move in until early May 1935—"I have another car." On the other hand, I doubt if there are many people who, if asked without any warning in August 1948 what happened about the disposal of a car in 1935, could give any clear answer. It is not disputed that Hiss allowed Chambers to have the use of the car. But it is a fact that it did not legally pass out of the possession of Hiss until July 1936, more than a year after Chambers had left the 28th Street apartment.

The circumstances of its disposal to the Cherner Motor Company reveal a remarkable state of affairs. The Cherner Motor Company is a responsible trading organisation in Washington. In July 1936 Hiss signed a document transferring his old Ford, which had very little value, approximately $25 according to his own evidence, to the Cherner Motor Company. He had his signature witnessed by a Mr. Marvin Smith, who was a notary and at that time was working with Hiss in the Department of Justice. The document did not pass through the ordinary books of the Cherner Motor Company. It would seem that they had some Communist servant who took it upon himself to transfer the car directly to one William Rosen. Rosen was called at the trial but declined to testify on the ground that he might incriminate himself. All he would say was that he did not know Hiss and had never met him. Now, of course, this transaction, if Hiss was responsible for it, would be enough to stamp him as an avowed Communist. If, on the other hand, the details were fixed up by Chambers, any such conclusion would be unfair. Hiss stated that he regarded himself as being committed to give the car to Chambers. He had got the Plymouth in September 1935. He had no need for two cars. They were sitting around on the streets of Washington, and the old Ford was a responsibility and of no use to him. If it be a fact that Chambers suggested that Hiss should transfer the car to the Cherner Motor Company, Chambers could quite easily have done the rest. He could have seen that the documents did not go directly through the company's books and that the car was transferred to William Rosen. If Chambers had wanted for any reason to build up a case against Hiss and to demonstrate his Communist affiliations, he must have welcomed this simple opportunity. I cannot help feeling it odd that Hiss, if he was engaged in a discreditable transaction with a Communist, should have selected as his notary a well-known figure in the Justice Department.

That is how the matter rests, and the whole incident may well have affected the jury's mind adversely to the case of Hiss. He had been proved wrong in his original recollection. He had not transferred the car until long after Chambers left his apartment, and when he did transfer it, it got into the hands of this man Rosen, who claimed privilege from answering questions.

It is interesting to note that in his recently published book *Witness* Chambers says that either Peters gave the address of the Cherner Motor Company to Hiss or "he [Peters] gave me the address which I passed on unread to Alger." He there says that he was present when Hiss drove the car away and when he came back after having turned it over. Chambers adds that he would have been "shocked" had he realised that Hiss had got Mr. Marvin Smith[1] to notarise the transfer.

But the story of the automobiles does not rest only on the history of the old Ford. We must now turn to consider the history of the cars which Chambers owned. There is no doubt that on the 23rd November 1937 Chambers bought a new de-luxe Ford four-door sedan from the Schmidt Motor Company. He bought it in the name of his wife. He traded in his old car, which was a 1934 Ford sedan, for $325 and paid $486.75 in cash.

What was the history of this old car which Chambers traded in? It proved impossible at the trial to establish this in any sort of detail. Chambers was quite vague and uncertain about the whole affair. He said he had bought it either in 1935 or 1936; he thought it was in the summertime. He could not remember the name of the firm from whom he had bought it; the nearest he could go was that he thought it was purchased in New York. He did not know how much he had given for it, but he did know that the money had been provided by J. Peters, who was head of

[1]Later Mr. Smith committed suicide for reasons which Chambers states in *Witness* to have been, according to his information, "purely personal."

the Communist underground movement. One might have hoped that with the unlimited opportunities for reflection, and the aid of the F.B.I., who left no stone unturned in their search for documents relating to all the cars, Chambers would have been able to reveal more facts about the purchase of this Ford. But, alas, this was not so, and in his book *Witness*, running into 800 pages, there is nothing to throw any light on the mystery of the purchase of this car which he turned in on the 23rd November 1937. If we assume that Chambers was a witness of truth, honouring his oath to reveal all the relevant facts, here indeed is proof how difficult it is to remember details about the purchase of a car which had taken place more than ten years ago. But whatever may have been the circumstances, there is no suggestion that Chambers ever informed Hiss that he had a car of his own, and it would be odd that he should have borrowed the old Ford belonging to Hiss if at that time he had had one of his own.

Far more important, however, than the turning in of the old car which was of such mysterious origin was the payment by Chambers of the sum of $486. From what source had he obtained this money? All through the hearing before the House Committee no suggestion was made indicating that Hiss was in any way responsible for providing this money or any part of it. It was only at a later date that Chambers alleged that $400 was provided by Hiss as a loan for the express purpose of enabling him to buy the car. Hiss had a banking account with the Riggs National Bank in the name of himself and his wife, and it is an undoubted fact that on the 19th November 1937, only a few days before Chambers had purchased his car, Mrs. Hiss withdrew $400, thereby leaving only a very few dollars in the account. This fact, unless explained, obviously tends to corroborate the story of Chambers that Hiss had lent him $400, and if this is in fact true, it goes a long way to show that there must still, as late as November 1937, have been a very close association between the two men. Mr. Murphy, Counsel for the Prosecution, was at pains to point out that when Chambers, during the first trial, asserted that Hiss had lent him $400, he could have had no access to Hiss's passbook. This may well be true, but it is possible that Chambers could have got the information as to the withdrawal of the $400 from the F.B.I. The passbook is the document kept by the customer of the bank; the bank also keeps accounts. The F.B.I., in the course of their investigations, had obtained access to the books of the bank by February 1949, and at this very time Chambers was in daily association with the F.B.I. If, as Mr. Cross suggested, they had revealed to Chambers that Hiss had withdrawn $400 only four days before Chambers purchased his new car, the significance which Mr. Murphy sought to attach to the fact that Chambers had not seen Hiss's passbook seems to me to disappear altogether.

In *Witness*, Chambers says that after Hiss had offered to lend him $400 towards the purchase of a car he went to Bykov to obtain his consent to the acceptance of the loan. He used this offer, so he says, in his "campaign with Bykov." This, if it be true, reveals an extraordinary state of affairs. Chambers, be it remembered, desired to purchase a car as one of his preparations for leaving the Communist Party. He thought it necessary to acquire "mobility," so that he might perfect his break. He was, of course, according to his account, representing the matter in a very different light to Hiss. But why on earth should he need Bykov's consent before he accepted a loan from Hiss with which he intended to buy a car to enable him to leave the Party? Why, indeed, should he start a campaign with Bykov at all at a time when he regarded himself as a deserter from the Communist Party? Chambers tells us that his own car, bought with Communist money, was old and ailing and that for purposes of flight it seemed a serious handicap. He says that he had begun a systematic campaign to get Bykov to finance a new one. But even so, if Hiss offered the money to him, it is a mystery to me why Bykov's consent was necessary to its acceptance.

There remains Hiss's explanation of what happened, and this was a matter which the jury might well have taken into their consideration. Hiss said that the money had been withdrawn in anticipation of their move into a house in Volta Place which was larger than any they had previously occupied. The $400 was needed for the purchase of furniture and fittings.

The actual move to the house in Volta Place did not take place until the 29th December 1937, and it was asked with great force by the Prosecution: Was it the least likely that Hiss would have withdrawn $400 on the 19th November 1937, in order to buy furniture and fittings for a house, when it was at that date by no means certain that he would succeed in securing a tenancy of it? Moreover, he had various charge accounts with firms who dealt in furniture and fittings. Would he not in any case have exhausted these charge accounts before withdrawing this money? It is an undoubted fact that the owner of the Volta Place house had not finally agreed to let it to Hiss on the 19th November, the day on which he withdrew the $400. Evidence was allowed to be given in rebuttal, and an advertisement was produced which appeared in the Washington *Post* on Sunday, the 5th December 1937. It read:

> Georgetown, 3415 Volta Place, Northwest. Remodeled six-room house with attic, automatic heat, insulated, walled garden, terrace, sun deck, two stairways, open fireplaces, large living room, open for inspection Sunday from 10 A.M. to 6 P.M.

That advertisement was put in by a Mrs. Tally on behalf of her mother, Mrs. Flanagan, who had recently had a stroke. Mrs. Tally explained the circumstances at the trial. She and her husband had been living with her mother at this Volta Place house, and as Mr. Tally was being transferred from Washington to Philadelphia, they wanted to dispose of the house. They employed two real estate men, one of whom was a Mr. Gilliat. It was not until shortly after the appearance of the advertisement I have just quoted that Mr. Gilliat told Mrs. Tally that he had a client, who turned out to be Mr. Hiss. Mrs. Tally remembered meeting Mrs. Hiss and having a conversation with her about a washing machine and built-in bookshelves. It was not until the 8th December that the first cheque for $100 for the rent was paid. I think it is clear that this was a case in which, owing to the illness of Mrs. Flanagan, which had more or less incapacitated her, the wires had been badly crossed. Mrs. Tally had taken it upon herself as a kind of agent of necessity to act for her mother, but Mr. Gilliat still regarded Mrs. Flanagan as his client. In actual fact, the lease of the premises was signed by Mrs. Flanagan, by Mr. Gilliat and by Alger Hiss on the 2nd December 1937, three days before the advertisement appeared on the 5th December. The conversation about the washing machine and the built-in bookshelves, therefore, undoubtedly took place after the lease had been signed.

If it be a fact that Hiss advanced $400 to Chambers in 1937, it is clear that Hiss was not speaking the truth in saying that his association with Chambers had terminated at about the end of the year 1936. Though it does not prove directly that Hiss turned over documents in or about February or March 1938, it does bear in a most striking manner on the credibility of his evidence. Yet the whole transaction reveals Chambers, if we accept his story, in an unfavourable light. For Chambers said that the purchase of the new car in November 1937 took place at a time when he was contemplating breaking with the Communist Party—he had, he said, at that time seen the error of his ways; he had ceased to be an atheist. Indeed, he stated that the purchase of the car, in order to secure his mobility, was one of the steps taken by him with the express object of effecting his break with the Communist Party. He went to Hiss, according to his own account, telling him that he wanted to buy a car, not to break with the Communist Party but in order more effectively to carry on his work for the Communists; and Hiss, the ardent Communist—as Chambers depicts him—thereupon found $400 of his own money, which he lent to Chambers so as to further the Communist cause. The reader will not be surprised to hear that Chambers never paid back or attempted to pay back any part of this loan. It may be thought that any trick is good enough to beat the Communists, but no man with any active sense of honour could possibly have behaved as Chambers on his own showing did behave about accepting a loan from his friend under these circumstances.

There is one further odd fact which must be stated. Mrs. Chambers, in whose name the purchase of the car was made, had said that her recollection of the source of the $400 was that it was provided by Mrs. Chambers, her husband's mother; the mother was not called at the trial and her bank account was not produced.

It remains to consider the question of the gift of the rug—a rug of substantial value—which Hiss regarded as being in part payment for the use of the apartment and the gift of the old

Ford which had belonged to him. I should myself draw no inference whatever against Hiss from the mere fact that Chambers gave him a rug. After all, Hiss had in all conscience made enough concessions to Chambers to justify some return either in meal or in malt.

A great deal of time and energy was spent in dealing with the question of this rug. Its size, its colour, its pattern—all formed the subject of much discussion and many questions. The one point which was of real importance was left obscure; namely, the date at which the rug was given.

The evidence of Chambers on this is quite clear. He said that on the instructions of Colonel Bykov he had told Professor Schapiro to buy four rugs and had paid for them with money provided by Bykov. He gave Professor Schapiro instructions to send the rug to George Silverman in Washington. Chambers said it was brought in George Silverman's car and transferred from that car to Hiss's car at a restaurant on the Washington–Baltimore road. Chambers had told Hiss that the rug was a present from the Soviet people in recognition of the work of the American Communists. Professor Schapiro stated that he had bought the rugs from the Massachusetts Importing Company at the request of Chambers at the end of 1936, and he produced a cheque for $600, dated the 23rd December 1936, made out to the Massachusetts Importing Company. He also produced a delivery receipt signed by his wife, dated the 29th December 1936. He said that he sent the rugs to Washington shortly after their arrival, addressed to a man named Silverman.

Unless, then, there were two lots of rugs—and this has never been suggested—it cannot have been before the beginning of January 1937 that the rug, if it formed one of those bought through Professor Schapiro, was presented to Hiss.

It is undoubted that Hiss left the P Street house in June 1936. It is obvious, therefore, that if the rug was not given until about the 1st January 1937 it can never have been at the Hisses' house in P Street. Yet Mrs. Hiss clearly remembered that the rug was given when they were still in occupation of the P Street house and described in detail the difficulty in finding a suitable place for it. In her evidence in chief she stated that they put it down in Timmy's playroom on the top floor of the P Street house, that they then had it at the 30th Street house, and that finally it was stored. In cross-examination she was asked these questions:

> You had the rug when you were at P Street?
> *Answer:* Oh yes.
> *Question:* As a matter of fact, you had it for a number of months prior to that?
> *Answer:* That is right.

She further stated in cross-examination that she remembered Chambers coming to visit them in P Street, and remembered in particular the occasion when he came alone, bringing a rug, saying that it was a gift to them and that it had previously been a gift to him. She never seems to have been challenged on the simple point that if it was one of the rugs bought through Professor Schapiro it could not possibly have been at P Street, a house which they had left in June 1936.

Hiss, in his direct examination, testified that he saw Crosley in the spring of 1936 at the P Street house when he brought the rug, saying that it had been given to him and he in turn was making a gift of it to Hiss. In cross-examination long extracts of his evidence before the House Committee and at the first trial were read over to him, in which he stated that it was a rug with an oriental pattern, about 9 by 12, that it had been received by him whilst still at P Street, and that he received only one rug from Chambers. He was reminded of his evidence before the House Committee. Then he was asked this question:

> When you received a rug from Chambers, when you were living at P Street, you say that was considered by you as payment of the rent?
> *Answer:* I think it could be regarded, not payment of the rent, but as payment in kind, part payment.
> *Question:* Did Chambers say to you: "Here is a rug worth so many dollars which I would ask you to consider as payment in kind for the obligation of rent that I owe you"?
> *Answer:* No, he did not. He did not say that he wanted me to consider the rug as payment in kind.

Later on in his evidence he stated that they had the rug in February, March or April of 1936, not very long before they left the P Street house, and he described how they put it down in the playroom on the top floor of the P Street house.

Clidi Catlett, the coloured servant who worked for the Hisses in the P Street house, gave evidence that she well remembered the red rug in the back room there. It was, she said, in Timmy's playroom. She was not challenged in any way in cross-examination.

It seems clear that neither Hiss nor his wife, nor his servant, was ever challenged as to the fact that the rug was in the P Street premises, which Hiss left on the 15th June 1936. Nothing can be more certain than this, that if the rug was in fact in the P Street premises it was not one of those bought by Professor Schapiro, which were only delivered to him on the 29th December 1936. It may well be that it was the practice of Chambers to get rugs provided for him by Communist money and to dispense them as he thought best, and it may be that the rug which Hiss undoubtedly had as a gift from Chambers was one of an earlier consignment. There is, however, no evidence of this. The matter was not pursued by either side, and we are left with the plain impossibility of a rug which was not delivered to Professor Schapiro until December having been in a house which Hiss finally left in June of that same year. I could have wished that one half of the energy which was expended in trying to find out when the Hisses sent the rug to storage, as they did from time to time, had been devoted to clearing up the question of when the rug came. I see no relevance whatever in the question pursued at great length as to the rug being placed in storage, but I do see some relevance in finding the date on which it was given. I see it for these reasons: First, because if the gift of the rug did not take place until January 1937, it is improbable that it could have been regarded as part payment for any obligation for rent which might have been incurred in respect of the months of May and June 1935. Secondly, because if a rug was being given and received in January 1937, it destroys the idea that the relationship between Hiss and Chambers had come to an end in 1936. Thirdly, because if the rug had been given before July 1936, the somewhat dramatic evidence of Chambers relating to the way in which the rug was given must be wrong; for Chambers had said that it was brought up in Silverman's car in January 1937 to a restaurant called the Yacht, that it was there transferred from Silverman's car to the car of Hiss, though Silverman and Hiss did not meet each other, and that he explained it to Hiss by telling him that it was a gift to him from the Soviet people in recognition of the work of the American Communists.

Mr. Murphy, in his closing speech, made some play with the fact that the rug was never produced, and suggested that Hiss dared not show it lest it should be identified as one of those bought by Professor Schapiro. There was, however, nothing to prevent Mr. Murphy from asking to see it, and it would have been impossible for Hiss to refuse to produce it if he had been asked to do so. I cannot see, therefore, that there is any substance in this complaint.

When the jury retired in the second trial they came back to ask Judge Goddard for further directions as to the degree of certainty—or perhaps I should say the absence of doubt—that they must have before arriving at a verdict. I think that the matters which I have dealt with in this chapter may have influenced them in coming to a conclusion adverse to Hiss. For these facts, though not directly relevant, I suspect just tipped the balance.

Let me then briefly summarise them. There was the fact that Hiss allowed Chambers to occupy his apartment for at most the mere cost that Hiss was paying for it, and that Chambers got the free use of the furniture left behind and the benefit of the utility services, for which Hiss continued to pay. Moreover, Chambers was allowed the use of the old car which was finally made over to the Cherner Motor Company and then assigned by some person in their employment to Rosen, a Communist. There was the fact that Hiss, when first asked to recall the circumstances in 1948, was in error in supposing that he had a second car before September 1935.

He must, therefore, have been wrong in saying that he "threw this car in with the apartment." More important still is the fact that Hiss did not part with the legal title to the car until July 1936. He explained that he regarded himself as being committed to give the car to Chambers, and that he therefore gave it, notwithstanding the fact that Chambers had by July 1936 plainly defaulted in his obligation to pay rent.

If Hiss had intended to give the car "to some poor Communist organizer" (as Chambers asserted), he would perhaps not have chosen Mr. Marvin Smith as his notary. Were the Cherner Motor Company suggested by Peters or by Chambers as being suitable nominees? Certain it is that the car was passed on to Rosen, who declined to testify on the ground that he might incriminate himself, although he did state that he had never met Hiss.

There was also the payment of the $486 in cash by Chambers for the purchase of his car on the 23rd November 1937, and the story of the loan of $400, which had been withdrawn by Hiss from his account on the 19th November 1937. There was, finally, the gift of the rug—and if it was not given until January 1937, it was given at a date by which Hiss said his relationship with Chambers had ended.

All these incidents afforded ample scope for cross-examination; and Mr. Murphy, Counsel for the Prosecution, made the most of his opportunities in a searching but quite proper manner.

For myself, I consider that, of all of these incidents, that of the withdrawal of the $400 from the Hisses' account at a time just before Chambers made a part payment of $486 on his new car to be the most significant, more especially because the rival explanation which Hiss gave for this withdrawal was unconvincing.

I have said that I think Mr. Murphy put his case too high in claiming that Chambers could not have known of this withdrawal before testifying at the first trial because he had not seen the passbook.

In his closing speech, Mr. Murphy characterised the point of Mr. Cross that Chambers might have heard of the withdrawal from the F.B.I. as a suggestion "of suborning-perjury sort of evidence." I do not agree; indeed if the F.B.I. decided, as they did, to enlist the help of Chambers to unravel the mystery, they would have been acting sensibly and with perfect propriety in asking him whether he could inform them of any facts which would account for this withdrawal.

The significance lies in the fact of the withdrawal, and not in the question whether or nor Chambers knew about it.

CHAPTER X

OF THE VISITS, TRIPS, ETC.

On the 7th August 1948, when giving evidence before the House Committee, Chambers spoke of the various trips by car which he had taken with Hiss or sometimes with Hiss and Mrs. Hiss. He was then asked whether he had ever stayed overnight on any of these excursions, and he replied that he never had. It is important to remember this answer, which was recalled at the second trial, as it may throw light on the truth of the story which Chambers told about his numerous trips.

I think the first in order of date was a journey which he said he made with Hiss to Erwinna, Pennsylvania. They left Washington on the Saturday before Easter 1935. Erwinna is over 150 miles away, and they spent Saturday night at a tourist home near Center Square, Pennsylvania. Chambers could not remember the name of the house, nor could he identify it. He thought that the proprietor had a Polish name, and he felt sure that they had registered there. He admitted that he could not remember the object of the visit, but he recalled that in Norristown on Easter Sunday they had noticed a policeman carrying an Easter lily. He said that this incident pleased Hiss, though it may be thought strange that such a sight would have delighted the heart of a Communist atheist. Chambers could remember nothing more—he could not, for example, remember where they had meals; indeed, he had forgotten the incident until about a month before the second trial; it was not mentioned in his evidence at the first. Hiss denied the whole story, and it is obvious that it is much too vague to be of any importance in the case.

In the early days of 1935 Chambers said that he went with Hiss to see a farm near Westminster, Maryland. They drove over together in the Ford roadster. It is an undoubted fact that Hiss thought of buying this farm and actually made a down payment to a Mr. Edward Case, the agent for the sale; but ultimately he withdrew from the transaction by a letter written in May 1936. It is another fact that at a much later date, namely in 1937, Chambers himself bought this very farm in his wife's name. It may well be true that Chambers and Hiss did visit this farm together and that it was on the basis of this inspection that Chambers eventually decided to purchase it. This would certainly account for the odd coincidence that one negotiated for its purchase and the other finally bought it. In 1935 Chambers, under his name of Crosley, and Hiss were seeing something of each other, and I see no inherent improbability in the story which Chambers told about this trip, though he may have been in error about the date. Hiss denied that he had ever been with Chambers to see the farm. He said that he first became interested in it in November 1935, as a result of seeing an advertisement in a Baltimore paper. He then went to see the place, made a deposit, and signed a contract to buy it. If this is right, Chambers must, I think, be wrong in describing the visit as "in the early days of 1935."

Mr. Murphy placed some reliance on these facts in his closing speech and found corroboration for Chambers' story in the identity of the farm. I think it fair to assume either that Hiss told Chambers in or after November 1935 that he was contemplating buying this farm or that Chambers went with Hiss to inspect it at about this time. If either of these assumptions is made, I cannot see any significance in the fact that Chambers purchased a farm for which Hiss had formerly negotiated.

There was another trip, to New York. Hiss was going to drive there from Washington in his Ford in about April or May 1935. He said that he told Chambers that he was making this journey, and Chambers asked for a lift. There is nothing remarkable in this incident—except perhaps the fact that Hiss and Chambers were in agreement about it.

Chambers spoke of a trip in June or July of 1935 when he accompanied Mr. and Mrs. Hiss. They drove from New York to a place called Long Eddy, about 150 miles away, to look at a bungalow. It was, said Chambers, quite unsuitable, and they were there only a few minutes. This again was denied by Hiss and his wife.

Next in order of date comes the supposed visit which Mrs. Hiss paid to the Chambers at Smithton, and this is of more importance. It is an undoubted fact that in the summer of 1935 Chambers, his wife and his friend Maxim Lieber rented a cottage from a Mr. Boucot at Smithton, a place about six miles south of Frenchtown, New Jersey. They were there for two or three months. The Chambers at that time were passing as "Mr. and Mrs. Breen" and their daughter as Ursula Breen. Chambers asserted that Mrs. Hiss spent about a week or ten days with them in this cottage in the fall of 1935. Mrs. Chambers supported her husband's evidence. She said that Mrs. Hiss had come over to "help her with her painting." She recalled that she gave Mrs. Hiss a landscape which she painted from the porch of the cottage during the visit and that she had later seen this painting in the Hisses' house in 30th Street. The Hisses occupied this house from July 1936 till December 1937. Mrs. Chambers said that at this time she used to call Mrs. Hiss "Pros" and Mr. Hiss "Hilly." She said that Mrs. Hiss called her "Liza." At the end of the visit, Mrs. Chambers said that Hiss came over in his car to fetch his wife, and they drove back together to Washington. Hiss and his wife both swore positively that no such visit had ever taken place.

It seems clear that one side or the other must have been lying about this, for I cannot believe that a visit of such length could have completely escaped the memory of an honest witness. Maxim Lieber was not called at the trial. He had been a close friend of Chambers in his Communist days. It was he who helped Chambers to get a Government job at the end of 1937.

We look, therefore, to see if there was any independent evidence of this supposed visit. Mr. Boucot, from whom Chambers had rented the cottage, and his sister Mrs. Brown were themselves living at Smithton and, indeed, were occupying a cottage only about a hundred feet away. Chambers testified that he had met Mr. Boucot on many occasions and that Mr. Boucot occasionally used to come over to their cottage. When testifying on the 5th November 1948, Chambers had said: "I am quite sure he [Boucot] met Mrs. Hiss there, and I believe that Boucot's sister, Mrs. Brown, also met Mrs. Hiss." Both Mr. Boucot and Mrs. Brown testified at the trial that during the entire time Chambers and his wife had stayed at Smithton they had never met Mrs. Hiss. No doubt in intelligent anticipation of this evidence, Chambers at the second trial said that he did not know whether Mr. Boucot or his sister had in fact met Mrs. Hiss during her supposed visit. Mrs. Chambers, however, was even at the trial clearly of the opinion that Boucot had met Mrs. Hiss, and remembered that she had introduced them to each other. Asked what name she used to introduce Mrs. Hiss, she agreed that she probably would not have used the name "Hiss" and said that she must have invented a name for the occasion. She could not remember for certain what this was, but said that the name "Rogers" at one time had had "a ring for her." But whatever name was used, she was certain in her own mind that Boucot had met Mrs. Hiss, for "he used to come in for coffee quite frequently."

Mrs. Hiss, in her direct evidence, said that she had never been in the Boucot cottage in her life, and she was asked no questions about it in cross-examination.

Chambers deals with this visit in his book *Witness*. He says that Mrs. Hiss drove over in the Ford roadster and that she came to help Mrs. Chambers with the baby, so that Mrs. Chambers could be free to devote herself to painting. He says that he drove the Ford roadster back to Washington and was acutely conscious of the difficulty that arose because the windscreen wiper was only hand-operated.

Mr. Murphy did not refer to this visit in his closing speech. And there the matter rests; the only independent witnesses, Mr. Boucot and Mrs. Brown, were certain that they had never met Mrs. Hiss, and Mr. Lieber was not called.

The next and most important of all the supposed visits was that made to Bleak House, near Peterborough, New Hampshire. Chambers said that on the 9th August 1937 he joined Mr. and Mrs. Hiss on this trip. His recollection was that he came over from Baltimore that day, and that they started early in the morning in the Plymouth car from the house where the Hisses were then living on 30th Street, Washington. This was a strange beginning, for the route which the Hisses would have had to take from Washington lay through Baltimore, and if, as Chambers said, the trip was arranged on the telephone, it would surely have been simpler to pick him up at Baltimore and save him this unnecessary journey.

The total distance to be covered was over 500 miles, so they had to spend a night on the way, and this they did at a tourist home at Thomaston, Connecticut. They arrived there after dark, and Chambers thought that they registered.

The object of the trip, Chambers said, was so that he could visit Harry Dexter White, who was spending the summer at a house near Peterborough. He admitted that he never told the Hisses anything about White, either in the course of the drive there or on the way back. It appears that Chambers asked Hiss to stop outside a lane which led to the house but from which the house was not visible. Chambers then got out of the car and walked quite a short way up the lane, when he came upon Harry White, who was playing with his children. He and Mr. White talked for some twenty minutes and then together walked back to within a few yards of the place where the Hisses were standing in the road. White could have seen the Hisses but did not come up to them and instead turned round and walked back. White, in his evidence before the House Committee, had said that he had never known Chambers and, when shown a photograph of him, said that he did not recognise it as being of a man he had ever known. But White was never asked about this incident, and this for the simple reason that Chambers never said anything about it until after his death.

I find this whole story quite extraordinary. It is surely inconceivable that nothing would have been said as to the reason for the stop, that Chambers would have given no explanation at all and would have said nothing about the man who had walked back with him down the lane. Here I should say that White and Hiss were, of course, known to each other. Moreover, to reach the lane that led to White's house, they had to leave Route 202, upon which they had arranged to travel; but nothing was apparently said as to the reason for this departure.

After this unexplained stop upon an unexplained route, the journey to Peterboro was resumed. Chambers said that they spent the night of the 10th August at Bleak House, one bedroom being occupied by the Hisses and another by himself. He was unable to remember whether they had anything to eat at that house or where they got any of their meals. They left Bleak House on the following morning—the 11th August—to drive to New York, some 350 miles. Asked about the reason for visiting New York, Chambers said that he could not remember why he wanted to go there, but that the Hisses had told him they wanted to stay at a little hotel where they had spent their honeymoon. It is an undoubted fact that the Hisses did not honeymoon in New York.

Both Hiss and his wife testified that this whole story was an invention; and so again it was hard swearing on one side against hard swearing on the other—but with this difference, that there was one important independent witness called for the Defence, a Mrs. Davis. Mrs. Davis said that she had taken a lease of Bleak House in July 1937 for three years and that she had opened it as a guesthouse on the 1st August 1937. On that date she started to keep a visitors' book, and it was her practice to see that guests registered. She was in charge of the house, lived there and was on the premises all day long. She had some fourteen bedrooms and served meals. She was confident that she had never seen Mr. or Mrs. Hiss or Mr. Chambers before the trial, and their names were not recorded in the visitors' book, which was produced in evidence. Chambers admitted that he could not recognise Mrs. Davis as the hostess of Bleak House. I should add that he had made two trips to Thomaston when working with the F.B.I. before the trial and had not been able to locate the house there where they spent the night.

I used the phrase "working with the F.B.I." advisedly, for in the course of his cross-examination Chambers was asked about these visits to Thomaston:

Mr. Chambers: I had been in New York talking with the F.B.I. every day except week ends for a matter of some months, and during that process we took a trip to Thomaston, Connecticut—in fact, we made two trips to Thomaston and one trip to Peterborough, New Hampshire.
Mr. Cross: You say you were staying in New York and spending practically the entire time with the F.B.I. for a matter of months except for week ends.
Mr. Chambers: I believe that is correct.
Mr. Cross: Beginning when?
Mr. Chambers: Beginning during the Grand Jury proceedings of December 1948.
Mr. Cross: And extending down to what period?
Mr. Chambers: Extending to about some time in March 1949.
Mr. Cross: And of course you have spent a considerable time with them since?
Mr. Chambers: I have seen them from time to time.
Mr. Cross: During that time would it be fair to say that you were spending some five or six days a week with them?
Mr. Chambers: Five, I believe, would be a liberal estimate.
Mr. Cross: The entire day?
Mr. Chambers: From about ten-thirty in the morning until about four to four-thirty in the evening.
Mr. Cross: Over a period of three and a half months?
Mr. Chambers: Yes, with time out for lunch.

Exceptional cases do sometimes arise in which it is necessary for the Prosecution, if they are to do their job properly, to rely on information revealed by some particular witness and therefore to remain in close and continuous touch with him: no doubt it seemed to the authorities that this was such a case. Any experienced person would, however, resort to this course with reluctance, since he would know that it might give rise to the suspicion that the witness had been "coached," and therefore tend to lessen the weight which a jury would attach to his evidence. On the other hand, once it has been decided to adopt such a course, the witness should surely be asked for his help on all relevant matters, whether concerning the peculiar circumstances of the withdrawal of the $400 or of the trip to Peterborough.

I can find no corroboration of the story Chambers told about this visit. Mr. Murphy suggested in his closing speech that the fact that a photograph of White's house, taken at some unspecified time, was produced was some sort of corroboration. I quote his words: "He [Chambers] showed you a picture. No contradiction about that. Ladies and gentlemen, that is corroboration." I cannot understand this; if the photograph corroborated anything, it corroborated the fact that White had a house; and I do not think it even corroborated that, since it did not follow that the house belonged to White or that he had been there at the time in question. Chambers could not, even after two visits with the F.B.I., identify the house at Thomaston; the story about meeting White is wildly improbable and was not told during White's lifetime; he never took the F.B.I. to the place where the Hisses waited outside the lane whilst he walked up the lane to talk to White; Mrs. Davis had no recollection of the party, and Chambers could not recognise her, and the names were not registered in her visitors' book; and lastly, Chambers had testified to the House Committee that he had never spent a night on any trip.

Mrs. Hiss said that she was spending the month of August 1937 at a place called Chestertown on the Eastern Shore of Chesapeake Bay, where she had lodgings with a Mrs. Wickes at 117 Front Street. Hiss was with her until the middle of the month, when he had to go back to Washington, but he continued to come out for week ends. She had two nieces, Ruth and Cynthia Fansler, and her son Timmy in camp nearby. Ruth

Fansler, whose parents were in Europe, got pneumonia and was taken to a hospital, where she was kept until 1st August. Mrs. Hiss was visiting the children at their camp every day in August and was able to say with certainty that she was not away from Chestertown for a single night that month; she most certainly did not visit Peterborough on the 10th August. Apart from Chambers' story, there seems no reason to doubt her evidence on this point.

The evidence of Thomas Fansler, the father of Ruth Fansler, if it were correct, would prove conclusively that the Hisses cannot have started on the Peterborough trip early on the 9th August. He had returned from Europe on the *Bremen*, which arrived in New York on Monday, the 2nd August 1937, the last day of his leave. On Friday, the 6th August, he went to Chestertown to see his daughter Ruth. On Monday, the 9th August, he had to return to New York and was driven by the Hisses to Wilmington, some forty or fifty miles from Chestertown, to catch a train at what he described as a leisurely hour. If his story of the journey to Wilmington is correct, it is certain that the Hisses cannot have been driving Chambers to Bleak House on that morning.

Why, then, the reader may ask, should Chambers have taken the trouble to invent such a tale; and to that question I certainly have no answer. It is often said that George IV talked so much of his experiences at the Battle of Waterloo—he had, in fact, been in England when it was fought—that he finally came to believe that he had been there. There is no doubt that memory—even in the case of the most normal men—can play strange tricks. It may well be the fact that Chambers had on some occasion gone to visit White. It may be he had heard something which made him think that the Hisses had attended the performance of *She Stoops to Conquer*. The date of the performance—as a glance at the files of the newspapers would show—was the 10th August 1937. The date was of some importance, for it was at a time when, according to Hiss, his association with Chambers had long ended. If it had turned out that the Hisses had been present at the performance and had stayed at Bleak House and had registered, it would not have been difficult for Chambers to explain away his non-registration, for Communist agents do not care to record their movements. Had things so turned out, Chambers would have claimed them as corroborating his story—but they did not so turn out.

Still the mystery remains: Why should Chambers invent such a bizarre story? It was a mystery which plainly oppressed the Defence. They tried to meet it by the medical evidence that Chambers had a "psychopathic personality." I understand nothing of such matters, and I confess I think psychologists are sometimes given to constructing theories on inadequate material. But, whatever the explanation may be, experience has taught me that witnesses do sometimes tell long and detailed stories which on examination prove to be mere figments of the imagination. I have, at any rate, set out the relevant facts, and the reader must decide for himself whether Chambers' story was such an invention or not.

There were certain other visits between the Hisses and the Chambers, of which evidence was given, and these deserve mention. For example, at one stage Chambers said that he had slept at the 30th Street house when the Hisses were living there. (They were there from July 1936 to December 1937.) This must have been a mistake, because there were only two bedrooms, one of which was occupied by the Hisses and the other by Timmy Hobson. Chambers was challenged in his cross-examination and said that he had been trying to recollect but found he could not remember the layout of the 30th Street house, which led him to the conclusion that he had not spent a night there.

There was, however, other evidence of two visits paid by the Chambers to the 30th Street house. On one occasion Mrs. Chambers deposed that in the summer she and her husband had driven up to the house and parked their car a little distance away. Chambers went to investigate if there were any visitors. They went in for quite a short time, but the incident was impressed on the mind of Mrs. Chambers because her baby had "an accident" and wet the floor, and she said that Mrs. Hiss gave her an old, soft towel.

The second occasion was a New Year's party at the 30th

Street house at the close of the year 1936 or the beginning of 1937. That was impressed on Mrs. Chambers' mind because her husband was violently sick after drinking some port; and as he was, as all good Communists, so he stated, should be, a strict teetotaller, this is perhaps understandable. Chambers, in his evidence to the House Committee, had explained that he was strictly forbidden by the Communist Party to taste liquor at any time, and said that he never drank. Hiss and his wife denied that there had been any such party, and there is no evidence to show, apart from that given by the Hisses and the Chambers, where the truth lies.

There was another occasion which Mrs. Chambers remembered, of a wedding anniversary in December 1937. She said that the Hisses came to visit her at her house in Mount Royal Terrace, Baltimore. They brought with them, so she said, as their contribution to the feast, a bottle of American champagne, and this time Mrs. Chambers said that she was sick. She had previously said that this celebration took place at the Volta Place house of the Hisses and that her husband had been sick. She explained the discrepancy by saying that she had been confused.

Hiss and his wife both said that they had never visited the Chambers at Baltimore, and here we do get some independent testimony. For at Baltimore the Chambers had a servant, a Mrs. Edith Murray, who testified at the trial. She was called in rebuttal. She had been available throughout the trial, and if she was to be called at all (her evidence would have been inadmissible in England), I should have thought she ought to have been called by the Prosecution during their case. Mrs. Murray testified that she remembered an occasion when Mrs. Hiss came over to visit Mrs. Chambers at Eutaw Place, Baltimore. Mrs. Chambers was pregnant at the time and had gone to her doctor in New York. Mrs. Hiss, whom she called "Miss Priscilla," came over to help with the baby. Mrs. Murray had left the service of the Chambers in the spring of 1936, so that any visits which Mrs. Hiss paid whilst she was there must have been before that date. She said that she remembered Mrs. Hiss coming about four times and Alger Hiss coming at least once. Her recollection, of course, was challenged. She had not been asked about the matter until November 1949, when she was taken by the F.B.I. to see Chambers at his farm. She there had a three-hour interview with Chambers and his wife (whom she had known as Mr. and Mrs. Lloyd Cantwell). It would not be surprising if she was making a mistake about events which had taken place some thirteen years before. She had been in the doctor's hands and explained that she never read the papers.

If she was right in her recollection and was speaking the truth, it does show that the Hisses were wrong in their recollection or were not speaking the truth in saying that they had never visited the Chambers' home. The jury saw Mrs. Murray and were in a position to decide just how much weight to attach to her evidence.

Such, then, in broad outline, was the evidence given about the association between the Hisses and the Chambers. It is, of course, possible that the Hisses were concerned to represent this as being slight and casual, and the Chambers to represent it as being close and continued; and it is further possible that —as so often happens—the truth lies somewhere between the two extremes.

CHAPTER XI

OF THE SUPPOSED COMMUNIST GROUP

I think there can be no doubt that nothing prejudiced the case of Hiss more in the minds of the public, and probably of the jury, than the belief that he was associating with a nest of Communists. There is an old Latin proverb—"*Noscitur a sociis*" —which, being interpreted, means: "You can tell a man by the company he keeps." The jury, of course, did not know, or at any rate should not have been influenced by, anything which had taken place at the House Committee hearings, even though that evidence had been published and discussed in the newspapers before the case came before them. In any event, what mattered was not whether persons who associated with Hiss were in fact Communists, but whether he knew, or ought to have known, that they were Communists. But be that as it may, one cannot help feeling that he was singularly unfortunate in some of his associates.

Before I go further, it is only fair to remember that we are dealing with events which took place between the years 1935 and 1938. In the year 1952, when I am writing this book, we know much more about Communists and Communism than we knew then. In those early days we had an expression, "drawing-room bolsheviks," for describing people with vague Left-wing sympathies who thought Communism was, on the whole, a promising development on democratic lines. Events since then have opened the eyes of all but the wilfully blind, and I should imagine that "drawing-room bolsheviks" have now ceased to exist. It is fairly obvious that the same sort of people existed in America. In Mr. Chester Wilmot's brilliant book, *The Struggle for Europe*, there is a most revealing passage outlining the views held by no less a person than President Roosevelt at the time of the Yalta Conference. He says that the President anticipated that he would have no difficulty in developing a satisfactory relationship with Stalin, and that he feared that the British people in general and Mr. Churchill in particular might prove a far greater source of trouble to him. I confess I read this part of the book with amazement.

In the years 1935–38 the unworthy deal between Stalin and Hitler for the partition of Poland lay in the future; the Communist government of Russia was seen as a possible challenge and counterpoise to the frightful tyranny which Hitler had established. It was regarded, albeit quite wrongly regarded, as a development of democratic freedom after the harsh repression of the Tsarist government; it was even regarded by some as a development of Christian doctrine. It enlisted the sympathy of many intellectuals and writers on both sides of the Atlantic. Its full implications were unknown.

It is only fair to remember this when considering the history of Chambers himself; and it is to his credit that after the Hitler-Stalin pact had been revealed he decided to make a partial—a very partial—disclosure to Mr. Berle of the extent to which Communism had infiltrated into high places in America. The names of the men whom Chambers mentioned to Mr. Berle and to Mr. Ray Murphy were in the main repeated in his evidence before the House Committee.

First and foremost stands Harold Ware. Chambers said that he was the organiser of an underground Communist group in Washington of which Alger Hiss was a member. Chambers told Mr. Berle in 1939 that Pressman was a member of the "underground organized by the late Harold Ware," and that he had been in Ware's group from 1932 to 1933. Ware was killed in a motor accident in 1935. He figures prominently in the history of this case. Chambers gave evidence that he met Ware, whom he had previously known in New York, when he first went to Washington in about May or June 1934. He was introduced to Ware, said Chambers, by J. Peters, the head of the whole underground of the American Communist Party; and it was Ware who in June or July of the same year introduced him to Alger Hiss. I have already described this latter meeting which, according to Chambers, took place at a restaurant in Washington. It will be remembered that this was the occasion when it was announced, so Chambers said, that Hiss was to leave Ware's apparatus and join that of Chambers. I shall refer later to the evidence Chambers gave before the House Committee on the 3rd August 1948. He was then asked what Harold Ware's real name was and replied: "As far as I know, 'Harold Ware.' I never knew him." I understand that the answer as recorded in the transcript is incomplete. The full answer was, "I never knew him to use any other name."

This explanation, of course, accounts for the absence of any cross-examination on this point, which struck me as surprising until I learned that the recorded answer was incomplete.

There seems no reason to doubt that Ware had been a Communist organiser, and in particular that he had been in charge of some apparatus in Washington. Chambers in his book asserts that he met Ware on many occasions, and in fact took over the leadership of the apparatus in Washington from him.

Hiss was asked in direct examination whether he had known Harold Ware, and replied that Ware had come into his office in the Department of Agriculture on one or two occasions, but that that was the only contact he had had with him. Cross-examined by Mr. Murphy, Hiss was reminded that he had told the Grand Jury in March 1948 that he had met Harold Ware only very occasionally and knew very little of him.

Hiss was questioned about Lee Pressman; he explained that they had been together in the same class at Harvard Law School and had both become members of the editorial board of the *Harvard Law Review*. Pressman had gone to the Agricultural Adjustment Administration before Hiss, and they had served together on the staff of Mr. Frank. Hiss said that since he left the Department of Agriculture in April 1935 he had not seen Pressman to speak to. He had recently heard statements that Pressman was either a Communist or a fellow-traveller, but he had never had any reason to suppose this at the time he knew him.

When asked about John Abt, Hiss said that he had worked with him in the Department of Agriculture, that Abt had visited his home, but that he had had no contact with him since then. He gave the same evidence about Witt and about Kramer, whom he had known as Krivitsky. He had seen none of them since the old days in the Department of Agriculture. With regard to Victor Perlo, Hiss said he had met him in 1934 but could not remember him very well and had had no further contact with him since. He admitted that he had known Henry Collins and that they had been close friends since childhood. They shared an interest in bird-watching.

Pressman, Witt, Abt, Collins and Kramer were all called to give evidence before the House Committee in 1948, but they all objected to answering questions on the ground that their answers might incriminate or degrade them. Each of them, indeed, had given this answer to the precise question: "Did you know Alger Hiss?" Each read a statement denying that he had been a member of a Communist group—statements on which I should myself have found it difficult to place much reliance, in view of their refusal to answer questions. These answers given before the House Committee were presumably not present to the mind of the jury, although they must have been struck by the fact that none of these men was called at the trial to deny the statements that had been made about him. It would surely have been natural for Collins, the lifelong friend, to come forward in the defence of Hiss, unless there had been some strong reason to prevent him. I feel that the jury might well have come to the conclusion that there was good foundation for the statements that these men were Communist sympathisers.

Two years later, namely in August and September 1950, Pressman, Witt, Kramer and Abt were once more summoned before the House Committee. The last three adhered to their previous refusal to answer questions, but—to his credit—Pressman was more forthcoming. He admitted that he had joined a Communist group in Washington, D.C., in 1934, and said that he had given up all active participation in the following year. He had been asked to join by Harold Ware. He said that there were three other persons—and only three other persons—in the group, namely Witt, Kramer and Abt. He said that Alger Hiss was not a member of the group. He described the functions of the group, saying that they received literature of a Communist nature and met to discuss the problems covered by the literature. He had paid his dues to Ware and, after Ware's death, on one occasion at least to Peters, but not to Chambers.

The position appears to rest as follows: Chambers had testified before the House Committee that these men were members of a Communist group. Pressman, when he testified before the House Committee in 1950, admitted that he had been a member of a Communist group. The others—with of course the exception of the Hiss brothers—refused to affirm or deny the accusation. I see no reason why the uncontradicted evidence of Chambers on this matter should not be accepted, more especially since it is, to some extent, corroborated by the evidence which Pressman gave in 1950. This would lead to the conclusion that Pressman, Witt, Abt and Kramer had been members of such a group; and the same may well apply to Perlo and Collins, since these two, unlike Donald and Alger Hiss, never, so far as I am aware, contradicted the statement.

But what were the functions of the group—whatever its membership may have been? Originally there was no question of its being concerned with espionage. Indeed, if Alger Hiss was guilty of turning over documents, he was the only member of the group—if he was a member—to have done any such thing. The evidence of Mr. Berle, given on the 30th August 1948 before the House Committee with regard to his interview with Chambers in September 1939 was as follows: He said that Chambers had told him that the Communist Party had been trying to develop a group of sympathisers who might be of use to them in the United States Government. "This was not," as he put it, "any question of espionage. There was no espionage involved in it." He stated that their object was to get some people who would be sympathetic to their point of view. With that in mind apparently, a strong group of some sort had been formed of men who were interested in knowing something about Russia and Russian policy and the general Communist way of life. Mr. Berle then added that Chambers had told him that the membership had finally come down to four men—Alger Hiss, Donald Hiss, Nathan Witt and Pressman.

Chambers himself repeatedly stated that the object of the group was infiltration rather than espionage, and, indeed, I find it difficult to make the idea of a group fit in with espionage. Stealing documents is, I should have thought, one of those businesses which must be run strictly on an individualistic basis, and the collective activities of a group seem strangely out of place.

Practically nothing about the group was said at the second trial, but the names of the men concerned were rolled out and Hiss was asked about his association with them. There was an undoubted danger that these names might have become familiar to the jury, since the proceedings before the House Committee had been so fully reported.

In the cross-examination of Alger Hiss at the second trial, there was read to the jury pages from the evidence he had given before the Grand Jury in March 1948 concerning Kramer, Ware, Collins, Pressman and Abt, and the names Witt and Perlo were also mentioned. Hiss explained the extent of his knowledge of each of these men, which, with the exception of Collins, appears to have been very limited; but if the names in the rogues' gallery are enumerated one by one, the impression may be created that the man under examination is himself a rogue. But before this inference can be drawn, it must be shown that he knew them to be rogues. Hiss had denied when before the Grand Jury in March 1948 that he knew, or had any reason to suppose, that any of these men were Communists, and Mr. Murphy—as in fairness he was bound to do—read out both the questions which had been put to Hiss and the answers which he then gave.

There are other names which appear from time to time. In the notes taken by Mr. Berle of the 1939 conversation with

Chambers, it is recorded, "Duggan and Field supposed to have been both members of Party," and Field is said to have introduced Duggan to one Hede Massing, who was a witness at the second trial. In his book *Witness*, Chambers states that the Fields and Duggans lived in the same apartment house and that Hiss was conducting an active campaign to admit them to the Party. Duggan's name was also mentioned in the closing speeches at the second trial, and the position which Chambers desired to adopt with regard to Duggan was then made clear. He said that he had no personal knowledge as to whether or not Duggan was a member of the Communist Party, and Mr. Murphy made it plain that there was no ground for saying that Chambers had ever accused Duggan of having been a member. It would appear that Field accepted a position with the League of Nations in Switzerland and that he left the State Department to take up this post. Chambers says in *Witness* that during the Hiss case Field left Switzerland and disappeared into Soviet-controlled Europe, and that Duggan[1] had a "fatal fall from his New York office window," also during the case.

Hiss was asked in his direct examination about Noel Field and said that he had had an excellent reputation in the State Department; that he (Hiss) had recommended him to Mr. Sayre, along with others, for employment in the Philippines; and that he had seen him on one or two occasions after he had gone to the League of Nations when he was home on vacation. In his cross-examination Hiss stated that in the spring of 1948 Duggan had sent him a copy of a letter he had received from Field; Hiss said he had written a letter to Field in reply. A carbon copy of this letter was produced at the trial. It was a photostat of the carbon copy which was in the files at the Carnegie Endowment.

We shall hear of Field again when I consider the evidence of Hede Massing—although I must confess that I think he is as far removed from the real issue in this case as is Switzerland from the United States.

[1]It is only right to state that on 24th December 1948 the Attorney General of the United States made a further statement to the effect that there was no evidence that Mr. Duggan had ever been associated with the Communists; on the contrary, the statement continued, he was a loyal employee of the United State Government.

CHAPTER XII

OF THE EARLY STATEMENTS MADE BY CHAMBERS

It is always a matter of the first importance in determining the truth of evidence given by a witness to consider the circumstances and the details of the story as he first told it. Broadly speaking, it is true to say that the English law—and I think the American law is similar—allows as evidence against an accused person only acts done or things said in his presence. Yet complaints made by a person wronged may throw such a flood of light on the truth of his evidence that our law in certain cases allows them to be given in evidence. Thus, if a man is accused of rape or attempted rape, the fact that a girl makes a prompt complaint to her mother, even though this complaint is not made in the presence of the accused, may be given in evidence. Such a complaint proves at least this, that the story which the witness tells is not a mere afterthought. It is not something elaborated after long and searching interviews with the police and lawyers. By comparing the contents of the complaint with the contents of the later evidence, one can form an impression as to whether the later evidence is genuine and spontaneous or a mere afterthought.

It is therefore important to compare the early statements which Chambers made with his later evidence in order to judge the truth of his story.

First I must reveal how the interview with Mr. Berle came about. It is, I think, certain that Chambers, after his break with the Communists, was not the sort of person to remain silent. Reticence and discretion were not among his strong points. He undoubtedly talked, and one of the people to whom he talked was Mr. Isaac Don Levine. We learn from *Witness* that Mr. Levine was a well-known journalist who had for years been carrying on a private war against Communism; and Chambers, no doubt in the endeavour to earn some money of which at that time he stood desperately in need, was minded to write some articles on the Communist underground movement and approached Mr. Levine in 1938 to obtain his assistance. Mr. Levine, on hearing Chambers' story, at once advised him to take it to the proper authorities, but Chambers was "wary." When, however, Mr. Levine proposed that he should arrange a private meeting between Chambers and President Roosevelt himself, Chambers immediately said he would co-operate. It seemed to him that this was the "appropriate level" on which his observations should be considered. But months passed, in the course of which Chambers obtained employment with the magazine *Time*, and he had, so he says in his book, become so preoccupied in learning his job that he had forgotten all about President Roosevelt; and perhaps the President, if indeed he had ever heard of Mr. Chambers and his proposed disclosure, may well have taken a different view as to the "appropriate level."

At last, on the morning of the 2nd September 1939, Mr. Levine told Chambers that he had succeeded in securing an appointment with Mr. Berle, an Assistant Secretary of State in charge of security matters, for that very evening. It was thus that Chambers, accompanied by Mr. Levine, took the plane for Washington that day. Chambers, in his book, describes his reflections in the course of that journey. It was at that very time that the Nazi Panzer divisions were spreading death and destruction in Poland. Chambers felt that this was the prelude to a new world war, in which the ultimate struggle would prove to be between the Axis and the Communists; but he thought that in the immediate future it was only too probable that the German and Russian intelligence services would join forces. Did he, I wonder, fear that in this changing and uncertain situation his past activities would be brought to light? Did he think it would be wise to put himself right with the authorities by making some disclosure about the activities of others, without revealing too much of his own activities? We cannot find any answer to these questions in his book; but we do find a statement that on getting back to New York, after he had made his disclosure to Mr. Berle, he expected an immediate arrest. As we know now, his worst fears were not realised. Plainly he had not told too much about himself. He would have us believe that his reticence—for reticence it was if his later story be true—was due to his desire to spare Hiss and was in no way caused by a wish to save his own skin. Anyhow, he must have had the feeling that he had assisted the authorities—which is always comforting to a man awaiting arrest.

Let me now try to reconstruct what took place at the interview between Chambers, Mr. Levine and Mr. Berle. Chambers recalled in his evidence that after dinner he and Mr. Levine went into the garden, where they had a long discussion with Mr. Berle. Afterwards they returned to the house and Mr. Berle made notes of the conversation. These notes[1] were introduced at the trial after a good deal of sparring between the respective Counsel. Neither Mr. Berle nor Mr. Levine was called at the second trial, and Mr. Cross, Counsel for Hiss, was of course entitled to object to Chambers giving an account of his conversation with Mr. Berle, at which Hiss had not been present; yet I venture to think that this might have been greatly to Hiss's advantage. For Mr. Berle had given evidence on the 30th August 1948 before the House Committee in executive session. These proceedings were released on their publication later the same year, so that they could have come to the knowledge of the jury at both the first and second trials. He there gave the following account of what took place:

> Mr. Chambers stated that he wanted to disclose certain information about Communist activities in Washington. He

[1]Appendix I.

related a story to me that he had been a member of the undercover Communist group from 1934 to the end of 1937, as nearly as I can recall; that at that time, and apparently as a result of the purge activities which had been going on, he had decided to cut clear of the whole thing. He stated that he had then lived in hiding for a year or more under various names. He appeared to be even then in fear of some sort of reprisal and was obviously under some emotional strain.

He said that in addition to the New York core, the Party policy, the Communist Party policy, had been to try to develop a group of sympathizers who might be of use to them later in the United States Government.

This was not, as he put it, any question of espionage. There was no espionage involved in it. He stated that their hope merely was to get some people who would be sympathetic to their point of view. With that in mind apparently, a study group of some sort had been formed of men who were interested in knowing something about Russia and Russian policy and the general Communist theory of life, and so on. He said that in that group there had been various people at one time or another, but that it had finally come down to four men who had been named at that time as being in or about the Government service, and he mentioned Alger Hiss, Donald Hiss, Nathan Witt and Pressman, who had previously been in the Department of Agriculture and at that time had got out and was counsel to the C.I.O. I don't recall the names of these other men. They were not in the Government service, in any event.

He said that these men, it was hoped, would go, as they called it, "underground"; that is to say, that they would not appear as part of the well-known or open Communist group, but that they would simply be there and be sympathetic.

In one respect, what he told me omitted something that he has told you: he did not make the direct statement that any of these men were members of the Communist Party. They were apparently, from what I then gathered, men who were sympathetic to their general point of view and to whom they might have access and perhaps a sympathetic approach in case anybody brought a request there.

> You have in mind that when Mr. Chambers talked to me in 1939 he was talking about something that was then two years old at the time when there was no strain on relations. A man might be very much interested in Russia, and most people in the State Department were. I was myself, so far as that is concerned, so that about all you had to go on was that —and I must add that Chambers did not state to me that he was a member of the Communist Party; merely that this was a group that was hoping to be sympathetic, so that was all you had to go on.

In his book, Chambers gives us further details of what took place. He remembers going into the garden with Mr. Berle and Mr. Levine, and he remembers the Negro servingman bringing drinks. He says frankly that he knew two or three glasses of scotch and soda would give him a liberating exhilaration and that he welcomed any aid that would loosen his tongue. Gradually, he says, he felt the alcohol take hold. The conversation lasted two or three hours. In these circumstances, it is not likely that he withheld any material information.

Unfortunately the jury were not given these interesting background facts. They were not made directly aware of the statements which Mr. Berle had made to the House Committee. They had only the notes he made of the conversation.

It is clear from these notes that Chambers mentioned a considerable number of people in addition to Alger and Donald Hiss, Witt and Pressman. Donald Hiss is listed in the following way:

> Philippine Adviser—Member of C.P. with Pressman and Witt—Labor Dept.—Asst. to Frances Perkins—Party wanted him there—to send him as arbitrator in Bridges trial—Brought along by brother.

Then follows a note on Alger Hiss:

> Asst. to Sayre—C.P.—1937—Member of the underground Com.—Active Baltimore boys.

Priscilla Hiss is described as a "Socialist," which is odd if one recalls Chambers' later testimony. At the trial he said that when it was suggested that the system of typing documents should be introduced it was Mrs. Hiss who said that she sought some activity for herself, that she had been restless in underground work, and that this typing would give her an opportunity to satisfy the need which she felt. There is no mention at all of Harry Dexter White.

Did Chambers believe in the truth of the statements he had made to Mr. Berle? I can well believe that he did. He was a highly emotional man who had become as enthusiastic a devotee of the anti-Communist cause as he had previously been of the Communist cause. He oversimplified the problem, as he makes it clear in his book. In his opinion, there were two mighty forces—those for revolution and those for counterrevolution. There was no middle course. Those who were not for him in his new-found role were against him. Liberals, Socialists and New Dealers were all, he felt, against him.

I should think it quite possible that Hiss had indicated to him in the course of their conversations sympathy with Left-wing views and perhaps, too, a sympathy with Russia; for as Mr. Berle implied in his evidence to the House Committee, many people before the war were interested in Russia, and many looked to her as a possible bulwark against Nazi aggression. Certainly Mrs. Hiss, in their early married life, seems to have had some Socialist sympathies. Then, too, Chambers would have learned that Hiss had, to a greater or less extent, associated with men like Pressman and Collins. Give this material to an emotional man of Chambers' outlook: would there not here appear to be something to support his allegation? No doubt the story he told to Mr. Berle may have been embellished; that would have been natural enough to a man of Chambers' temperament, even without the alcohol. "The study group of some sort" may, for example, have been one of the embellishments. It seems to me that on any view of the case Chambers may well have believed in the truth of the broad outline of the story he revealed to Mr. Berle. In saying this, however, I must make one exception. I cannot find any justification for his statement about Donald Hiss, and I shall review all the evidence about him in a subsequent chapter.

Nothing happened as a result of this disclosure to Mr. Berle —rather, I gather, to Chambers' chagrin; and, indeed, Alger

Hiss went on rising rapidly in the public service. Perhaps Chambers came to realise that if he wanted action to be taken he must cast his revelations in a more striking and sensational form.

His chance came in 1945; and it came apparently through Mr. Berle's having put his notes at the disposal of the authorities. Mr. Ray Murphy, State Department security officer, after this long interval of time, got in touch with Chambers, who made two statements to him, the one on the 20th March 1945[2] and the other on the 28th August 1946.[3] At the first of these interviews Chambers disclosed that he was the Washington representative of J. Peters, who was located in New York. He was charged with the task of trying to enlist the active support of those not openly identified with the Party, but whose background and training might make them useful affiliates under the guise of advancing reform legislation. He described a group, working under Harold Ware, of promising, ambitious young men with advanced social and political ideas, amongst them being Alger Hiss. The purpose of the group was for each member to rise as high as possible in the Government in order to shape legislation favourable to the programme of the Communist Party. Chambers made it plain that he left the Party at the end of 1937. He remembered several conversations with Alger Hiss in the early part of 1938, during which Hiss was adamant against the plan of breaking with the Party. He described Hiss as a man "with a charming personality, absolutely sincere in his convictions and motivated by the idea that he was on the right track." Donald Hiss, he said, was a later adherent of the Party. The statement ends with this paragraph:

> Eleanor Nelson ran a low-grade but important Communist group in the Government. More of a trade-union group, but its members had access to Government files which would be made available to the Party. Hiss was a member of this group.

I have not been able to find anything in *Witness* to connect Hiss with Eleanor Nelson.

The second interview with Mr. Ray Murphy took place on the 28th August 1946. Once again Chambers made it quite clear

[2]Appendix II.

[3]Appendix III.

that he left the Party at the end of December 1937. He said that Alger Hiss's function was "never to make converts. His job was to mess up policy. . . . This was an elite policy-making, top-level group. This group did not exchange secret documents from Government departments, but did give sealed reports on the membership of the groups and on policy. It was not a spy ring, but one far more important and cunning because its members helped to shape policy in their departments." Harry White is mentioned as being a member of one of the cells, not a leader.

These three documents, the notes of the conversation with Mr. Berle in August 1939 and the notes of the conversations with Mr. Ray Murphy in 1945 and 1946, make most remarkable reading.

By now the reader will be aware, or I shall have hopelessly failed in my task, that the accusation against Alger Hiss was that he had lied on oath in denying that he had delivered secret documents to Chambers and denying that he had seen and conversed with him in or about February or March 1938. The reader will also be aware that the essential elements in the case Chambers made against Hiss at the trial were that at a meeting between Bykov and Hiss in about January 1937, at which Chambers was present, Bykov asked Hiss to bring out documents and that Hiss consented to do so. Then, according to Chambers, there was a further meeting between himself and Hiss in the summer of 1937 at which it was arranged that documents should be typed or copied, and Chambers said that thereafter, until some time in April 1938, Hiss supplied him with these secret documents.

Now let us see how these allegations square with the statements made to Mr. Berle and Mr. Murphy. In the first place, the reader will observe that there is no suggestion whatever, either in the statement made to Mr. Berle or in the statements made to Mr. Murphy, that Hiss delivered any documents either in or about February and March 1938, or indeed at any other time. There is no account of the critical meeting between Bykov and Hiss at which Hiss undertook to deliver documents. Too much must not, I think, be made of these omissions, for it is the undoubted fact that Wadleigh did deliver documents, and this is also unrecorded. The reason for this reticence is not, I think, far to seek. At the time when the statement was made to Mr. Berle there would have been no statute of limitations protecting those who had been guilty of any such act of treachery. If at that date Chambers had said that he had received documents from Wadleigh or Hiss or anyone else, and had passed them on to the Communists, he too might have found himself expiating his crime behind prison bars. The story, moreover, which he elected to tell to Mr. Berle in 1939 had, as he doubtless intended, been passed on to the security officers, and he found himself anchored to it, with the result that in 1945 and 1946 he was still telling the same story, though with substantial embellishments, to Mr. Murphy as he had previously told to Mr. Berle. As I shall show presently, throughout the hearing before the House Committee Chambers made it clear that he brought no charges of espionage. It was not until he found himself confronted with a libel action and a demand for $75,000 damages that he for the first time revealed the existence of the documents, thereby making it quite plain either that he had acted in a conspiratorial fashion by suppressing the fact of their existence when being questioned by Adolf Berle, Ray Murphy, and the House Committee, or that his later story was a complete fabrication to escape from the difficulties of the libel action. His explanation of his conduct seems singularly unconvincing. Let me record it in his own words:

> I told Mr. Marbury [Mr. Marbury was the counsel cross-examining Chambers in the Baltimore libel action] that I had had a twofold purpose in testifying up until that time: one part of the purpose was to destroy or paralyze the Communist conspiracy within the country and the Government; the other part of my purpose was to do as little injury as possible to the human beings involved in that conspiracy.
>
> I pointed out that in my own case a kind of grace had been given me to find the strength to break, and time had been given me in which to work out a new life.
>
> I pointed out that in breaking with the Communist Party time is a most essential factor. Therefore I had wanted to give these people some of the same opportunity which had been given to me. But I had now been forced into a position where

> I had no choice but to introduce those documents into evidence.

It is difficult to reconcile some of the passages in the early statements with the assertion that in making them he wanted to do "as little injury as possible to the human beings involved." From his interview with Ray Murphy in 1945 I extract the following:

> The persons listed below are said to have disclosed much confidential information and to have arranged among themselves a program committing this Government to a policy in keeping with the desires of the Communist Party.

Or from the 1946 conversation:

> Alger Hiss was never to make converts. His job was to mess up policy.

And again from the same document:

> This group did not exchange secret documents from the Government departments, but did give sealed reports on the membership of the groups and on policy. It was not a spy ring, but one far more important and cunning because its members helped to shape policy in their departments.

The most likely explanation of the failure of Chambers to disclose the true facts, always assuming that the facts to which he deposed at the trial were true, was that he did not want to reveal them at a time when he might have found himself the subject of a charge, and that having committed himself to this story in 1939 in his statement to Mr. Berle, he adhered to it in 1945 and 1946 in his statements to Mr. Ray Murphy, and in 1948 in his evidence before the House Committee, only revealing the true facts when he found himself confronted with a claim for heavy damages.

There are other facts, however, in these documents which are very remarkable. In his statement to Mr. Berle and in both his conversations with Mr. Ray Murphy, Chambers stated definitely that he broke with the Communist Party at the end of 1937. In the 1945 interview it is thus stated:

> The informant dealt with these people from 1934 till the

> end of 1937, when he broke with the Party and attempted to persuade various of these contacts to break also. He remembers several conversations with Alger Hiss in the early part of 1938, during which Hiss was adamant against the plan of breaking with the Party.

And in the notes of the 1946 conversation:

> My informant entered into the Washington picture in the summer of 1935 and left it and the Party at the end of December 1937. . . . My informant asked Alger Hiss personally to break with the Party in early 1938, but Hiss refused with tears in his eyes and said he would remain loyal to the Party.

If the fact was that he had broken with the Party in 1937, how came he to go round to Hiss to collect secret documents "in or about February and March 1938"? A possible answer to this question—if it be the fact that Hiss was handing over documents—may be that Chambers was concerned at this time to build up his "life preserver," that is to say, to obtain incriminating documents which might stand him in good stead in the future.

I have often heard the question asked: "What possible motive had Chambers for chucking a $30,000 editorial job to stand as the accuser?" Any such question is based on a series of inaccuracies. The fact is that he volunteered his resignation from *Time* because he feared that his continued presence on their staff would do the business harm. The president of Time, Incorporated, accepted his resignation with the greatest regret and the proprietors made him a most generous settlement. He had had one serious breakdown in health and may not have been sorry to retire to the more perfect surroundings of farm life. Moreover, as I have pointed out, once he had had the interview with Mr. Berle—just after he had joined *Time*—he was committed to the necessity of giving evidence later on. Indeed, he was practically committed when in the year 1938 he took the advice of Mr. Levine and consented to discuss the matter with the President. At that time he had no job either with *Time* or with anyone else, but was dependent on his translations for a livelihood.

CHAPTER XIII

OF THE HOUSE COMMITTEE ON UN-AMERICAN ACTIVITIES

This Committee was set up by Public Law 601 of the Seventy-ninth Congress and House Resolution 5 of the Eightieth Congress. Public Law 601 states in part that the "Committee on un-American Activities as a whole or by sub-committee is authorized to make from time to time investigations of:

(1) the extent, character and objects of un-American propaganda activities in the United States;
(2) the diffusion within the United States of subversive and un-American propaganda . . . ; and
(3) all other questions in relation thereto that would aid Congress in any necessary remedial legislation."

Accordingly, in 1948 the Committee were conducting an investigation into Communist infiltration into the Federal Government, and the operation within the Government of persons who were collecting information to be turned over to foreign governments.

It behoves any Englishman to speak with great discretion of

such an august body as a committee of the Congress of the United States. He should be prepared to respect—even if he does not entirely comprehend. Occasions must arise in the working life of any democracy when it is necessary, in order that some topic may be investigated, to employ extra-judicial methods.

In this country we have an act, called the Tribunals of Inquiry (Evidence) Act, 1921, which provides for the setting up of such an enquiry. If both Houses pass the necessary resolution, such a tribunal can be established, and it can be given the further powers of summoning witnesses and of calling for the production of documents. I can recall two cases since I entered political life where this procedure has been adopted; the one some twenty years ago to enquire into certain allegations of leakages of budget secrets; the other, a year or so ago, to enquire into certain alleged corrupt or improper practices concerning in particular the Board of Trade. The former tribunal was presided over by Lord Porter, then a judge of the High Court, assisted by two very distinguished members of the Bar. The latter tribunal was presided over by Mr. Justice Lynskey, who in his turn was assisted by two equally distinguished barristers. In each of these cases the tribunal was carefully selected, and no member of either one had up to the time of his appointment ever taken part in any political activities. This was, I feel sure, a wise precaution, since, in the words of the old adage, not only must justice be done, but it must be manifestly seen that justice is done.

We are, of course, familiar with the proceedings of the Committee of Privileges of the House of Commons, whose jurisdiction relates solely to the privileges of the House. Such a committee is of necessity comprised of active politicians, though in my experience its members forget their political loyalties and affiliations in their single-minded desire to see that a fair conclusion is reached.

It is inevitable, owing to the fundamental differences in the two constitutions, that the method adopted in the United States must be radically different from that adopted here. In that country, speaking broadly, there is a far greater degree of separation of the executive, of the legislative and of the judicial functions than exists here. In this country the executive cannot continue unless it has the support of the House of Commons, and directly that support is withheld the Government falls. In the United States the President is elected for a fixed term, and he may or he may not have the support of Congress throughout his term of office.

If the United States legislature thinks that the executive is not being, for example, sufficiently active and astute in investigating or suppressing Communist agencies in the Government, they may appoint a committee to investigate with the intention, if the facts seem to justify it, of enlisting public opinion so that the executive may be forced to take the necessary action. Such a committee, if it is fairly to represent Congress, must be comprised in some part of those who support the administration and in some part of those who oppose it. This must give rise to the risk that it will be said, whether truly or not, that some members of such a committee are at least as much concerned with bringing the administration into discredit as with protecting the rights and privileges of an individual citizen.

It is, of course, true that no person summoned before such a committee is compelled to answer any question if he can assert that he might thereby be incriminated. *Nemo seipsum prodere tenetur* is an ancient principle of our law, and I fancy it is even more liberally applied in the courts of the United States than it is here. It undoubtedly applied to proceedings before the House Committee, just as it applies to any court. Yet it affords a quite inadequate protection to a man in a prominent position in public life, for if such a man claims protection on the ground that an answer might incriminate him, he thereby discredits his position in such public life. How impossible, for example, it would have been for a man who held the important post of President of the Carnegie Endowment to decline to answer questions on any such ground, if he sought to retain that post.

I have often thought the position of a judge, when a witness declines to answer a question on the ground that he might be incriminated, a little unreal. He has, of course, to tell the jury that they must not draw any conclusion adverse to the witness from his refusal. Yet, when his judicial robes are removed, he would certainly himself take an unfavourable view of such a witness. If, for example, when his work in court was over, he attended some committee of his club to select new candidates, and he found the name of that very witness put forward for membership, I feel tolerably certain that he would not support his candidature.

I assume, but without adequate knowledge, that the same position would prevail in the United States. But the situation was, in fact, very different; for it would seem that some of the witnesses based their objection upon much wider grounds: namely, that it was no part of the function of a committee of the legislature to embark upon an investigation of the conduct of a citizen of the United States. That, so they seemed to assert, was the function of the judiciary and not of the legislature. Not a few of the witnesses attended with counsel who formulated objections on behalf of their clients. It was said, for example, that the matter under investigation was outside the scope of any enquiry under the First Amendment of the Constitution, and that the whole investigation was outside the scope of any Congressional enquiry, as it was an intrusion upon the judicial function. Sometimes it was stated that the Committee or subcommittee was wrongly constituted, and sometimes additional objections were raised under the Fifth or Sixth Amendment.

I am in no way competent to express any opinion as to the validity of such objections; certain it is, though, that neither Hiss nor White ever raised any. The principle does seem to me to have been carried to ridiculous lengths. For instance, Ullmann, a friend of Harry Dexter White, when asked whether he played tennis, answered that he objected to answer on the ground that he might be incriminated—at which there was laughter in the committee room. There was more laughter when Pressman was asked whether he was a member of the American Legion and declined to answer on the same ground. It is right that a judge should not probe too deeply into the reasons which prompt a witness to say that he fears self-incrimination, but I cannot imagine any judge in this country allowing this objection to prevail to such a ridiculous extent.

It is desirable that a committee of Congress should wield great powers, for otherwise it could never do its job in a complete and satisfactory manner. To them surely Shakespeare's words might be applied:

O, it is excellent
To have a giant's strength; but it is tyrannous
To use it like a giant.

When I reflect that any citizen may be summoned before such a committee and be cross-examined about any passage of his private life, of which he has had no previous notice, without having had the right to hear everything that has previously been said to the committee to his discredit, and without having the advantage of any advocate to speak for him or present his case, I realise that these great powers must be used with the utmost discretion. It is true that witnesses were allowed to have counsel with them, with whom they were allowed to consult before answering questions, but this is a poor substitute for the right to have all facilities for representation such as are allowed in any court of law.

It is, of course, an exaggeration to refer to the Committee as a Court of Star Chamber, for that court would not only investigate the conduct of some individual, but would try and punish him as well; it would certainly not have been astute to adopt any regular procedure or established rules of evidence. Moreover, it would have conducted its entire proceedings in secret or, to use the American expression, in executive session. The Committee on Un-American Activities merely investigates; it does not try; it does not punish; but the results of its investigations may be to bring an individual into grave public discredit. Its activities are divided into executive sessions, and public sessions which in the present instance naturally attracted immense publicity; it would appear, however, that the proceedings in executive session did not always remain private.

There was an occasion when Hiss was asked in an executive session whether he would be prepared to submit to a lie-detector test. I must make it clear that I have no knowledge of such mechanical contrivances—we have nothing of the kind in our courts—but I should have thought that at best such a test could only record the emotional reaction existing at a given moment. I can well imagine that some timid witness, when asked for a name and address, would at once have a lie registered; but I can equally imagine a brazen-faced liar telling the most shocking untruths without turning a hair or having a lie registered against him. I have no doubt that attempts have been made to adjust the machine to the idiosyncrasies of the witness, and it is possible, I suppose, that some satisfactory system may have been worked out. Judges of the future may have all sorts of contrivances denied to those of us who carry on the judicial function today. Lie-detecting tests may be perfected, and the administration of the so-called truth drugs may become a matter of common practice. I should not myself think it desirable that an investigating committee should ask the person whose conduct is being investigated and who is not represented by Counsel to submit to such a test; but if such a question is thought to be right and is asked in private, it is wholly lamentable—and in this every member of the investigating committee would agree with me—that the fact that such a question had been asked should become public. I may add that I should myself have answered that question in exactly the way that Alger Hiss answered it. The fact remains that Hiss was asked in a private session whether he would take a lie-detector test, and the fact that he had been asked such a question leaked out and appeared in the press.

There is a passage in Whittaker Chambers' recent book, *Witness*, which suggests that this Committee was not influenced solely by its desire to come to a right and just conclusion upon the evidence brought before it.

The author there, in language far more graphic than I can hope to emulate, describes the position of the Committee after Hiss had given his evidence. He tells us that they stood for some time in mute gloom until one of the members said, "We're ruined." Chambers points out that their terror was fully justified, for it was an election year and the seat of every member was at stake. There had already been considerable hostile clamour in the press about the activities of the Committee, as a result of which, he says, its members were, both individually and collectively, so apprehensive that they were in a state approaching anxiety neurosis.

How dangerous it is that anyone exercising a judicial, or even a quasi-judicial, function should feel such personal apprehensions about the outcome of his conclusions. Yet if the whole matter had come to nothing, it might have proved a veritable boomerang.

Such is the substance of the statement made by Whittaker Chambers.

I cannot, of course, assert that this statement is true, but, as a witty judge once observed, "Truth will out even in an affidavit"; and it is possible that this statement may contain the germs of truth. If so, I feel bound to say that the luckless individual who appears before such a committee may find himself rather in the position of the shuttlecock between two expert wielders of the battledore. If it be true that political considerations are to influence the conduct of such a committee, if he is to be used as the *corpus vile* whereby the legislative branch is to put pressure on the executive branch to activate the judicial branch, his lot is indeed unhappy. The administration of justice and the participation in political life are surely two useful and praiseworthy activities. It is a mere platitude to say that they should be kept, so far as possible, in watertight compartments, for when politics comes in by the door justice tends to fly out by the window. When we set up a tribunal of investigation in this country, we always arrange that anyone whose conduct is under investigation shall have the right to be represented by Counsel and to hear all that can be said against him. This seems to me to be a useful precaution, and I trust we shall never depart from it.

No doubt the Committee did much to make the American people alive to the very real danger of Communist infiltration and to enlighten public opinion as to the extent to which Communist sympathisers had succeeded in getting into federal employment. In calling attention to these facts, the Committee rendered what may well have been a most useful service; but the method adopted seems to involve the risk of unfairness to individuals, particularly when there is added a submission to a grand jury, followed by a trial on an indictment found by such a grand jury. For however clear and impelling may be the admonition given to the jury at the trial to disregard all facts which have not been adduced in evidence before them, it is, I should think, only too probable that the jurors, albeit unconsciously, may have at the back of their minds the proceedings before the House Committee, which must have been discussed and rediscussed at many American breakfast tables.

Every government must have the unquestioned right to dispense with the services of any of its officers and to make such enquiries as it thinks appropriate to ascertain whether there is ground for supposing that any of its employees are or have been Communist sympathisers. In the light of our present-day knowledge every government would, I should think, be well advised to see that those suspected on reasonable grounds do not continue in its service, at least in positions in which they might have access to confidential documents. But are not such enquiries all the better if they are made discreetly and quietly? Such, at least, has been our practice. If the majority in the House of Commons thought that the Government of the day was disregarding the elementary precaution of seeing that it was not employing Communists in positions of trust, the Government would fall. But our constitution is so different from the American that our procedure might be quite inappropriate there; and the appeal to public opinion, which in the last resort is the governing factor in any democracy, can only be made in the most public manner possible. It was for this reason, no doubt, that all the devices of broadcasting and of the camera were so fully employed to publicise the proceedings of the House Committee.

After the conclusion of the second trial, and at a time therefore when comment could properly be made, Mr. Nixon, who had been an active member of the House Committee, gave an interesting account of its work.[1] He made it clear that in his opinion the administration had been lax in not probing more thoroughly into the allegations which Chambers had made in the early days to Mr. Berle and to Mr. Ray Murphy. This raises a political question; and I feel it would be inappropriate that I should express any opinion about it.

In the course of his speech Mr. Nixon revealed the nature and the contents of the documents which Chambers had pro-

[1]Speech in the House of Representatives on Thursday, the 26th January 1950.

duced, and which Chambers said had been given to him by Harry Dexter White. Mr. Nixon explained that he had in his possession photostatic copies of eight pages of documents[2] which were in the handwriting of White, which formed part of the documents which Chambers had produced in the course of the pre-trial proceedings at Baltimore on the 17th November 1948. Mr. Nixon then said that he felt that the public was entitled to "see and consider the evidence." I respectfully agree with the course Mr. Nixon then took and with the reasons which actuated him in so doing.

It was, of course, a most unhappy fact that these documents were not revealed during White's lifetime; for White would then have had an opportunity of explaining their nature and origin, and of giving such explanation as he could of the undoubted fact that these documents, written in his own handwriting and dealing with confidential matters, were in the possession of Whittaker Chambers. Unhappily we can never know what explanation he would have given. We are driven to make our own deductions from a consideration of these documents.

On the face of them they would appear to be either some sort of diary, or the raw material from which a diary could be constructed, or else they may be letters which White intended for some friend of his in the Treasury who was presumably absent from Washington at the time they were written.

Although, as I have said, they deal with confidential matters, yet they seem to deal with these matters from such an internal point of view that I should have thought it unlikely that they were prepared by White with the intention of handing them over to an outsider, be he Chambers or indeed anyone else outside the Department. Consider, for example, the first and second paragraphs; and here let me say that the letter "M" obviously stands for Mr. Morgenthau, who was Secretary of the Treasury at the relevant time.

The first paragraph makes it clear that Mr. Morgenthau was not disposed to hurry about a settlement of the Hungarian indebtedness, and that he did not want to fix at that time a pattern which would probably tend to become applicable to

[2]Appendix VI.

other debt settlements. I can well understand that the Communists might have been interested in this piece of information.

But the second paragraph contains a reflection in the following terms:

> What is behind Taylor's, and possibly Feis', desire to press M into a debt-settlement arrangement of that character at this time? Why didn't Taylor try to convince Secretary directly instead of surreptitiously via Feis?

This seems to me to be a reflection concerning internal Treasury matters; and I cannot think that the Communists would be interested in knowing whether the approach to Mr. Morgenthau had been made directly or surreptitiously. I doubt, too, whether they would care to have the information that Mr. Morgenthau had been interested in reading *Red Star over China*. Such things would no doubt be interesting to a Treasury colleague whom White wished to keep fully informed about the current affairs of the Department.

These considerations have, I think, some bearing on the question whether these documents were stolen from White by some Communist agent or whether they were handed by him to Chambers. It would, I should have thought, be especially interesting to know whether other documents, similar to those now under consideration, were found amongst White's papers. If they were some sort of material for a diary, they would presumably have continued notwithstanding the fact that after April 1938 Chambers no longer called to collect documents; and if they were letters to a colleague, they would presumably have continued so long as that colleague was absent. I have, of course, no means of knowing whether any researches on these lines were ever instituted, nor what conclusions would have been reached if they had been made.

The true facts concerning the "White" documents may, I think, have some bearing on the documents written in the handwriting of Hiss which Chambers said were given him by Hiss. For if documents which had in fact been stolen from White were stated by Chambers to have been given to him by White, there is revealed a certain pattern of behaviour. If this be the fact in relation to White, it makes it easier to infer that Chambers may also have said that documents had been handed to him by Hiss when the real fact was that the documents had been stolen from Hiss. Unhappily, we do not possess sufficient material to carry this matter further. I could wish it had been more deeply explored.

I must now resume the sequence of my narrative and consider the proceedings of the House Committee in so far as they bear upon the case of Alger Hiss.

CHAPTER XIV

THE PROCEEDINGS BEFORE THE HOUSE COMMITTEE

At the second trial of Alger Hiss, with which this book is concerned, repeated reference was made to the proceedings which had taken place before the House Committee, and long extracts were read to the jury. It becomes necessary, therefore, for me to give some short sketch of these proceedings.

It was on the 3rd August 1948 that Whittaker Chambers first appeared to give evidence. He asked leave to read a written statement, in which he said that he had joined the Communist Party in 1924 and had left it in 1937. The statement continued that on leaving the Party he feared that the Communists would try to kill him. He said that there had been an underground organisation in Washington which had been formed by Harold Ware; that at one time Nathan Witt had been the head of that organisation, and that later John Abt became its leader. Pressman and Alger Hiss were members of this group, the purpose of which, he explained, was not primarily espionage but infiltration of the Government. On being questioned by Mr. Stripling, the chief investigator of the Committee, he said that Donald Hiss, Victor Perlo, Charles Kramer and Henry Collins were also members of the group, and that group meetings were normally held at the apartment of Henry Collins.

I omit for the moment the question of the payment of dues, with which I deal separately; but I must call attention to the fact that in these proceedings, of which I now set out the more material passages, Chambers clearly implied that the group was not concerned with espionage.

He was asked these questions:

> When you left the Communist Party in 1937 did you approach any of these seven to break with you?
> *Mr. Chambers:* No. The only one of those people whom I approached was Alger Hiss. I went to the Hiss home one evening at what I considered considerable risk to myself and found Mrs. Hiss at home. Mrs. Hiss is also a member of the Communist Party.
> *Mr. Mundt:* Mrs. Alger Hiss?
> *Mr. Chambers:* Mrs. Alger Hiss. Mrs. Donald Hiss, I believe, is not. Mrs. Hiss attempted while I was there to make a call, which I can only presume was to other Communists, but I quickly went to the telephone and she hung up, and Mr. Hiss came in shortly afterwards, and we talked and I tried to break him away from the Party.
> As a matter of fact, he cried when we separated; when I left him, but he absolutely refused to break.
> *Mr. McDowell:* He cried?
> *Mr. Chambers:* Yes, he did. I was very fond of Mr. Hiss.
> *Mr. Mundt:* He must have given you some reason why he did not want to sever the relationship.
> *Mr. Chambers:* His reasons were simply the Party line.
>
> *Mr. Stripling:* Is Harry Dexter White a Communist? Was he a Communist to your knowledge?
> *Mr. Chambers:* I can't say positively that he was a registered member of the Communist Party, but he certainly was a fellow-traveler so far within the fold that his not being a Communist would be a mistake on both sides.
> *Mr. Stripling:* Did you go to Harry Dexter White when you left the Communist Party and ask him also to leave the Party?

Mr. Chambers: I did.
Mr. Stripling: You considered him to be a Communist Party member then?
Mr. Chambers: Well, I accepted an easy phrasing. I didn't ask him to leave the Communist Party, but to break away from the Communist movement.
Mr. Stripling: What did he tell you?
Mr. Chambers: He left me apparently in a very agitated frame of mind, and I thought I had succeeded. Apparently I did not.

Mr. Stripling: Who was the actual head of the group?
Mr. Chambers: The actual head of the group—well, the elected head of the group was either Witt at one time or Abt, and the organizer of the group had been Harold Ware. The head of the whole business was J. Peters.
Mr. Stripling: Harold Ware was employed in the A.A.A., was he not?
Mr. Chambers: I don't know whether he was or not. If I have known, I have forgotten. My impression is he wasn't.
Mr. Stripling: Do you recall what happened to Harold Ware?
Mr. Chambers: He was killed in an automobile accident.
Mr. Stripling: Here in Washington?
Mr. Chambers: No. I think in Pennsylvania.
Mr. Rankin: What was his real name?
Mr. Chambers: As far as I know, Harold Ware. I never knew him [to use any other name].[1]

Mr. Chambers: After I had been in Washington a while it was very clear that some of the members of these groups were going places in the Government.
Mr. Hébert: What year is this?
Mr. Chambers: I should think about 1936. One of them clearly was Alger Hiss, and it was believed that Henry Collins also might go farther. Another was Lee Pressman. So it was decided by Peters, or by Peters in conference with people whom I don't know, that we would take these people out of that apparatus and separate them from it physically—that is, they would have no further intercourse with the people there

[1]See p. 121.

—but they would be connected still with that apparatus and with Peters through me.

It was also decided to add to this group certain other people who had not originally been in that apparatus. One of those people was Harry White.

Mr. Chambers: I should perhaps make the point that these people were specifically not wanted to act as sources of information. These people were an elite group, an outstanding group, which it was believed would rise to positions—as, indeed, some of them did—notably Mr. White and Mr. Hiss—in the Government, and their position in the Government would be of very much more service to the Communist Party.

Mr. Stripling: I want to get clear the status of this select group that infiltrated the Government.

Would you say the purpose was, on the part of the Communists, to establish a beachhead or a base from which they could move further into the Government and obtain positions of power, influence and possible espionage?

Mr. Chambers: I would say power and influence were the paramount objectives.

Mr. Stripling: At that time?

Mr. Chambers: Yes, at that time. You must remember you are dealing with the underground here in a formative stage, with Communists many of whom had not been in the Party more than a year or so.

Mr. Mundt: Mr. Chambers, I am very much interested in trying to check the career of Alger Hiss. I know nothing about Donald Hiss; but as a member of the Foreign Affairs Committee, the personnel committee, I have had some occasion to check the activities of Alger Hiss while he was in the State Department.

There is reason to believe that he organized within that Department one of the Communist cells which endeavored to influence our Chinese policy and bring about the condemnation of Chiang Kai-shek, which put Marzani in an important position there, and I think it is important to know what happened to these people after they leave the Government. Do you know where Alger Hiss is employed now?

Mr. Chambers: I believe Alger Hiss is now the head of the Carnegie Foundation for World Peace.

Mr. Mundt: That is the same information that had come to me, and I am happy to have it confirmed. Certainly there is no hope for world peace under the leadership of men like Alger Hiss.

At the close of the day's proceedings, Chambers was sincerely thanked for the "splendid" testimony he had given. Those who were going to be called to controvert the statement of this "splendid witness" were going in to bat on a very sticky wicket, and Hiss, in particular, must have anticipated trouble in view of the statement made before he had been called as a witness that there was no hope for world peace under the leadership of men like him.

Two days later, on the 5th August 1948, Hiss appeared before the House Committee and also read a statement, in which he denied that he had ever been a member of the Communist Party or that he had ever followed its line; he said that to the best of his knowledge none of his friends was a Communist. He explained the extent of his acquaintance with Abt and Pressman and the others who had been mentioned. He said that he had first been asked about Whittaker Chambers by representatives of the Federal Bureau of Investigation in 1947; so far as he knew, he had never seen Chambers, and he wished he could have seen him before he testified. Mr. Stripling showed him a recent photograph of Chambers, explaining that Chambers was much heavier now than he had been ten years ago; and Hiss replied that he could not recognise the photograph. He recalled that "last winter" he had heard indirectly that a man called Chambers was calling him a Communist; and he recounted how, at the instance of Mr. Justice Byrnes, the then Secretary of State, he had submitted himself in the spring of 1946 to the F.B.I. for investigation, on the strength of the rumour that he was a Communist. He said that he had been an Episcopalian all his life and that his wife was a Quaker.

Hiss was then asked about the part he had played at the Yalta Conference, and stated that he had been opposed to the particular clause by which the United States had agreed to support

Russia's application for votes in the Assembly and for membership in the U.N.O. for her two satellites. Mr. Mundt congratulated him on his attitude to these questions. This incident serves to illustrate the striking difference that exists between the position of a civil servant in this country and that of his opposite number in the United States.

At this stage I feel it would have been much better to arrange forthwith for a confrontation of Chambers and Hiss. It would, I think, have been fairer to both of them and would have saved the Committee a lot of unnecessary evidence. But it was decided otherwise, and on the 7th August 1948 the Committee heard Chambers in executive session—that is, in private.

Chambers gave evidence of various facts which proved conclusively that he had known Hiss and, indeed, that he had stayed in his house. For example, he spoke of the interest which Hiss had in bird-watching (his house contained many bird pictures) and related how Hiss had once seen a rare bird called a prothonotary warbler. Chambers said that he had stayed with Hiss for as long as a week and, indeed, had made the Hiss home a kind of informal headquarters. He described various intimate family matters which would have become known only to a person who had stayed in the house. I would point out that all this evidence would have been quite unnecessary if Hiss had at this stage been given the opportunity of being confronted with Chambers and had been able to recognise him as a man who had stayed in his house.

Chambers said that when he first knew him Hiss had an old Ford car, and he described how Hiss had given it away—against the advice of Peters and himself—for the benefit of some poor Communist organiser. Chambers explained that the Communist Party had in Washington a service station—or, at any rate, that they had some Communist working in a service station—and that Peters either took Hiss there or else gave him the address. He continued: "He left the car there and simply went away, and the man in charge of the station took care of the rest of it for him. I should think the records of that transfer would be traceable." The last sentence about the records of the transfer is not, I think, without significance. They proved to be traceable.

In conclusion, Chambers said that he was willing to submit to a lie-detector test.

On the 16th August 1948 the Committee met again in executive session to hear Hiss. Hiss said he was anxious to meet Chambers in the flesh and to hear what Chambers had said about him, for he feared that Chambers might come to hear what he (Hiss) had told the Committee and might make use of that information to prove an acquaintanceship. Hiss was shown another photograph, and said that the face was definitely not unfamiliar, but he said that he was not prepared to testify on the basis of a photograph.

He said that he had been thinking it over and remembered meeting a free-lance journalist called George Crosley when he was working for the Nye Committee; he recalled that he had let Crosley occupy his apartment and had "thrown in" an old Ford with the apartment; but he could not make out from the photograph whether George Crosley and Whittaker Chambers were the same person. He recalled further that George Crosley had given him a rug, but that he had never made any other payment for the use of the apartment, and that he had from time to time borrowed small sums of money. Thus the rug was first mentioned by Hiss. It was at this meeting that Hiss was asked about his willingness to take a lie detector test.

I have dealt with these matters briefly because the evidence relating to them was in most cases textually reproduced during the second trial. The reader who has followed me thus far will have observed the statement by Chambers: "These people were specifically not wanted to act as sources of information," and he will have observed, too, that when Mr. Stripling, the chief investigator, added "possible espionage" to a list of group purposes, Chambers so framed his answer as not to include this amongst the activities of the group.

I must now relate what happened when the two chief actors in this drama, Alger Hiss and Whittaker Chambers, were—at long last—confronted with each other before the House Committee. The evidence of the confrontation was read to the jury at the trial, and they were asked to judge from it whether the doubts and difficulties which Hiss expressed in recognising the man with whom he was so confronted were genuine or assumed.

Further proceedings took place before the House Committee after the confrontation, but as all the important matters then elicited were brought out again when the case came before the jury, it is not, I think, necessary for me to refer to them here. I shall set out the full account of the confrontation, and thereafter the evidence which Chambers gave before the House Committee relating to the payment of dues. This matter of the payment of dues was not referred to at the trial.

CHAPTER XV

THE CONFRONTATION OF ALGER HISS AND WHITTAKER CHAMBERS BEFORE THE HOUSE COMMITTEE

It was on the 17th August 1948 that the two men were at last confronted with each other. The following dialogue took place:

Mr. Nixon: Sit over here, Mr. Chambers. Mr. Chambers, will you please stand? And will you please stand, Mr. Hiss? Mr. Hiss, the man standing here is Mr. Whittaker Chambers. I ask you now if you have ever known that man before.
Mr. Hiss: May I ask him to speak? Will you ask him to say something?
Mr. Nixon: Yes. Mr. Chambers, will you tell us your name and your business?
Mr. Chambers: My name is Whittaker Chambers. [At this point Mr. Hiss walked in the direction of Mr. Chambers.]
Mr. Hiss: Would you mind opening your mouth wider? . . . You know what I am referring to, Mr. Nixon. Will you go on talking?
Mr. Chambers: I am senior editor of *Time* magazine.
Mr. Hiss: May I ask whether his voice, when he testified before, was comparable to this?

Mr. Nixon: His voice?
Mr. Hiss: Or did he talk a little more in a lower key?
Mr. McDowell: I would say it is about the same now as we have heard.
Mr. Hiss: Would you ask him to talk a little more?
Mr. Nixon: Read something, Mr. Chambers. I will let you read from——
Mr. Hiss: I think he is George Crosley, but I would like to hear him talk a little longer.
Mr. McDowell: Mr. Chambers, if you would be more comfortable, you may sit down.
Mr. Hiss: Are you George Crosley?
Mr. Chambers: Not to my knowledge. You are Alger Hiss, I believe.
Mr. Hiss: I certainly am.
Mr. Chambers: That was my recollection. [Reading] "Since June——"
Mr. Nixon (interposing): Just one moment. Since some repartee goes on between these two people, I think Mr. Chambers should be sworn.
Mr. Hiss: That is a good idea.
Mr. McDowell: You do solemnly swear, sir, that the testimony you shall give this Committee will be the truth, the whole truth, and nothing but the truth, so help you God?
Mr. Chambers: I do.
Mr. Nixon: Mr. Hiss, may I say something? I suggested that he be sworn, and when I say something like that I want no interruptions from you.
Mr. Hiss: Mr. Nixon, in view of what happened yesterday, I think there is no occasion for you to use that tone of voice in speaking to me, and I hope the record will show what I have just said.
Mr. Nixon: The record shows everything that is being said here today.
Mr. Stripling: You were going to read.
Mr. Chambers (reading from *Newsweek* magazine): "Tobin for Labor. Since June, Harry S. Truman had been peddling the labor secretaryship left vacant by Lewis B. Schwellen-

bach's death in hope of gaining the maximum political advantage from the appointment."

Mr. Hiss: May I interrupt?

Mr. McDowell: Yes.

Mr. Hiss: The voice sounds a little less resonant than the voice that I recall of the man I knew as George Crosley. The teeth look to me as though either they have been improved upon or that there has been considerable dental work done since I knew George Crosley, which was some years ago. I believe—I am not prepared without further checking to take an absolute oath—that he must be George Crosley.

Mr. Nixon: May I ask a question of Mr. Chambers?

Mr. Hiss: I would like to ask Mr. Chambers, if I may.

Mr. Nixon: I will ask the questions at this time. Mr. Chambers, have you had any dental work since 1934 of a substantial nature?

Mr. Chambers: Yes, I have.

Mr. Nixon: What type of dental work?

Mr. Chambers: I have had some extractions and a plate.

Mr. Nixon: Have you had any dental work in the front of your mouth?

Mr. Chambers: Yes.

Mr. Nixon: What is the nature of that work?

Mr. Chambers: That is a plate in place of some of the upper dentures.

Mr. Nixon: I see.

Mr. Hiss: Could you ask him the name of the dentist that performed these things? Is that appropriate?

Mr. Nixon: Yes. What is the name?

Mr. Chambers: Dr. Hitchcock, Westminster, Maryland.

Mr. Hiss: That testimony of Mr. Chambers, if it can be believed, would tend to substantiate my feeling that he represented himself to me in 1934 or 1935 or thereabouts as George Crosley, a free-lance writer of articles for magazines. I would like to find out from Dr. Hitchcock if what he has just said is true, because I am relying partly—one of my main recollections of Crosley was the poor condition of his teeth.

Mr. Nixon: Can you describe the condition of your teeth in 1934?

Mr. Chambers: Yes. They were in very bad shape.
Mr. Nixon: The front teeth were?
Mr. Chambers: Yes, I think so.
Mr. Hiss: Mr. Chairman.
Mr. Nixon: Excuse me. Before we leave the teeth, Mr. Hiss, do you feel that you would have to have the dentist tell you just what he did to the teeth before you could tell anything about this man?
Mr. Hiss: I would like a few more questions asked. I didn't intend to say anything about this, because I feel very strongly that he is Crosley, but he looks very different in girth, and in other appearances—hair, forehead, and so on, particularly the jowls.
Mr. Nixon: What was Crosley's wife's name?
Mr. Hiss: I don't think I recall.
Mr. Nixon: You did testify that she on several occasions was in your home overnight.
Mr. Hiss: That is right.
Mr. Nixon: And that you have ridden with her in a car as well as with him.
Mr. Hiss: I don't recall testifying to that.
Mr. Nixon: Do you testify she didn't?
Mr. Hiss: I don't recall.
Mr. Nixon: But she did stay overnight in your home on several occasions.
Mr. Hiss: She did. I don't think I said several occasions.
Mr. Nixon: How many times did you say?
Mr. Hiss: My recollection is that at the time George Crosley sub-rented my apartment on 29th Street his wife and he and infant spent two or three or four consecutive nights in my house because the van had not come with their furniture, and we left only certain pieces of furniture behind to accommodate them.
Mr. Nixon: In regard to the rental agreement that was entered into with Mr. Crosley, do you recall approximately the rental that was charged and agreed to?
Mr. Hiss: My recollection is that I said I would be glad to let him have the apartment for the cost to me. It was a rather moderate rental.

Mr. Nixon: Could you say within certain limits?

Mr. Hiss: My recollection—I can't remember just what I paid for the apartment that far back—my recollection is it was under $75 a month. It was a very reasonable rental. That is one of the reasons I had taken it.

Mr. Nixon: For how long was this rental agreement?

Mr. Hiss: I think I went into this yesterday in the testimony. Some time in the spring, according to my recollection, of 1934.

Mr. Nixon: Or did you say 1935?

Mr. Hiss: I am looking at notes I made trying to remember the dates. Some time in the spring of 1935 I leased the house on P Street. Having both a house and an apartment on my hands, I was looking for a way of disposing of the apartment on sublease, and on the occasion of one of the talks I had with Crosley, he said he was planning to spend the summer in Washington carrying on the researches he had been doing in the field of the Munitions Committee investigations. I asked him if he would like to sublet my apartment during that period of time, that it was not too cool, but that it was up on a hill and had a very decent location as Washington goes, that I would let him have it for the cost to me. In the course of the negotiation he referred to the fact that he also wanted an automobile.

Mr. Nixon: How many months, Mr. Hiss, approximately, was that?

Mr. Hiss: Just the summer months.

Mr. Nixon: Three months?

Mr. Hiss: I don't remember how long the lease ran. I think to September. Maybe it ran to October. I think this conversation probably took place in June.

Mr. Nixon: When did your lease on this apartment run out?

Mr. Hiss: I think in the fall, September or October, and I had several months still to go after the time I had taken the other place.

Mr. Nixon: You think this lease on the apartment ran out in the fall?

Mr. Hiss: That is my best recollection.

Mr. Nixon: You are testifying, as I understand, that the lease to Mr. Crosley was for the three summer months approximately.
Mr. Hiss: As long as he wanted to stay during the summer period while I still had the use of that apartment.
Mr. Nixon: It was beyond the month of July? Did it include the month of July, do you know?
Mr. Hiss: I think it included July and August.
Mr. Nixon: You say it did include July and August?
Mr. Hiss: Yes. We are talking about something that occurred thirteen years ago. It is my best recollection.
Mr. Nixon: I understand. Was it a lease for longer than two months?
Mr. Hiss: Mr. Nixon, I have testified that I think it took the summer months. It might have been June, July, August and September. It depends on how long I had the disposition of the apartment.
Mr. Nixon: Then the total rental value for the period was, if it were for two months, it would have been approximately $150; three months, approximately $225.
Mr. Hiss: It was contingent upon the number of months he would occupy the remaining unexpired term under my lease.
Mr. Nixon: How long did he stay there?
Mr. Hiss: As far as I know, he stayed there all summer. He certainly never said he didn't.
Mr. Nixon: Your lease did not run out after the end of the summer?
Mr. Hiss: That is right.
Mr. Nixon: He didn't stay there after that?
Mr. Hiss: Not to my knowledge.
Mr. Nixon: Did he ever pay any rent at all?
Mr. Hiss: My recollection is that he paid no cash, that he once paid in kind.
Mr. Nixon: No cash at all?
Mr. Hiss: He also borrowed some cash in addition.
Mr. Nixon: How much did he borrow, approximately?
Mr. Hiss: I don't think it got over $35 or $40, in different transactions, not all at once. I hope it didn't.
Mr. Nixon: Did you enter into a written contract?

Mr. Hiss: I think it was oral. It wasn't easy to sublet an apartment during the summer in those days in Washington.

Mr. Nixon: How did you first meet Mr. Crosley?

Mr. Hiss: My best recollection—I was thinking over this yesterday morning on the way down to the Committee hearing—is that Mr. Crosley came into my office in the Senate Office Building, where I was serving as legal assistant to the Senate Munitions Committee, as a pressman making inquiries about the investigation, as many dozens of other press people, authors, students, researchers did.

Mr. Nixon: That is the first time you had ever seen him in your life?

Mr. Hiss: The first time I had ever seen him.

Mr. Nixon: Did you immediately discuss this rental contract?

Mr. Hiss: No.

Mr. Nixon: The agreement that you were entering into?

Mr. Hiss: No.

Mr. Nixon: When did that first come into the conversation?

Mr. Hiss: I think that came into the conversation in the spring of 1935 after I knew that I was going to have a house as well as an apartment.

Mr. Nixon: How long had you known Mr. Crosley?

Mr. Hiss: I don't remember which stage of the Munitions Committee investigation I first met Mr. Crosley, and haven't even had time to check when I actually went to the Hill. I think it was in the fall of 1934, but I am not sure.

Mr. Nixon: You had known Mr. Crosley, your testimony is, for about eight months before you entered into this agreement?

Mr. Hiss: Five or six months.

Mr. Nixon: Then you had had several conversations with him during that period?

Mr. Hiss: I think I must have seen him as often as I did any other newspaperman who was particularly interested. I think I saw him ten or eleven times.

Mr. Nixon: Never saw him socially during that period?

Mr. Hiss: Never saw him socially.

Mr. Nixon: Only in the course of your business?

Mr. Hiss: Only in the course of my business.

Mr. Nixon: Then in 1935, the spring of 1935, Mr. Crosley discussed this matter of getting your apartment for the summer with you?
Mr. Hiss: Would you like me to state how I think it originated?
Mr. Nixon: Certainly.
Mr. Hiss: It originated by his saying he was planning to spend the summer months in Washington to complete his research and investigation of the series of articles which he had been engaged upon at the time I first met him.
Mr. Nixon: Would you refresh me on where this apartment was?
Mr. Hiss: This was on 29th Street.
Mr. Nixon: This is the 29th Street apartment?
Mr. Hiss: That is correct.
Mr. Nixon: And from that apartment you had moved to P Street?
Mr. Hiss: 2905 P Street.
Mr. Nixon: House?
Mr. Hiss: House.
Mr. Nixon: That was a house?
Mr. Hiss: That is correct.
Mr. Nixon: Go ahead with your recollection.
Mr. Hiss: You asked me how it originated.
Mr. Nixon: I understand.
Mr. Hiss: That I described. What else did you want?
Mr. Nixon: That completes——
Mr. Hiss: As to how it originated. He mentioned he was planning to spend the summer months consistently in Washington. My understanding had been before he came down to Washington from New York for various hearings of the Committee, for talking to the staff, for getting material, and he said he intended to spend the summer in Washington completing his researches and was looking for a place to live, and I said I happened to have a place I would be very glad to get rid of.
Mr. Nixon: So you agreed with him that he could move into your apartment for three months approximately?
Mr. Hiss: That is correct.

Mr. Nixon: Which would be for a consideration of, say, $225, roughly?

Mr. Hiss: Whatever the actual cost to me was.

Mr. Nixon: And then there was some conversation about a car. What was that?

Mr. Hiss: There was. Mr. Crosley said that while he was in Washington he wondered if he could get a rented car or something, because he would like to have it while his family were with him, get out week ends, something like that. I said, "You came to just the right place. I would be very glad to throw a car in because I have been trying to get rid of an old car which we have kept solely for sentimental reasons which we couldn't get anything on for trade in or sale." I would be very glad to let him have the car because we wanted somebody to make real use of it. We had had it sitting on the city streets because we had a new one.

Mr. Nixon: It was a '29 Ford?

Mr. Hiss: One of the first Model A Fords.

Mr. Nixon: The year of this transaction would be 1935?

Mr. Hiss: That would be my best recollection.

Mr. Nixon: A six-year-old Ford?

Mr. Hiss: That is right.

Mr. Nixon: You just gave him the car with this $225 rental?

Mr. Hiss: As part of the total contract. That is my best recollection.

Mr. Nixon: The rent was simply the going rate, as you indicated?

Mr. Hiss: That is right.

Mr. Nixon: And you just threw in this six-year-old car with it?

Mr. Hiss: That is my best recollection. I don't think it figured as a financial element in the transaction.

Mr. Nixon: Do you know the Blue Book value of a 1929 Ford in 1935?

Mr. Hiss: I certainly don't. I know what the going rate was with sellers of new cars. I think the most I had ever been offered for it was $25 or $30 at that time, a few months before that.

Mr. Nixon: So you gave him the car.

Mr. Hiss: As part of the whole transaction.

Mr. Nixon: Then before he moved into the apartment I understand that you allowed him and his wife to stay with you in your home?
Mr. Hiss: My recollection of that—and this is repetitious——
Mr. Nixon: We are repeating it for his benefit as well as to see if he can recall this incident.
Mr. Hiss: I am glad he has no other way of finding out about it, Mr. Nixon. My recollection on that point is that Mr. Crosley said since he was only coming down for the summer he didn't want to bring very many things. I said since we had rented a furnished house we had more furniture than we really needed. In fact, one of the rooms in 2905 P Street was perpetually used as a storeroom for furniture while we were there. We left several pieces of furniture in the apartment for several weeks or months, I don't remember how long, and I don't remember what pieces, but there was a bed and a bureau and a table and a couple of chairs. When the day came when Mr. Crosley was supposed to move in, his moving van hadn't arrived but his wife and baby had. We put them up the way one would be apt to try to be helpful to people you were sub-letting. You develop a kind of pseudo-friendliness over a transaction of that kind. Mr. Crosley, his wife and infant were put up in my house for two or three days while the moving van was coming; it may have been four, may have been two. It was more than one night. I imagine my wife would testify it seemed even longer than that.
Mr. Nixon: Were those the only two apartments in which Mr. Crosley saw you?
Mr. Hiss: To the best of my knowledge, yes.
Mr. Nixon: When did you see him after that period of the rental agreement?
Mr. Hiss: I saw him several times in the fall of 1935, as I recall it.
Mr. Nixon: What were the occasions of those visits?
Mr. Hiss: Some occasions—he would call—no; I think he came to my house once or twice after that because of this establishment of a personal relationship. I remember on one occasion he came and brought me a rug which was part payment. He hadn't yet sold his articles, he was hard up, he was

going to make payment. My recollection is I never got paid a single red cent in currency.

Mr. Nixon: What kind of a rug was it?

Mr. Hiss: It was about the color of this rug [indicating rug on floor]. I still have it. A fairly sizable rug. My recollection is Mr. Crosley said some wealthy patron had bestowed it upon him as a gift. It was not a very useful rug. It had been used in the nursery. It is in my youngest son's room now, he still being almost of nursery age. He was seven on the day I testified publicly before your Committee.

Mr. Nixon: On these other occasions on which Mr. Crosley stayed with you—did he ever stay overnight?

Mr. Hiss: I wouldn't be sure of my recollection. It is quite possible he may have said he couldn't get a reservation. Mr. Crosley was apparently in the habit of having difficulties. He may very well have said that he couldn't get a hotel reservation, could I put him up. Mr. Crosley, not being someone who paid his debts, may very well have added to his obligations in that way. That I wouldn't be sure of.

Mr. Nixon: You testified on one occasion you took him on a trip, as I understand it, ferried him to New York.

Mr. Hiss: My recollection is that on one occasion when my wife and I were going to drive to New York in any event, Mr. Crosley asked for a ride. I may have mentioned when I was talking to him that I was going to New York, or he may have said he was going to New York, and I said so was I. My recollection is I drove him to New York on one occasion. Whether my wife was present or not, I am not sure. I rather think she may have been. I would have to ask her, and I haven't asked her.

Mr. Nixon: Was that after the time of this rental agreement?

Mr. Hiss: I am afraid I can't recall.

Mr. Nixon: No further questions of Mr. Hiss at this time.

Mr. Stripling: Mr. Hiss, you say that person you knew as George Crosley, the one feature which you must have to check on to identify him is the dentures.

Mr. Hiss: May I answer that my own way rather than just "yes" or "no"?

Mr. Stripling: Well, now, I would like to preface whatever you are going to say by what I say first. I certainly gathered the impression when Mr. Chambers walked in this room and you walked over and examined him and asked him to open his mouth that you were basing your identification purely on what his upper teeth might have looked like. Now, here is a person that you knew for several months at least. You knew him so well that he was a guest in your home.

Mr. Hiss: Would you——

Mr. Stripling: I would like to complete my statement—that he was a guest in your home, that you gave him an old Ford automobile and permitted him to use, or you leased him, your apartment and in this, a very important confrontation, the only thing you have to check on is this denture; is that correct? There is nothing else about this man's features which you could definitely say, "This is the man I knew as George Crosley," that you have to rely entirely on this denture; is that your position?

Mr. Hiss: Is your preface through? My answer to the question you have asked is this:

From the time on Wednesday, August 4, 1948, when I was able to get hold of neswpapers containing photographs of one Whittaker Chambers, I was struck by a certain familiarity in features. When I testified on August 5 and was shown a photograph by you, Mr. Stripling, there was again some familiarity in features. I could not be sure that I had never seen the person whose photographs you showed me. I said I would want to see the person.

The photographs are rather good photographs of Whittaker Chambers as I see Whittaker Chambers today. I am not given on important occasions to snap judgments or simple, easy statements. I am confident that George Crosley had notably bad teeth. I would not call George Crosley a guest in my house. I have explained the circumstances. If you choose to call him a guest, that is your affair.

Mr. Stripling: I am willing to strike the word "guest." He was in your house.

Mr. Hiss: I saw him at the time I was seeing hundreds of people. Since then I have seen thousands of people. He meant nothing to me except as one I saw under the circumstances I have described. My recollection of George Crosley, if this man had said he was George Crosley, I would have no difficulty in identification. He denied it right here. I would like—and asked earlier in this hearing—if I could ask some further questions to help in identification. I was denied that.

Mr. Stripling: I think you should be permitted——

Mr. Hiss: I was denied that right. I am not, therefore, able to take an oath that this man is George Crosley. I have been testifying about George Crosley. Whether he and this man are the same or whether he has means of getting information from George Crosley about my house, I do not know. He may have had his face lifted.

Mr. Stripling: The witness says he was denied the right to ask this witness questions. I believe the record will show you stated "at this time." I think he should be permitted to ask the witness questions now, or any other motion should be granted which will permit him to determine whether or not this is the individual to whom he is referring.

Mr. Hiss: Right. I would be very happy if I could pursue that. Do I have the Chair's permission?

Mr. McDowell: The Chair will agree to that.

Mr. Hiss: Do I have Mr. Nixon's permission?

Mr. Nixon: Yes.

Mr. McDowell: Here is a very difficult situation.

Mr. Nixon: The only suggestion I would make in fairness to Mr. Chambers is that he should also be given the opportunity to ask Mr. Hiss any questions.

Mr. McDowell: Of course.

Mr. Hiss: I will welcome that.

Mr. Nixon: Mr. Chambers, do you have any objection?

Mr. Chambers: No.

Mr. Hiss: Did you ever go under the name of George Crosley?

Mr. Chambers: Not to my knowledge.

Mr. Hiss: Did you ever sublet an apartment on 29th Street from me?

Mr. Chambers: No, I did not.

Mr. Hiss: You did not?

Mr. Chambers: No.

Mr. Hiss: Did you ever spend any time with your wife and

child in an apartment on 29th Street in Washington when I was not there because I and my family were living on P Street?

Mr. Chambers: I most certainly did.

Mr. Hiss: You did or did not?

Mr. Chambers: I did.

Mr. Hiss: Would you tell me how you reconcile your negative answers with this affirmative answer?

Mr. Chambers: Very easily, Alger. I was a Communist and you were a Communist.

Mr. Hiss: Would you be responsive and continue your answer?

Mr. Chambers: I do not think it is needed.

Mr. Hiss: That is the answer.

Mr. Nixon: I will help you with the answer, Mr. Hiss. The question, Mr. Chambers, is, as I understand it, that Mr. Hiss cannot understand how you would deny that you were George Crosley and yet admit that you spent time in his apartment. Now would you explain the circumstances? I don't want to put that until Mr. Hiss agrees that is one of his questions.

Mr. Hiss: You have the privilege of asking any questions you want. I think that is an accurate phrasing.

Mr. Nixon: Go ahead.

Mr. Chambers: As I have testified before, I came to Washington as a Communist functionary, a functionary of the American Communist Party. I was connected with the underground group of which Mr. Hiss was a member. Mr. Hiss and I became friends. To the best of my knowledge, Mr. Hiss himself suggested that I go there, and I accepted gratefully.

Mr. Hiss: Mr. Chairman.

Mr. Nixon: Just a moment. How long did you stay there?

Mr. Chambers: My recollection was about three weeks. It may have been longer. I brought no furniture, I might add.

Mr. Hiss: Mr. Chairman, I don't need to ask Mr. Whittaker Chambers any more questions. I am now perfectly prepared to identify this man as George Crosley.

The whole of the evidence relating to this confrontation was read to the jury at the second trial. They did not have the advantage of seeing Hiss and Chambers while the evidence was being given. It is, of course, possible to take the view that Hiss was staging an elaborate act in pretending not to recognise a man whom he must have known perfectly well. It must be remembered that, according to Chambers' account, he had not met Hiss since about Christmas 1938, and, if Hiss is to be believed, they had not met since about the end of 1936. By either account they had not seen each other for some ten or twelve years. Of course, if they had met very frequently, it is tolerably certain that Hiss would have had no difficulty in recognising Chambers, even though he had had considerable dental work done and had changed considerably in the meantime in other respects. But if, in fact, they had met only about a dozen times, it is possible that Hiss might have had genuine difficulty in recognising Chambers after a lapse of time.

I think it only fair to point out that Hiss's recollection was obviously at fault in many respects. He spoke of the apartment as though it were on 29th Street, when it was of course on 28th Street. But no one could suggest that this was anything more than a plain mistake. Equally, he spoke of the rent as being "under $75 a month," and of the period of his unexpired lease as though it included August and September; in fact, the rent was $60 a month and his lease came to an end on the 1st July. In making these mistakes he was saying something against himself and was tending to make the concession to Crosley more important than it in fact was. In the same way, when he dealt with the car and said: "I would be very glad to let him have the car . . . because we had a new one," I think it is fair to say that he was making an honest mistake, for he must have known that the date of the purchase of the new car could be checked.

Hiss made it plain that he was speaking according to his best recollection only, as to the events of some thirteen years back; he said that he had not checked up on the accuracy of his answers. I see no reason to disbelieve him or to attribute these replies to wilful perjury. I think Mr. Stripling's statement—"I certainly gathered the impression . . . that you were basing your identification purely on what his upper teeth might have looked like"—was erroneous. Hiss had said: "I feel very strongly that he is Crosley, but he looks very different in girth . . . hair, forehead, and so on, particularly the jowls." The teeth were no doubt one of the factors in the identification, but they were quite plainly not the only factor which Hiss took into consideration.

CHAPTER XVI

THE PAYMENT OF DUES

This matter was never mentioned at the trial, but it was of such importance that I should, I think, record it.

At the hearing before the House Committee on the 3rd August 1948, Chambers said that he had met the members of the group of which he said Hiss was a member at Collins' apartment; then followed this question:

> *Mr. Stripling:* When you met with these people at Mr. Collins' apartment, did you collect Communist Party dues from them?
>
> *Mr. Chambers:* I did not, but the Communist Party dues were handed over to me by Collins, who was the treasurer of that group.
>
> *Mr. Stripling:* When . . . he would turn over Communist Party dues would he turn over any other information to you, any other dues or information other than from these seven people?
>
> *Mr. Chambers:* Well, the dues were not simply from the seven people, I believe. Dues were from the whole apparatus, cells which were headed by these seven people.

Mr. Stripling: How much money was turned over to you from time to time?

Mr. Chambers: That I don't know.

Mr. Stripling: Was it a considerable sum?

Mr. Chambers: My impression was that it was, and I believe I heard that because at that time the dues were 10 per cent of whatever the individual's salary was.

On the 7th August the following questions were asked:

Mr. Nixon: Did you obtain his [Hiss's] Party dues from him?

Mr. Chambers: Yes, I did.

Mr. Nixon: Over what period of time?

Mr. Chambers: Two or three years, as long as I knew him.

Mr. Nixon: Party dues from him and his wife?

Mr. Chambers: I assume his wife's dues were there; I understood it to be.

Mr. Nixon: You understood it to be?

Mr. Chambers: Mr. Hiss would simply give me an envelope containing Party dues which I transferred to Peters. I didn't handle the money.

Mr. Nixon: How often?

Mr. Chambers: Once a month.

Mr. Nixon: What did he say?

Mr. Chambers: That was one point it wasn't necessary to say anything. At first he said, "Here are my dues."

Mr. Nixon: And once a month over a period of two years, approximately, he gave you an envelope which contained the dues?

Mr. Chambers: That is right.

Mr. Nixon: What did you do with that envelope?

Mr. Chambers: I gave it to Peters.

Mr. Nixon: In New York?

Mr. Chambers: Or Washington.

Mr. Nixon: This envelope contained dues of Hiss and other members of the group?

Mr. Chambers: Only Hiss.

Mr. Nixon: You collected dues from the other members of the group individually?

Mr. Chambers: All dues were collected individually.

Mr. Nixon: I see. So this money could not have been money from anybody but Hiss?
Mr. Chambers: Only from Hiss.
Mr. Nixon: Couldn't have been giving you dues for his wife and not for himself?
Mr. Chambers: I suppose it is possible, but that was certainly not the understanding.
Mr. Nixon: The understanding was it was his dues?
Mr. Chambers: The understanding was it was his dues. Not only that, but he was rather pious about paying his dues promptly.

Then, as regards Donald Hiss, the following questions were asked:

Mr. Nixon: Donald Hiss—what relation did you have with him?
Mr. Chambers: A purely formal one.
Mr. Nixon: He knew you as Carl?
Mr. Chambers: Yes.
Mr. Nixon: Did you collect dues from him?
Mr. Chambers: Yes.
Mr. Nixon: Did you meet his wife?
Mr. Chambers: I think I met her once, not very often.
Mr. Nixon: Where did you collect the dues from him, at his home?
Mr. Chambers: Probably in Alger's house. He frequently came there.
Mr. Nixon: He came there to see you?
Mr. Chambers: Yes.

On the 25th August Chambers was asked these questions:

Mr. Nixon: Did you yourself have occasion at any time to take dues from Mr. [Alger] Hiss for the Communist Party?
Mr. Chambers: I did.
Mr. Nixon: You did?
Mr. Chambers: Yes.
Mr. Nixon: On one occasion or more occasions than one?
Mr. Chambers: At least on one occasion, and I would think on at least three occasions.

Mr. Nixon: Could it have been more or less than that?

Mr. Chambers: It could have been more than that.

Mr. Nixon: It could have been more than that. Who collected dues for Mr. Hiss generally?

Mr. Chambers: Henry Collins.

Mr. Nixon: Henry Collins?

Mr. Chambers: Henry Collins was the treasurer of that group.

Mr. Nixon: Did J. Peters ever collect dues from Mr. Hiss?

Mr. Chambers: Yes, he did.

Mr. Nixon: To your knowledge?

Mr. Chambers: To my knowledge.

It would have needed all the skill of Mr. Thomas Murphy, leading Counsel for the Prosecution at the second trial, to reconcile the statement that Chambers had received dues from Hiss once a month over a period of two years with the statement that he had taken these dues on at least one occasion, perhaps even three. He wisely did not try.

The absence of any reference throughout the trial to the payment of dues strikes me as the most extraordinary feature of an extraordinary case. A vast amount of time was expended in tracing the history of the cars, of the visits, of the giving of the rug, and so on. The relevance of all these things—in so far as they had any relevance—was to establish that there had been close and intimate relations between Chambers, the Communist agent, and Hiss. Then, the argument runs, this close and intimate relationship would never have existed unless Hiss was in sympathy with Chambers' views, and as Chambers' views were those of a Communist, it follows that Hiss must also have been at least a Communist sympathiser. Yet direct proof that Hiss was not only in sympathy with the Communist point of view, but was also a member of the Communist Party, lay in the fact—if fact it was—that he had paid dues; and this had been categorically stated by Chambers on his oath. Why was this direct proof never referred to throughout the trial? It would not be fair to blame Chambers; he was there to answer such questions as might be put to him, whether by Mr. Murphy or by Mr. Cross, the leading Counsel for the Defence. But when I read *Witness,* I did expect at last to have this mystery cleared up. I found no such thing. Chambers refers in several places to the fact that Hiss and the others were dues-paying members of the Communist Party. I turned over the pages eagerly, hoping to find when and to whom they paid their dues, but in all the 800 pages I found no answer to this question. I found a statement that Chambers is sure he is right in remembering that members of the group, to which he said Alger Hiss belonged, paid 10 per cent of their salaries in dues; and that Hiss, in particular, continued devoutly to pay exorbitant dues to the Party even after he had been transferred to the underground and it was no longer strictly necessary. But the questions I have propounded remain unanswered; they are wrapped in impenetrable mystery.

CHAPTER XVII
THE LIBEL ACTION

The libel action was filed on the 27th September 1948; that is, in the course of the month following the confrontation. Hiss was, of course, committed to bringing this action by the attitude he had adopted before the House Committee, when he challenged Chambers to repeat on a non-privileged occasion the allegation that he had been a member of a Communist group. Chambers repeated this allegation over the radio; and Hiss, after consulting his old friend Mr. Marbury, who acted as his Counsel, instituted proceedings claiming damages for defamation. Chambers put in his defence, stating that the allegations he had made were true; and Hiss then, through his advisers, made use of the procedure under which one party is entitled to cross-examine the other in "pre-trial proceedings."

Chambers was cross-examined at length during the 4th and 5th November 1948. It is interesting to read from the statement[1] which Hiss made to the Federal Bureau of Investigation on the 4th December 1948 that when on the 5th November Chambers was asked whether he had ever obtained any documents from

[1]Appendix IV.

Hiss for transmittal to the Communist Party, he replied that he had not. Further hearing was then adjourned until the 16th November, when the examination of Chambers was to have been continued. But shortly before that date Mr. Marbury was informed by the lawyers acting for Chambers that Chambers would not be available on the 16th November, but that Mrs. Chambers would take his place.

Accordingly, on the 16th November 1948 and on the morning of the 17th November, Mrs. Chambers was examined. Whittaker Chambers attended in the afternoon of the 17th November, and it was then that he produced the incriminating documents which he said had been handed to him by Hiss in the early months of 1938, nearly eleven years before.

I must now recount what Chambers had been doing in these days preceding the 17th November. On Sunday, the 14th November, he went to the house of Mr. Nathan Levine in New York; and in the afternoon Mr. Levine drove him round to his parents' home, 260 Rochester Avenue, New York. Here it was that in the summer of 1938 a sealed envelope had been deposited at the request of Chambers. He and Levine went up to the bathroom, and from a recess near a dumbwaiter shaft Levine retrieved the envelope which had remained there all those years. It is not surprising to hear that it was covered with dust. Levine handed it to Chambers, and Chambers took it down to the kitchen to open it. Levine, too, went into the kitchen, but only to get a brush to clear up the mess he had made in the bathroom; so it happened that when Chambers opened the envelope he was alone.

Chambers explains in his book how astounded he was to see the contents of the envelope. He had completely forgotten, so he says, that there were a large number of copied State documents and spools of microfilm. All these things had "sunk from his memory." He asks us to believe that until he opened the envelope he had completely forgotten their existence. If anyone had asked him, he says, what the envelope contained, he would have answered: "Two or three scraps of Alger Hiss's handwriting and perhaps something of Harry White's." He adds in his book that it was providential that he had not remembered, for had he done so he would probably have destroyed them so that he might never be tempted to use them. These seem remarkable statements. I do not know whether to be more surprised at Chambers saying that he had completely forgotten the contents of the life preserver or at his statement that if he had remembered them he would probably have destroyed them.

But having opened the envelope and seen its contents, he pushed back the papers "by a reflex of amazement." He held on to the edge of the table, for he felt the floor swinging round him and thought he was going to fall. That feeling passed quickly. He describes in *Witness* how he continued to grip the edge of the kitchen table, for he was experiencing that kind of "physical hush" that a man feels when an act of God has happened to him. But the hush was interrupted by the return of Levine.

On the night of that eventful Sunday, the 14th November 1948, says Chambers, he left New York for Baltimore. He stated in his evidence that the next day he went round to his lawyers and told Mr. Cleveland what he had found—except that he did not tell him about the film. He testified further that he told Mr. Cleveland that he would like a day to consider whether he would introduce the documents into the pre-trial examination. Thus Mr. Cleveland arranged with Mr. Marbury that on the 16th November Mrs. Chambers would take her husband's place.

Chambers describes in *Witness* how he went down to his farm while his wife was in Baltimore giving evidence in the pre-trial examination. He was all alone. He had to decide whether to produce the documents, and in his solitude, confronted with this problem, he contemplated committing suicide. But he then reached no decision as to suicide except as to the method he would employ if he later decided on this course. He determined, in that event, to use a gas-producing substance rather than his gun.

On the afternoon of the 17th November he resumed his evidence at the pre-trial examination and produced the typewritten and handwritten documents and made mention for the first time of the supposed meeting between Hiss and Bykov.

Hiss was not present when the documents were produced, and Mr. Marbury went to New York on the 18th November to show him the photographs of the documents which Chambers had produced and to ask for his instructions. The reaction of Hiss was immediate. He insisted that the Attorney General of the United States be promptly informed of what had taken place and that the documents be put at his disposal.

I can deal quite briefly with the history of the production of the films. Chambers said in his evidence that he did not give Mr. Cleveland the films; he had "read" the developed film but kept the undeveloped film in his house, thinking he would develop it himself. A few days later Mr. Stripling of the House Committee spoke to him on the telephone, and as a result Chambers called at Mr. Stripling's office and was served with a subpoena to produce documents. So it came about that on the 2nd December 1948 the investigators of the House Committee went with Chambers to his farm and were handed the two films, which he had hidden in a pumpkin. The undeveloped film, for some reason, turned out to have been spoilt, but the developed film contained what I have called the photographed documents.

It is, I think, unnecessary to deal with the further history of the libel action, but it is useful to consider at this stage whether there are any inferences to be drawn from the fact that such an action was brought and was conducted in the way it was. Of course, if Hiss was innocent of the charges which up to that time had been made against him, he would have acted as he did. He would have pressed his action and given no quarter; he would have insisted on any documents which were produced being put in the hands of the authorities. If he had in his younger days expressed his sympathies with Russia, or his desire to find out more about Russia, or even if he had been a member of a Communist study group, he might well have brought his action. Mr. Berle had given the House Committee his recollection of the statement Chambers had made to him in 1939: that there had been a "study group of some sort formed of men who were interested in knowing something about Russia and Russian policy and the general Communist theory of life, and so on"; that their aim was "merely to get some people who would be sympathetic to their point of view." If this was a fair representation of what Chambers said, and if this was the truth, I can understand the bringing of the action.

Views about Russia had changed between the early months of 1938 and the closing months of 1948; so much so that in 1948 Hiss would be reluctant to admit that he had ever—even as far back as 1935–38—been a member of such a group. By 1948 he had reached a great position. He had resigned from the Civil Service after having played a distinguished part in the public life of his country and had become President of the Carnegie foundation. Many men in later years are reluctant to admit even youthful indiscretions; and the word "indiscretion" is an unduly mild word to use of membership in a Communist group by a civil servant, even if that group were devoted merely to intellectual study. If this membership were to be admitted, his position in the eyes of his friends and of the public would be severely shaken; yet if the sum total of his offence were mere membership in a Communist group, there would be no awkward documents to explain away. He could explain his association with Chambers as a mere casual acquaintanceship and rely on his reputation to establish his point against the evidence of a man with such a record. He might, in short, well have adopted the line he did in fact adopt.

But supposing he had handed over secret documents to Chambers "in or about February and March 1938"—is it likely that he would under these circumstances have brought a libel action based on the accusation, a minor accusation on this hypothesis, that he had been a member of a Communist group; and if he had brought it, that he would have pressed it in the way he did? Assuming for a moment that he was guilty of handing over documents, let us pause to consider what his mental attitude and that of his wife must have been in the intervening years. It must have occurred to them that Chambers had broken with the Communist Party, for he no longer came round to collect documents. As week followed week and he still did not come to collect the accumulated documents, they must have realised that he had broken; and then they must have realised that the loan of $400 which he had obtained from Hiss in November 1937 in order to buy a car for his work with the Communists had been obtained under false pretences. Surely they would have had some doubts as to the reliability of Chambers, and they must have known the frightful peril in which they stood. For the documents which Hiss had handed over had been in part written in his own handwriting and in part typed on his own ancient typewriter. During the next ten years this must have been a source of constant worry to him and his wife, for they were living on a volcano. If Chambers had retained any of these documents, and he might well have done so, what would be the position of Hiss? In any case, if Chambers had ever wanted to blackmail Hiss, it is plain that he had all the available material to hand.

Hiss was beyond question an exceptionally intelligent man even if, as Chambers would have us believe, he was a traitor to his own country. This intelligent man must have prepared himself for the line he was to take if ever the dreaded disclosure was made. What could that line be? If Hiss had been conscious of the existence of documents constituting such damning evidence against him, or even of the risk that they existed, would he have taken the course which he did in fact take? Would he in the first instance have challenged Chambers to repeat on a public occasion the allegation that he had had Communist affiliations, so that he could bring an action for defamation? It is of course possible that he might have determined that he was in such a difficult position that he must bluff the thing through. It is possible—but is it probable? If he had started such an action, is it probable that he would have had a pre-trial examination conducted which lasted many days, during which his Counsel, no doubt on his instructions, continued to press Chambers to produce documents? This was indeed a rash and foolhardy proceeding if he had been guilty of handing over documents and, be it noted, of handing them over to Chambers just before Chambers' desertion. Would he not rather have been content to rest on Chambers' evidence, which Hiss, on this hypothesis, must have heard with a sigh of relief, that he (Chambers) possessed no evidence of espionage? For, as I have said, Hiss must have known that he had deserted by the simple fact—if Chambers' story be true—that he no longer called at Hiss's house to collect documents. Indeed, Chambers asserted that Hiss already knew this in 1938 when Chambers called to ask him to break from the Party. If a man is living on a volcano, it is surprising to find him taking all the steps possible to bring about an eruption. It certainly seems to me that if Hiss was guilty he displayed an amazing lack of intelligence in this whole matter, and not least in that he cannot have taken his Counsel and old friend Mr. Marbury into his confidence.

It is difficult to determine from *Witness* the date on which Chambers made his attempt to commit suicide in the manner I have previously described. At first I thought—and wrote—that this attempt was made during the pre-trial examination. Further consideration of *Witness* has satisfied me that the attempt at suicide was made not during the pre-trial examination but during the proceedings before the Grand Jury in the first half of December 1948.

CHAPTER XVIII

WHAT'S IN A NAME?

It is one of the strange features in this strange case that Chambers was never prepared to admit frankly that he had used the name George Crosley. He said it was as "Carl," just plain "Carl," that he was known to Hiss.

If, as Chambers asserted, Hiss was a hardened and disciplined Communist when Chambers first got to know him, it is easy to understand the use of the name "Carl"; and Chambers, it will be remembered, said that when he was first introduced to Hiss by Peters and Ware, two leaders of the Communist underground, Hiss was already a Communist. If, on the other hand, as Hiss asserted, Chambers first came to know Hiss when the latter was with the Nye Committee, and introduced himself as a "free-lance journalist," then it is obvious that he would have had to adopt some name. Here I may point out that when Whittaker Chambers applied for a job with the Federal Government as one of his steps preparatory to leaving the Communist Party, he did describe himself as a "free-lance journalist"—a fact which Hiss could not have known when he testified that Chambers had thus described himself on the occasion of their first meeting.

Although the question whether Chambers made use of the name "George Crosley" and continued to use that name during the entire course of his association with Hiss is not, of itself, of great importance, yet it may serve as an indication of where the truth lies in the matter of the first introduction of the two men, which is of great importance.

The evidence of Hiss and of Mrs. Hiss was quite clear on this point. They had never heard the name "Whittaker Chambers" at any time when they were associating with him. They knew him throughout as "George Crosley." Whittaker Chambers agreed that they did not know him by his real name and that during these years they had never heard the name "Whittaker Chambers." He admitted the use of the name "Carl"; but when he was asked whether he had used the name "George Crosley," he said that it was "possible," that he "might have done so" or that he "couldn't remember"—but he never denied that he had used this name. I find this very hard to believe. I am quite unable to accept the statement that Chambers suffered from such a remarkable lapse of memory.

He may have used the name "George Crosley," or he may not, but to pretend that he could not remember whether he did or did not use that name is, I think stretching credulity to breaking point. Yet throughout the whole history of the case —from the first confrontation before the House Committee to the end of the second trial—he never gave a clear and positive answer to the simple question whether he was passing as George Crosley. At the confrontation he was asked by Hiss, "Are you George Crosley?" and he gave the strange answer, "Not to my knowledge." Some time later he was asked a similar question, "Did you ever go under the name of George Crosley?" and again he gave the answer, "Not to my knowledge." In his book *Witness*, Chambers says that is is "possible" that he used the name "George Crosley," though he has no recollection of it; and he adds that he thinks he has recalled all his other names "without effort." Perhaps with a little more effort he might have succeeded in recalling this name.

One of the disadvantages, of course, of not having a name must be that it makes an introduction to third persons so difficult. Mrs. Chambers experienced this difficulty when she had to introduce Mrs. Hiss to Mr. Boucot at the supposed visit to Smithton, and it will be remembered that she was unable to say how she had overcome this, though the name "Rogers" rang a bell.

There was an occasion in 1934 or early 1935 when Chambers was having a meal in the company of Hiss in a restaurant in Georgetown when in came a lady friend of the Hisses who rejoiced in the name of "Plum Fountain," to whom Chambers was introduced. Let me quote from the evidence:

Mr. Cross: You were introduced to her?
Mr. Chambers: That is right.
Mr. Cross: And you can't tell what name you used?
Mr. Chambers: That is right.
Mr. Cross: Well, you know it wasn't Carl, don't you?
Mr. Chambers: It certainly was not Carl.
Mr. Cross: Was it Mr. Crosley?
Mr. Chambers: I don't believe so.
Mr. Cross: Well, what name was it?
Mr. Chambers: I have no idea, as I have told you.
Mr. Cross: You wouldn't say it was not Mr. Crosley, would you?
Mr. Chambers: I think it very unlikely.
Mr. Cross: Well, you have testified here that it is possible that you used the name and they knew you as George Crosley, haven't you?
Mr. Chambers: Yes. To hasten matters, let us say that it is possible that they could have introduced me that way, but it is improbable.
Mr. Cross: Do you know how they did introduce you?
Mr. Chambers: I do not.
Mr. Cross: You know they did use the name?
Mr. Chambers: I believe they did.
Mr. Cross: And you know they did not use the name Mr. Chambers?
Mr. Chambers: That is definite.
Mr. Cross: That they did not use the name Mr. Chambers?
Mr. Chambers: That is right.

Mr. Cross: You know they did not use the name Breen, don't you?
Mr. Chambers: That is also definitely right.
Mr. Cross: And you know they did not use the name of Dwyer, don't you?
Mr. Chambers: That they did not know.
Mr. Cross: Did they use the name Lloyd Cantwell?
Mr. Chambers: I don't think so.
Mr. Cross: You can't help at all beyond what you have said, that you can't remember?
Mr. Chambers: I am sorry, I cannot help.

Then again Chambers was asked in his cross-examination what name he had used when he was staying at the 28th Street apartment, and he answered: "I have never been able to remember. It may have been Crosley."

Mrs. Chambers was in the like difficulty when she was asked how the maid Julia Rankin, whom the Chambers had "inherited" from the Hisses, addressed her during their occupancy of the 28th Street apartment. She replied that she did not know. She was quite certain the maid did not call her "Liza"; that name, she said, was "for the consumption of Mr. and Mrs. Hiss." She was quite certain that Julia Rankin had addressed her by some name, but she had no idea what it was. In fact, I believe that even in the best Communist circles it is quite impossible to indulge in the luxury of a servant unless you have some name, no matter what it may be; but it was strange that, like her husband, she had forgotten what the name was.

In the course of her cross-examination Mrs. Chambers was further reminded of the evidence she had given at the first trial. She had been asked what the Hisses called her and her husband, and she replied: "Carl and Liza; we never had a last name to them." The name Liza, she said, had been invented at the second meeting of herself, Chambers and the Hisses. It was invented "by all four of us." She could not remember how she was introduced to Mrs. Hiss at their first meeting. She also said that the Hisses used to call round and see her and her husband whilst they (the Chambers) lived at St. Paul Street. She rather thought the name "Cantwell," under which they were then passing, was not on the doorbell. Pressed as to what would have happened if the Hisses had in fact called, had rung a bell which was common to all the apartments, and could do no more than ask, "Is Liza at home?" she answered that she would have known approximately when they were coming.

If, as Chambers asserted, he and Hiss made several trips together and stayed overnight at tourist houses, it is quite inevitable that Chambers must have had some name other than Carl. To allege as he does that he became a close friend of Hiss and to pretend that Hiss knew no name other than Carl is ridiculous.

The matter of the name can be summarised as follows: Hiss and his wife swore positively that Chambers was introduced as, and always used the name of, George Crosley. Chambers himself said that he "may" have used that name. Mrs. Chambers said that they never had any names except Carl and Liza, though she later admitted that there must have been some other name.

It seems clear that there is no reason to disbelieve the evidence of the Hisses on this point; but why was Chambers so reluctant to be candid? Was it not because he feared that an admission that he had used such a name might tell against him alike in the manner of the introduction and on the question whether Hiss was a Communist at that time? "Carl" sounds so Communistic, but "George Crosley" is positively bourgeois.

CHAPTER XIX

AFTER THE FIRST TRIAL

The first trial, which had started on the 31st May 1949, before His Honour Judge Kaufman, ended on the 8th July 1949 in a disagreement; thus it became necessary to try the case again. It was commonly believed that four of the jurors were in favour of an acquittal and the remaining eight in favour of conviction.

The case had excited very great public interest, which indeed was inevitable, since Alger Hiss occupied a prominent position in the public life of the United States. Then, too, it had in some sense originated from the disclosures made before the House Committee, which had received the widest publicity and had created great anxiety amongst a large section of the American public. There had, moreover, been so many dramatic incidents in the case which would have attracted attention even if the accused had not been a public figure—the production of the rolls of microfilm from a pumpkin and the confrontation of Hiss and Chambers had afforded full scope to the American press. The fact that the first trial ended in a disagreement had in itself given rise to comment and controversy; for it seems clear that the doctrine of contempt of court, which forbids that anything shall be reported except what actually takes place in open court, is not so strictly enforced in the United States as it is in England.

It was natural in the circumstances that the Counsel who were acting for the Defence should feel anxiety lest those who would be selected to serve as jurors at the second trial might have become influenced by what they had heard or read of the case—and it was almost certain that they would have read about it in the newspapers. It was therefore decided to ask for a change of venue; that is, that the second trial should take place somewhere in the United States other than the Southern District of New York. The application was based on an affidavit by Mr. McLean of Counsel, and asked that the second trial should take place in Vermont on the ground that the publicity given to the case there had been "more limited in scope and more temperate in tone" than that in the Southern District of New York. The affidavit contained the following statement:

> The trial before Judge Kaufman was reported with a fullness which deponent verily believes to be unprecedented in this district. The case was first-page news in practically every metropolitan paper throughout the six weeks of the trial. The testimony was reported in detail and some newspapers reproduced large portions of it verbatim.
>
> Not only did the New York newspapers give minute attention to what transpired in the courtroom, but many of them also devoted considerable space to collateral aspects of the case apart from the trial itself. Columnists and feature writers made extended comment on the case. At the conclusion of the trial, considerable comment was forthcoming from certain members of Congress and others, all of which was reported in full in the press. Even during the interval between the conclusion of the trial and the present time, articles on the case have continued to appear in New York newspapers.
>
> Many of these manifold newspaper articles were, in deponent's opinion, of a nature highly prejudicial to the defendant. These articles will be referred to in detail hereinafter. In general, they fall into certain definite classifications:

1. Publication during the trial of alleged evidence that was not submitted to the jury and which, in some cases, had actually been excluded by the trial judge.

2. Attacks upon certain witnesses called by the defendant.

3. Attacks upon the trial judge and upon the integrity of this court.

4. Attacks upon certain jurors and interviews with jurors setting forth their comments upon the trial and their opinions of the court and their fellow jurors.

The affidavit set out extracts from newspapers showing that during the trial articles had been written contradicting evidence which had been given at the trial and adducing new "evidence" which had not been given at the trial. A particularly glaring illustration of this was afforded in the case of one Hede Massing, whose evidence had been rejected by Judge Kaufman as incompetent. An article was published in the press on the 1st July 1949—that is, during the first trial—setting out the evidence which she would have given if her testimony had been admitted.

It also appears from the affidavit that attacks had been made on two of the defence witnesses who had given evidence as to Hiss's character—apparently on the ground, which indeed seems strange to us, that they were Justices of the United States Supreme Court.

Four articles appeared in the press criticising Judge Kaufman's conduct of the case while it was still pending. After the jury disagreed and were discharged, the jurors were immediately interviewed by reporters, and their opinions on the trial, including pronouncements on questions of law involved in rulings of the trial judge, were given wide publicity. Members of the House Committee also gave voice to their views on the case and its conduct, which were critical of the trial judge. One congressman said that "a full investigation should immediately be made of the fitness of Judge Kaufman to serve on the Bench in view of his conduct during the trial." Another gave his version of what the excluded testimony of Mrs. Massing would have been. A third remarked, referring to the trial: "That thing in New York stank to high heaven."

A Mr. Du Bois, a member of the American Association for Public Opinion Research, also made an affidavit, from which it appeared that he had taken a poll of public opinion both in New York City and in Vermont. He had had about 200 people selected at random and interviewed in both places. The result showed that over 40 per cent of those in New York had formed an opinion one way or the other on the case; of these, nearly half thought that Hiss was guilty, and the other half was divided between those who thought he was innocent and those who would not express any opinion. The four jurors who had been in favour of an acquittal also made affidavits setting out anonymous and abusive post cards which they had received.

Mr. Murphy, the Counsel in charge of the Prosecution, made an affidavit in opposition to the motion for a change of venue. He said that he had had an analysis made of all the news stories published during the course of the trial and had found that 68 per cent were completely factual, 8 per cent pro-Hiss, 6 per cent anti-Chambers, and 17 per cent pro and anti the trial judge. Mr. Murphy said that, although the news coverage had been on a national basis, only an insignificant percentage had been virulent, and that not towards the defendant. He was supported by an affidavit of a Mr. Babcock, who had had experience in taking public opinion polls. He pointed out that according to the conclusions of Mr. Du Bois the proportion of people in Vermont who had formed the opinion that Hiss was guilty was even higher than in New York.

On the basis of these affidavits the judge decided against the motion for a change of venue. I cannot but think that the effect of the articles attached to Mr. McLean's affidavit might well have been to make it difficult to achieve that calm attitude of mind which is so essential if the jury system is to work at its best.

CHAPTER XX

OF TRIAL BY JURY

Hiss was, of course, tried by a jury; and before I begin to review the evidence in this particular case, I should like to make some general observations on the subject of trial by jury.

Juries are not infallible; no human system is proof against error. But I think that the risk that an innocent man will be convicted is smaller under the system of trial by jury than under any other that has yet been devised.

There are, however, certain dangers against which we must be on our guard if the system is to work satisfactorily. There is the risk that the jury will have heard about the case before the trial starts, and some members of it may even have preconceived ideas before the accused is put in their charge. The less, therefore, that a jury know about a case beforehand, the more likely are they to succeed in deciding only on the evidence adduced before them in court.

There is a second risk that the jury may be influenced by the opinion of other people who have not their responsibility. Sometimes, in extreme cases, a juror may even try to give a decision which will command popular support or will best accord with his conception of the public weal. It is for this reason important to observe the principle that there should be no comment on a pending case—a rule which can best be reconciled with the equally important principle of freedom of the press by preserving the right of the press to report fully all the proceedings in a court of justice, but forbidding any comment until after a final conclusion has been reached. Once the verdict has been pronounced, then judge and jury alike should be given over to the most complete and searching criticism.

Thirdly—and here I realise I am on much more debatable ground—I think the judge should help the jury to come to their decision. He should, of course, direct them on the law, but, in my opinion, he should also assist them by reviewing the evidence.

How far have we succeeded in securing the observance of these three principles?

I have sometimes wondered whether our system of criminal trial is the best that can be devised to secure that so far as humanly possible the jury know nothing about the case save what they hear from the witnesses. In England proceedings start before a magistrate, and if he thinks that a prima facie case has been established, he commits the accused for trial. These proceedings before the magistrate are fully reported in the press in any case which excites public interest.

I can recall a case which happened not very long ago where a man was accused of committing two murders. They were separated in point of time by a short interval of about a week or ten days. They were somewhat similar in point of fact. Each seemed to have been a brutal murder of a young woman, and each case seemed to have some kind of sexual background. The man was accused before the magistrate of having committed the two murders, and the proceedings were very fully reported in the press. He was committed for trial on both cases. When the case came before the assizes the judge quite rightly ruled, since the two cases were separate, that the accused should be tried in respect of one case only. He was duly tried in respect of the first murder and was convicted and sentenced. In this particular case no harm would have been done if the jury had had the story of the second murder, as revealed to the magistrate, in their minds; for the defence was a defence of insanity, and Counsel for the accused himself brought out the facts of the second murder to help him in establishing his defence of insanity. But it might well have been otherwise, and indeed would have been otherwise, if the defence had been that the accused had never committed the murder. In such a case the judge would have directed the jury that they must shut out from their minds anything they had heard about the case before the trial started and have regard only for the evidence which had been given during the trial. I feel sure that the jury would have tried loyally to follow the judge's direction; yet would they not have been confronted with an almost impossible task? It is very difficult for a mind untrained in considering evidence so to control and check the processes of thought. If the jury had been aware of the second murder, must there not have been a grave risk that that knowledge would —albeit unconsciously—have influenced them in coming to a decision?

This risk cannot be avoided under the system prevailing in England unless the enquiry before the magistrate relating to a case which may be committed for trial is to be held *in camera*, or at any rate not reported in the press. I realise that there are objections to any such limitation of publicity. Yet, on the other hand, I am conscious of the danger of allowing a jury to embark on the hearing of a case with such background information. We seldom challenge a juror in this country on the ground of possible bias. It will strike my American friends as a strange fact that throughout my long practice at the Bar I have never myself seen a juror challenged in a criminal case. Yet if the jurors in the case I am discussing had been asked, "Have you read about this case in the papers?" or "Are you conscious of the fact that the accused is charged with a second murder?" they would have answered, I do not doubt, they they were aware of these facts and that they had read about them. It is difficult for me to imagine a different answer, unless of course the juror was prepared to give a dishonest answer or was illiterate.

Let us contrast this system with the system which prevails in Scotland. All prosecutions in Scotland are under the control of the Lord Advocate, who in practice acts through his subordinates, the procurators fiscal. In any difficult case these procurators would apply to the Lord Advocate for his instructions and advice. There is no preliminary hearing before a magistrate. There is nothing for the press to report. When the case begins, no opening statement by counsel on either side is allowed. It is considered essential that the jury should hear the charge against the accused through the mouth of witnesses and in no other way. This system has been devised in order to ensure that the jury cannot be led astray by having regard to any facts which are not brought before them in evidence. There has recently been brought before the Parliament of Northern Ireland a bill to prohibit the report of any proceedings in a case until it has become clear that the accused will not be committed for trial before a superior court. In the general run of cases in America this principle is most carefully observed; for, if I understand their system aright, a man accused of a crime is first brought before a grand jury, where the proceedings are not reported.

In the particular case of Alger Hiss, it so happened that there had been a prolonged hearing before the House Committee. The allegation that Hiss had been a member of the Communist Party—though not the allegation that he had handed over documents—had been canvassed at great length before this Committee, whose proceedings had inevitably attracted the widest publicity. It is difficult to imagine that anyone called to the jury in the second trial of Hiss had not already read a great deal about the case both in the proceedings before the House Committee and in the accounts of the first trial. But it is equally difficult to see how in this wholly exceptional case such a result could have been avoided—unless the House Committee had conducted the whole of their investigation in "executive session" or, as we should say, in private.

The system we have established in England secures that once a case has started nothing may be reported save that which has actually taken place in open court. Any comment, any speculation, any expression of opinion made publicly either in the press or elsewhere is rigorously forbidden. It is regarded as a contempt of court and is punished most severely. In this way we seek to observe the principle of full publicity for our judicial proceedings and yet try to prevent the possibility of a jury being prejudiced by knowledge of circumstances other than those disclosed in evidence. In a case where the jury disagreed I feel certain that our courts would treat the case as still pending unless and until it became clear that the accused would not be put on trial again, with the natural consequence that no comment could be made. I understand that the same result is achieved in Scotland and Northern Ireland.

I think that the American courts are less strict than our courts in preventing comment on a pending case, and it may be that they lack the necessary powers. Certain it is that during and after the first trial of Alger Hiss, when the jury had been discharged on the ground of their disagreement, a flood of comment broke forth in the press, even though it must have been known that Hiss would be placed on his trial again. I hope I shall be forgiven by my good friends of the American Bar Association for making this criticism. I believe that many of them would welcome a stricter application of a doctrine on the lines of our principle of contempt of court and would not be in the least averse to a rule that all comment must be barred until the conclusion of the case, and that reports, once the trial has begun, should be limited to an account of the proceedings in open court.

My third principle brings me to the most striking difference between the trial of Alger Hiss and a comparable trial in England; it relates to the summing up by the judge. In England, as in Scotland, the judge will expound the law to the jury, who must take the law as expounded as being correct. If the judge makes an error in law, the Court of Criminal Appeal can correct him and, if they think the error sufficiently serious, will quash the proceedings. But once the judge has directed the jury upon the law, he will then turn to the facts, prefacing what he has to say by some such statement as this: "You, members of the jury, are the sole judges of the facts. What I say with regard to the facts you may if you so desire completely disregard. I merely sum up the facts to you to assist you in the task which is yours, and yours alone." In a lengthy and complicated trial it is, in my opinion, of the greatest assistance to the jury that the judge should thus review the facts, pointing out to the jury those which he thinks important and separating those which are comparatively immaterial.

That is not the system which prevailed at the trial of Hiss, and here, if ever, was a case where a summing up of the facts would have been of the greatest assistance to the jury. The evidence had lasted for weeks and covered many matters which, in my humble opinion, had little bearing on the issues involved. Counsel in America, I should guess from reading the report of the second trial, is allowed a far greater latitude than he would be allowed in England. It was essential to arrive at a true decision, to distinguish between those facts which bore directly upon the guilt of the accused and those facts which had but a remote relevance to his guilt. Yet Judge Goddard was not required to make any such review. I admit at once that there is a danger in allowing a judge to review facts, since facts are the province of the jury. There is a danger lest the judge should press unduly his particular point of view so that the trial may become in reality a trial where the judge pronounces on the facts by swaying and influencing the jury to follow his own point of view. Judges, after all, are only human. They have been trained as advocates. The temptation to a judge to try to induce the jury to take the course which he thinks justice demands is, of course, very strong. I have known cases—I have civil cases in mind at the moment—where judges have completely failed to resist this temptation. There is a school of thought in this country which holds that for this reason we should adopt the system which prevailed at the Hiss trial and prevent the judge from commenting on the facts at all. Nowhere has this been more clearly brought out than in a recently published book called *The Last Sergeant*, written by Sergeant Sullivan, for whom I have a great regard both as a man and as an advocate. His view, derived in the main from his experience at the Irish Bar, is expressed as follows:

> In many of the American states the judge is by statute prohibited from indicating his opinion on the issues of fact in the case. I thoroughly approve of this. Speeches on behalf of the prosecution delivered from the Bench in my

own country had created a rampart against the conviction of guilty men. It is no concern of a judge whether a man be convicted or acquitted. With the standard of duty everywhere evidenced by the British juror, I have no hesitation in saying that he is far more likely to arrive at a true conclusion of fact left to his own judgment than he is when influenced by the exhortations from the Bench. I once gave some offence to one of my judicial friends at the Old Bailey when I suggested to the registrar of the court that he should ask the foreman of the jury, did they find for His Lordship or against him? But in truth that is the issue left to the jury when the judge takes sides for the prosecution. Either the jury must do as the judge has implored or they must slap him in the face, and they are deprived of moral freedom to exercise their unfettered judgment when doing so might involve a slight upon a judicial officer.

If trial by jury is not to be trusted to do justice it ought to be abolished, but to waste the time of twelve men in order that they may ratify a verdict already indicated by the Bench does not afford to any accused person the constitutional protection to which he is entitled.

With the greatest respect to the learned Sergeant, I consider that in this passage he begs the question. I agree that the judge should not "indicate" his opinion on the issues of fact, and I certainly do not desire the jury to be "influenced by exhortations" from the Bench. But surely the judge may review the facts and marshal them to help the jury without laying himself open to the charge of exhortation or even of indicating his opinion. I concede, of course, that whenever you confer upon a man a discretion you run the risk of his committing an indiscretion. But experience has taught me that if a judge makes the mistake of being obviously one-sided, and if the jury take the view that he is being unfair, they will show their independence by promptly returning a verdict in the other sense. I am not aware of any criminal case in which the review of the facts by the judge has in fact failed to put fairly before the jury the case for the defence; and, indeed, if the judge failed in this respect the Court of Criminal Appeal would not hesitate to interfere.

Finally, before I leave the subject of trial by jury, let me set out what I conceive to be the parts which should be played by the respective Counsel in any criminal case. So far as the Counsel for the Defence is concerned, it is a truism to say that his duty is to endeavour by every legitimate means to secure his client's acquittal.

I do not think that the converse is true. I do not think that it is proper for the Counsel for the Prosecution to use every legitimate means to secure a conviction. He is playing a most important role in the administration of justice. The last thing he would desire is to secure a wrongful conviction, or even to secure a conviction in a doubtful case. It will often happen—especially in those cases where the Counsel for the Prosecution feels that some point has not been adequately dealt with by his opponent—that he will himself remind the jury of the answer which the accused could have made. He should, I think, eschew rhetoric and those various devices of advocacy which would not be inappropriate to the defending Counsel; and he should throughout so conduct his case as to avoid any risk of prejudice arising to the accused.

The responsibility of arriving at the right conclusion is the responsibility of the jury. The duty of the prosecuting Counsel is to assist the jury in the discharge of that responsibility by stating a plain unvarnished tale, unfolding the facts as they appear to him, and stating them to the best of his ability with meticulous accuracy.

I believe this to be the right canon which should be applied in England; and in England the judge reviews the facts after the speeches of Counsel have been concluded. How much more, then, should it be the right canon in those courts where the judge does not review the facts; for under such a system the Counsel for the Prosecution has the responsibility of having the last word upon the facts.

CHAPTER XXI

THE EVIDENCE AT THE SECOND TRIAL

I must now briefly review the evidence which was called at the second trial. I shall deal first with the evidence called on behalf of the Government, omitting merely formal witnesses and those with whom I deal under particular headings. I shall not consider further the evidence of Chambers or his wife.

Representatives of the manufacturers of the film on which photographs of the documents had been taken were able to show that the film had been made in or before 1937. Mr. De Lashmutt of the Riggs National Bank produced the Hisses' bank account and proved that the Federal Bureau of Investigation had had copies of that account shortly after January 1949. Miss Stafford of the University of Baltimore produced a letter which had been written by Mrs. Hiss on her typewriter to a Mr. Hillegeist; this was one of the standard letters which the experts used in determining that the incriminating typed documents had been typed on that typewriter. The letter concerned a course in inorganic chemistry which Mrs. Hiss proposed to, and did in fact, take. The course began on the 7th June 1937 and lasted eight weeks. Similar evidence was given about the other letters, including a report by Mrs. Hiss as President of the Bryn Mawr Alumnae Association of Washington, D.C. It was proved that she had passed a test in typewriting in 1927.

Mr. Appell, an investigator of the House Committee, described how he went with Mr. Chambers to his farm on the 2nd December 1948. He said that Chambers went into the house for a torchlight and then walked out to the pumpkin patch. After feeling two pumpkins he picked one up, and Mr. Appell and his colleague reached into it and removed three cylinders and some film in wax paper.

Professor Schapiro was called to prove that he had bought four rugs with money provided by Chambers from the Massachusetts Importing Company; that he had received them in December 1936; and that shortly afterwards he had despatched them to George Silverman in Washington. Mr. Touloukian, the representative of the importing company, stated that the approximate price of the four rugs was $894.

The purchase of the car by Mrs. Chambers in November 1937 and the down payment of $486 were proved. Miss Stearns gave evidence that *She Stoops to Conquer* was performed from the 10th to the 15th August 1937 at Peterboro, and that this had been advertised in the New York papers.

Nathan Levine testified that he had received an envelope from Chambers during the year 1938; that he had placed it in the dumbwaiter shaft of his parents' New York house; and that he had, in the company of Chambers, extracted it on Sunday, the 14th November 1948. He had not seen the contents of the envelope on either occasion.

Mr. Walsh of the F.B.I. spoke of a drive round Washington on the 1st February 1949, when Chambers pointed out the various residences which Hiss had occupied on 28th Street, P Street, 30th Street and Volta Place. He could not recall whether these houses did or did not have their numbers on them. A Mr. Callahan, another representative of the F.B.I., proved that Hiss with his solicitor came to the F.B.I. office in Baltimore on the 4th December 1948, and after four or five hours' discussion Hiss had signed a statement,[1] which was produced. Mr. Callahan said that Hiss had co-operated in every way. Mr. Sagona of the

[1]Appendix IV.

State Department proved that Hiss had taken his annual leave in the last fortnight of July and the first fortnight of August in 1937. Another representative of the F.B.I., a Mr. Francis O'Brien, proved that on the 7th December 1948 he had taken a statement[2] from Mrs. Hiss, who had been accompanied by her solicitor, Mr. McLean. Mr. McLean had then given to the F.B.I. a letter to the Equitable Assurance Company, which had been written on Mrs. Hiss's typewriter.

Mr. Anderson, who had been with the State Department for the past twenty-eight years, described the method of receipt and circulation of documents in the Department. When a code message came in, it first went to the code room, where it was decoded and put into English. It was then revised at a revision desk. The revised text was then typed on a stencil, and after checking, the operators would run off a number of copies. One of these copies was on yellow Government bond paper and was referred to as the action copy. This was sent to whatever branch might have the primary responsibility for dealing with the matter. Other copies on ordinary white paper were called information copies and were sent to other branches. The distribution clerk would settle how many copies were made. The copies to be distributed were taken by messengers in envelopes to the various departments and every Monday morning were collected and burnt, but there was no record kept of the number of documents collected or of the number burnt. He explained that it was possible to tell from the records to which departments the action copy and information copies of a particular document had gone. With reference to Exhibit 10 (this was the only one of the typed documents which had not been typed on the Hiss typewriter), he stated that the record showed that it had gone only to the Far Eastern Division. I do not think it necessary to deal further with the evidence of Mr. Anderson. He was necessarily examined and cross-examined at great length with regard to the various documents, and he gave his evidence very fairly. He admitted readily enough that according to the records certain of the documents had not gone to Mr. Sayre's office.

Mr. Mensh, the vice-president of the Cherner Motor Com-

[2]Appendix V.

pany, was called to say that he could find no trace in the books of the company of the transaction concerning the disposal of the old Ford which had belonged to Hiss. He said that he thought the words, "23rd July 1936," "Alger Hiss" and the other words in typescript, had been typed by some person in the employ of the company. The document, he said, purported to show a chattel mortgage for $25 in favour of his company; but it was not recorded in the company's books.

In complete contrast to Mr. Anderson was the next witness, Mr. Rosen. He was shown the assignment of a Ford from the Cherner Motor Company to himself on the 23rd July 1936 but declined to give information on the ground that he might be incriminated. In cross-examination he said he had never seen Hiss.

Miss Lincoln had been thirty years in the State Department and had been secretary to Mr. Sayre for a long time, including the period of 1933–39. She sat with Miss Newcomb in the reception room, from which doors opened to the rooms occupied by Mr. Sayre and Hiss. Outside the office sat a messenger, who would take errands both inside and outside the Department. Their office hours were from 9 till 4:30. She had a filing cabinet in her room, and Hiss also had one in his. It was common practice for both Mr. Sayre and Hiss to leave the office at night with a brief case containing documents. When they had gone, she would go into their rooms to see if they had left any papers on the desks. She believed that they used to lunch together from time to time. She recalled Wadleigh as being an infrequent visitor to the office. She said that when she was on vacation and during her lunch hour Miss Newcomb was present in the reception room. She was shown the handwritten documents and said that she could not recall ever before having seen documents of that nature. She was obviously a completely reliable witness of the type who could be counted upon to give the most loyal service to any department in which she was employed.

Mr. Feehan, of the Document Section of the F.B.I., had had very great experience in examining documents. I shall refer to his evidence later in considering the documents. He compared the incriminating typed documents with the standards, that is to say, with the letters which Mrs. Hiss had written on her typewriter—these were the letters to Mr. Hillegeist and others, and the Bryn Mawr report. He was able to say that the standards and the incriminating documents (with the exception of Exhibit 10) had all been typed on the same typewriter. There was a small defect on the bottom half of the letter g on that typewriter; the letter e, too, was malformed, either when the machine was made or else through an accident which had happened to it later; the small letter *i* rode slightly below the line of typing; the letter *o* was printed lightly on the left side and more heavily on the right; the serif (that is, the ending stroke) of the letter *u* had worn away; and there were other similar defects. He summarised his evidence as follows: "I reached the conclusion that the Baltimore exhibits 5 to 9 and 11 to 47 [these are what I refer to as the incriminating typed documents] were typed by the same machine, the Woodstock machine, that typed the four known standards." With regard to Document 10, he stated that he thought it had been typed on a Royal machine. It certainly had not been typed on that belonging to Mrs. Hiss.

Mr. Feehan was not cross-examined upon his conclusion as to the identity of the typewriter. His evidence was given most fairly, and is to my mind completely convincing; but nowhere did he ever suggest that there were any peculiarities which pointed to the identity of the typist. If he had been able to find any such peculiarities, it is surely certain that he would have drawn attention to them. He also gave evidence about the photographed documents.

There followed the testimony of Mr. Wadleigh and Mrs. Hede Massing, with which I shall deal separately.

Mr. Webb of the F.B.I. had also been concerned examining documents. He was able to prove that the photographed documents had been photographed by means of a particular Leica camera, which was identified as belonging to Mr. Inslerman. Inslerman was called and admitted that he owned the camera, but declined to answer whether he had taken any photographs of documents with it.

Mr. Philip Jessup, Ambassador-at-Large of the United States, who had held a large number of important appointments, was the first witness called for the Defence. He deposed that he had met Hiss for the first time in 1943, and that since that time he had remained in the closest touch with him, not only on an official basis, but they had also had close and friendly contacts. Mrs. Jessup also knew Mrs. Hiss; they had seen each other on a large number of occasions. He spoke highly of the reputation of Hiss for loyalty, integrity and veracity. In cross-examination he was asked whether his wife had been a member of the Directors of the China Aid Council and he replied that she had been. He stated that he was a member of the Institute of Pacific Relations. Whether these latter questions were intended to suggest some discredit to Mr. Jessup, I really do not know. If they were, they completely failed in that purpose.

Mr. Howland Shaw, who had been twenty-seven years in the State Department, spoke of various improvements which had been made since 1941 to ensure greater security. He had known Hiss since 1937, had had many reports concerning him, and said that he had an excellent reputation.

Mr. Hawkins had been head of the Trade Agreements Section in the State Department from 1936 to 1944. He said it was not the practice of his Department to send duplicates with action copies. He frequently reported to Mr. Sayre, and came in contact with Hiss when he did so.

Mr. Stanley Hornbeck, under whom Hiss had served for some time from 1939 when Mr. Sayre went to the Philippines, spoke highly of him. He said that he had heard some statement[3] from Mr. Bullitt that Hiss had been a fellow-traveller, but after thinking it over and talking to Hiss, he had come to the conclusion that there was no foundation for the allegation.

Mr. Duvall of the Far Eastern Division referred in particular to Exhibit 10, and said that there was nothing to support the view that it had ever gone anywhere except to the Far Eastern Division.

Mr. John W. Davis, a figure well known on both sides of the

[3]In the New York *Herald Tribune* of the 9th April 1952 it is reported that Mr. Bullitt, former U.S. Ambassador in Paris, testified before a Senate sub-committee to the effect that in 1939 M. Daladier, then French Prime Minister, had told him that he had read a French intelligence report which contained a statement that the Hiss brothers were Soviet agents. Mr. Bullitt said that he had told Mr. Hornbeck at a later date what M. Daladier had said to him.

Atlantic, as he was at one time Ambassador to the Court of St. James, was a member of the Board of Trustees of the Carnegie Endowment. He had, in fact, been one of the committee of three who had suggested nominations for the presidency of the Endowment. He had first met Hiss in 1946. He had talked to many people about him and had found that he had an excellent reputation. Similar evidence was given by Mr. Swope, who was a member of the New York law firm to which Hiss had at one time belonged.

Mr. Darlington of the State Department had been Wadleigh's superior in the Trade Agreements Section. He had noticed that Wadleigh had what he described as "a well-developed curiosity," and said that he would often come back to his room after lunch to find Wadleigh reading his papers. He never gave any particular thought to it at the time, as they had complete confidence in each other. He occasionally went round to Mr. Sayre's office, sometimes to see Hiss. He had noticed that Mr. Sayre's door was always kept closed, whereas the door to Hiss's room was always open. He said that he had seen Wadleigh in Mr. Sayre's office fairly frequently.

Mr. Green of the State Department spoke of the arrangement for supplying the Nye Committee with documents. I shall deal with his evidence in my next chapter.

Mr. Sayre described how he had arranged for Hiss to enter his office to take the place of Mr. Dickey. He said: "I used Mr. Hiss in a very personal way. In my work I tried to avoid formalities. He was my right-hand man, coming in and going out of my office constantly to perform these various duties as my assistant." He continued: "Hundreds of cables kept pouring in from all over the world. I could not possibly read every word. It was absolutely necessary to have someone to comb them through, to bring the important and significant ones to my attention, and summarize orally what the cables contained. That was part of his work." He said that there were occasions when Hiss would make some handwritten summary or some notation which would be sent in to him with a cablegram. They would often be written on small pieces of memorandum paper, frequently attached to the document itself. He had seen Hiss intimately for two and a half years and had never found him trying to influence American policy in regard to Russia. He did not remember the particular documents, the subject matter of the charge. He recalled that he left Washington on the afternoon of the 14th Januuary 1938 and was not in his office on Saturday the 15th.

Geoffrey May had lived next door to Hiss at 30th Street. The Hisses lived there from July 1936 to the 29th December 1937. The Mays got to know them very well and dropped in for informal visits in the evening. Their stairways adjoined and they could not help seeing each other's visitors. He never saw Chambers, nor did he hear typewriting going on in the Hisses' house. After Hiss moved from 30th Street, his house was occupied by a newspaper columnist. He noticed the change, because then he did hear the typewriter a great deal. After the Hisses left 30th Street, the Mays used to call on them at their new house in Volta Place.

Martha Pope worked for the Hisses from their early married life until after they moved to P Street. She remembered Pressman and Witt coming, but was quite confident that she had never seen Chambers. She was taken by the F.B.I. to see Chambers. He asked her various details about the furniture. She also remembered Mr. Frank coming to the house, but had never seen Collins or Ware.

Mr. Hall was a member of the law firm which Hiss had joined in Boston. He spoke of his regret at Hiss's leaving and of his high opinion of him.

Clidi Catlett started working for the Hisses in about September 1935, when they were living at P Street, and was with them until 1938. She remembered Chambers coming to the P Street house on one occasion and was able to identify him from photographs. Both Mr. and Mrs. Hiss were there when he called. She was taken by the F.B.I. to see Chambers in February 1949. Chambers had asked about tables and chairs and other furniture, and whether there was a red rug on the floor at 30th Street. She had told him they had grey rugs. She had told him that the red rug had been in the closet and not on the floor. Then he asked if she did not serve dinner for them at 30th Street and said: "You were the woman who used to mash potatoes?" She had answered: "No, it was not me. Anyone can mash potatoes. You never came to dinner at 30th Street, and you never were at P Street for dinner, and you were never at Volta Place." Chambers had told her that he had slept at 30th Street. Mrs. Catlett had said that he did not, because there were only two bedrooms. She had asked him, where would he sleep? He said: "I stayed there." Mrs. Catlett answered that there were only two bedrooms, and the room in which Timmy slept was only just big enough for a single bed. She was sure she had never met Mrs. Chambers. She said that she remembered the red rug in the back room at P Street. It was rolled up at the 30th Street house. At 30th Street there was a doorbell, and at Volta Place a knocker but no bell. She had said to Mr. Murphy that Chambers' name was something like Crosby. She was asked no questions in cross-examination. I could wish she had been, for she would have proved herself a foeman worthy of Mr. Murphy's steel. Her sons were called to deal with the disposal of the typewriter. I shall refer to their evidence when I consider that topic.

Thomas Fansler, the brother of Priscilla Hiss, said that he was a teacher at the University of Chicago. He was the father of Ruth Fansler, who spent the summer of 1937 at the camp at Chestertown. Ruth got pneumonia at that time. He returned from his visit to Europe, arriving in New York on the 2nd August. He went to stay with the Hisses, who were at Chestertown, on Friday the 6th, and stayed with them there until Monday the 9th August. On Monday the 9th August, Mr. and Mrs. Hiss drove him to Wilmington and put him on the train for New York. Wilmington is about forty-five miles away from Chestertown. He did not remember the time of the train, except that it was a leisurely time. Mr. Fansler was certain about his dates. He had checked that the *Bremen*, in which he travelled, arrived at New York on Monday the 2nd August, the day that his leave was up. He was certain that he had gone to Chestertown for the following week end, on Friday the 6th August. The importance of this evidence is that it shows that the Hisses cannot have accompanied Chambers in the early morning of the 9th August to see the performance of *She Stoops to Conquer* at Peterborough, on the 10th August. I have considered this matter in a previous chapter.

I have already considered the evidence of Mr. Boucot, the

owner of the cottage at Smithton, with that of his sister Mrs. Brown, and the evidence of Mrs. Davis of Bleak House in Chapter X.

Mr. Coleman produced the Hisses' banking account at Chestertown. Cheques were cashed on the 9th, 10th, 11th and 12th August 1937, and a deposit of $100 was credited to the account on the 9th August. This cheque was dated the 3rd August and was payable to Priscilla Hiss. As the account was in the name of Alger Hiss, it would require to be endorsed by him.

Mr. Collier was a builder who had done repairs to the Volta Place house. He had been asked by the F.B.I. to describe the house and to produce his plans. He was even able to describe the wallpaper that was used.

Mr. Cowley, who had been a writer for twenty-five years and had at one time had Communist sympathies—though he never became a member of the Party—spoke of a meeting with Whittaker Chambers on the 13th December 1940. The interview had been arranged by Chambers' secretary, as he (Chambers) was writing an article about writers who had "jumped off the Moscow express." Chambers had then told him that he had worked for the Communists in Washington and that there were two complete Communist undergrounds working in the Government, but that the only person who had lost his job for Communist activity was Nathan Witt. He mentioned Francis B. Sayre, and Cowley said: "Do you mean Woodrow Wilson's son-in-law, the High Commissioner to the Philippines?" Chambers had answered that that was the man, and had added that he was the head of a Communist apparatus in the State Department. Chambers had said that he was glad he had learned the Communist technique, as he was now going to use it against them in his fight for the Christian democratic counterrevolution. Mr. Cowley was so much impressed with this conversation that he made a memorandum of it that same evening.

Mrs. Kellog Smith helped her husband in running a children's camp at Chestertown. She was quite certain that Timmy Hobson and Ruth Fansler had been there in the summer of 1937. She remembered that Ruth had been ill and had been discharged from hospital towards the end of July. She said that Mr. Fansler had come to see his daughter as soon as he came back from Europe. She was quite certain that Mrs. Hiss was there throughout the month of August and that Hiss was there for as long as his vacation lasted.

Mrs. Tesone, whose maiden name had been Fountain, said that she had been a school friend of Mrs. Hiss at Bryn Mawr. She had there acquired the nickname of "Plum," which had stuck to her. She had no recollection of the incident when she was said to have met Hiss with Chambers at the restaurant in Georgetown, Washington. She had been interviewed by the F.B.I. on three occasions and had been asked a number of questions about the different houses in which the Hisses had lived.

Admiral Hepburn was one of the many character witnesses. As Commander-in-Chief of the United States Fleet, he had met Alger Hiss on many occasions, particularly in reference to the Dumbarton Oaks Conference. He had formed a high opinion of his character.

Karl Helfrich said that he had entered Williams College in 1920 and had had Whittaker Chambers assigned to him as a roommate. They had arrived two or three days before college opened and had busied themselves by going round Williamstown buying secondhand furniture. He described how the freshmen were going to meet as a body at a dinner the night before term started, but Whittaker Chambers had said he would not go. He had some problems to think out and would try to get some inspiration from the Scriptures. When Helfrich got back from the dinner, Chambers said he had decided to leave Williams College and went to catch a midnight train. Chambers thereafter wrote a number of long letters to Mr. Helfrich, who had thought it his duty to take them to Dr. Garfield, the then President of Williams College.

Dr. Eagleton, professor of international law at New York University, spoke of an occasion in the fall of 1939 when Hiss had got in touch with him. It appeared that Professors Hyde and Jessup had written a letter to the New York *Times* regarding the position of the United States as a neutral in time of war, to which Dr. Eagleton had replied. Hiss had then sent him a memorandum supporting the point of view that the United States were entitled to give aid to the Western powers without infringing the American Neutrality Law; since this was at the time of the Russian-German alliance, it would seem that Hiss, in taking this line, was adopting an anti-Russian attitude.

Mr. Marbury, Counsel for Hiss in the libel action, explained that he had been in Europe in August 1948 and had not got back until the 14th September. The libel suit was filed on the 27th September. He described the proceedings in the action.

Mr. Rabinavicius was called by the defendant in regard to the testimony of Mrs. Hede Massing, and I shall consider his evidence with hers in Chapter XXVI.

Dr. Shotwell, who had succeeded Hiss as President of the Carnegie Endowment, spoke of the annual dinner on the 12th December 1948, at which practically all the members of the Board had been present. Mr. John W. Davis was in the chair, in the absence of Mr. John Foster Dulles, who was in Europe. Dr. Shotwell said that Mr. Bullitt, one of the trustees, asked Hiss if he had told the House Committee that he had "specifically checked" with Mr. Justice Byrnes about his coming to the Carnegie Endowment. After answering this question, Hiss withdrew so that the trustees could be free to discuss the whole situation. Dr. Shotwell said that each member of the meeting was then asked to express his views, and Mr. Davis summed up. In the result, by a vote of the trustees, Hiss was given leave of absence with full pay. Dr. Shotwell concluded by saying that Hiss bore the highest possible reputation for integrity, loyalty and veracity.

Mr. Eichelberger, Director of the American Association for the United Nations, spoke of the valuable work which Hiss had done for this body since he first met him in 1937. He also spoke highly of his reputation.

Dr. Binger, an eminent psychiatrist, was then called. He had been present throughout the first trial and had observed Chambers while he testified at the second trial. He had also read and studied his literary works. He was asked to assume certain facts which, speaking generally, had been agreed upon at the trial. On the basis of these assumptions, and of Chambers' compositions, he said that he had come to the conclusion that he was suffering from a form of mental illness known as psychopathic personality. He explained that the symptoms of this disease included chronic, persistent and repetitive lying, a tendency to make false accusations, and generally amoral behaviour disregarding ordinary accepted conventions. He said that a psychopath is aware of what he is doing but does not always know why he does it. His acts are impulsive and very often bizarre; he has a conviction of the truth and validity of his own imagination, and feels a constant need to make his imagination come true. Dr. Binger was supported in this view by the evidence of Dr. Murray, a distinguished psychologist. I shall consider them in more detail when I have briefly reviewed the evidence called by the Government in rebuttal.

Dr. Nicholson, the first of the Government's witnesses in rebuttal, proved that Timmy Hobson came to consult her at her office in Washington on the 15th August 1937. Her evidence would seem to indicate that Mrs. Hiss left Chestertown at least for that day.

Sergeant Roulhac, who lived with the Catletts, gave evidence about the typewriter, as did also several other witnesses whom I need not here refer to. Mr. Henry and Mr. Hebb, two Washington estate agents, gave evidence about the location of the Woodstock Typewriter Company.

A Mr. Claessens proved that Mrs. Hiss had at one time been registered as a member of the Socialist Party. His evidence was objected to as immaterial and irrelevant, but was allowed as it impeached the testimony of Mrs. Hiss, who had said that she had not been a member of the Party. Its acceptance shows that there is a much greater latitude in calling evidence of this sort in the United States than there is in this country.

Mr. Grieb had been a counsellor during the year 1937 at the children's camp at Chestertown. He remembered Timmy Hobson and recalled that the Hisses came over frequently to see the boy. There was an occasion, he said, when Hiss told Timmy that he had to go to Washington on business, and in consequence neither of them came out for about a couple of days. He thought that this had been some time in the month of June 1937.

Mr. McCool, a special agent of the F.B.I., was called and asked to type a document on the old Woodstock typewriter, which he did without any apparent difficulty.

Mrs. Edith Murray said that she had worked for the Chambers at their house in Eutaw Place, Baltimore, in the fall of 1935 and the spring of 1936. They were then passing under the name of Mr. and Mrs. Lloyd Cantwell. Mrs. Cantwell had told her that her husband was a travelling salesman. She said that they hardly had any visitors; in fact, she could think of only two. She identified Mrs. Hiss, who was in court, as being one, and said that she had come and stayed overnight when Mrs. Cantwell had gone to New York to see her doctor. She described how she and Mrs. Hiss, whom she called "Miss Priscilla," had given the baby its bath. The other visitor she remembered was Mr. Hiss, whom she also identified in court. She remembered Mrs. Hiss coming about four times, and said that she seemed to be glad to see Mrs. Cantwell and the baby. On one of these occasions her husband came to fetch her, and that was the only time Mrs. Murray had ever seen Alger Hiss. She saw him then for a period of more than five minutes. She said that Mr. Cantwell—that is, Chambers—was at the house only for week ends, and she could not remember whether he had been there when Mr. or Mrs. Hiss called.

She described how representatives of the F.B.I. had come to see her in November 1949, some thirteen years after these events had taken place. They showed her photographs of Mr. and Mrs. Hiss and asked her if she could remember them. She said she had asked the representatives: " 'Is Mr. Cantwell back in Baltimore? Are they looking for me to work for them?' Because they were very nice people to work for, and I was all up in the air; I thought they were looking for me to work for them." Then on a Sunday three representatives of the F.B.I. called to see her and asked her questions; they stayed for about half an hour. On the Monday they took her down to see Mr. and Mrs. Lloyd Cantwell on their farm, and she spent three hours with them there.

Mrs. Murray explained that she had had a nervous breakdown and did not read the papers, though she was able to read a little. She had, however, heard about the pumpkin, and did ask whether the farm to which she was going was that on which they had found the pumpkin. When she first saw the pictures of the Hisses, she was inclined to think that they reminded her of people she had seen in the movies.

The next witness was a Mrs. Tally, who spoke of her efforts to dispose of the Volta Place house. I have dealt with her evidence in Chapter IX in connection with the $400 which Hiss is said to have lent to Chambers in November 1937.

The last important witness called in rebuttal was Mr. John Foster Dulles, whose evidence I shall consider in Chapter XXV.

I cannot conclude this chapter without making some further reference to the evidence of Dr. Binger and Dr. Murray. A vast amount of time was expended in the examination and cross-examination of these two witnesses—their evidence occupies nearly 450 pages of the transcript.

This evidence was tendered at the first trial and was there rejected as incompetent. It is not for me to express any opinion as to whether under the relevant law it should or should not have been admitted. It is quite certain that under English law no such evidence would be admitted; and I sincerely hope that it never will be. In saying this, I do not mean to imply the slightest criticism of the two eminent doctors who were called for the Defence; but I feel that we should at all costs maintain the principle that the responsibility for deciding where the truth lies rests with the jury. If doctors, of whatever eminence, are to be allowed to express their opinions as to the reliability of a witness—based in part on his demeanour at the trial—it seems to me that they are, in fact, trespassing on the province of the jury.

In the course of his evidence Dr. Binger appeared to find confirmation of his view that Chambers had a psychopathic personality in his observation of the fact that Chambers repeatedly looked up at the ceiling, and frequently in answering questions used such phrases as "I would say" or "It must have been." Mr. Murphy was not slow to take advantage of these points in his cross-examination of Dr. Binger. He arranged for a strict observation of the doctor himself, and as a result asserted that Dr. Binger had looked at the ceiling more often than Chambers.

As to the offending phrases, he asserted that a count showed that Hiss in his evidence had used such expressions more often than Chambers had in his. However this may be, these matters bear upon "demeanour," which surely is entirely a matter for the jury.

I have no specialist knowledge, and cannot therefore express any opinion as to the scientific value of this evidence; I can only say that my practical experience, acting upon an untutored mind, has led me to view evidence of this kind with considerable suspicion. I have thought sometimes that eminent doctors in this sort of case are apt to draw too generous conclusions from too slender premises; and the same thought has occurred to me in reading through this evidence. The premises had to be slender, for the doctors had to base their answers on a hypothetical question, which had to be so framed as to mention only those facts upon which there was agreement between the two sides; so that most of the facts, which were the subject of acute controversy, had to be omitted for this purpose.

The strange effect which his brother's suicide had upon Chambers, depriving him for a time of his desire—if not of his power—to move, and then turning him into a fanatical Communist, was one of the outstanding points on which the doctors reached their conclusion. The bizarre and somewhat sensational act of hiding the rolls of microfilm in a pumpkin was another. The repeated lies which Chambers told in his days as a Communist and in the days when he was breaking with the Communists; his many aliases; his failure to tell the whole truth to Mr. Berle, to Mr. Ray Murphy or to the House Committee—all these facts the doctors could and did take into consideration. They relied, too, on the strange story which Chambers told of his visit to Hiss at Christmas time 1938, when he said he went to ask Hiss to break with the Communist Party. He then described Hiss as a kind and gentle person, yet he said he was fearful of being assassinated. When Mrs. Hiss went to the telephone, he thought she was calling other Communists to her aid; yet almost immediately afterwards he decided to stay to dinner. The doctors found in this incident an abnormal fear of assassination which was quickly overcome and forgotten. They relied as well on his sudden and mercurial departure from

Williams College and the theft of the books from Columbia University.

It seems to me that all these matters added together still come within the description of "slender material." It would appear that lying and stealing are everyday practices to Communists and that they habitually use aliases. Yet no one would assert, I should suppose, that all Communists or all liars or all thieves have "psychopathic personalities." If only the doctors had had available to them the story set out in *Witness*, their material would have been vastly increased. No one can read the story of Chambers' attempted suicide without feeling sure that something is there revealed quite out of the ordinary.

I do not want, however, to infer that I have not been impressed by reading the evidence of Dr. Binger and Dr. Murray, particularly in their analysis of the books and poems which Chambers wrote. Dr. Murray stated that he found in these writings a higher proportion of verbal pictures that had to do with disintegration and destruction, with filth and dirt, with decay and decomposition and death, than in any writings he had ever examined. I can well understand that any competent critic examining the poetry of Chambers would find it morbid and unhealthy. I would express no sort of opinion as to whether these two doctors were right or wrong; but, having read their evidence, I must admit that I am sufficiently impressed no longer to be influenced in my judgment by the apparent absence of motive on the part of Chambers. Let me give an illustration from the story of the visit to Bleak House on the 10th August 1937. Here there is no sort of corroboration. The only available independent evidence seems to show that the story had no foundation. Why on earth, it was said, should Chambers invent such a story if it had no foundation in fact? I saw no possible answer to such a question as this, until I read the doctors' evidence. Having read it, I thought to myself perhaps they were right; and if they were, the absence of motive is explained.

I should be profoundly interested to hear the opinion of distinguished American psychiatrists and psychologists on all the new circumstances revealed in *Witness*. They would have available to them a wealth of material which was not known to Drs. Binger and Murray. I wonder what conclusion they would reach. Would they support the evidence of these doctors? Surely it should be put to the test.

Finally, I would remind the reader of the evidence of Mr. Cowley. If it be the fact that Chambers accused Mr. Sayre of being the head of a Communist apparatus, we have a perfect illustration of an absolutely wild and reckless allegation being made by Chambers without any shadow of justification.

CHAPTER XXII

THE FIRST ALLEGED ACT OF TREACHERY

Alger Hiss is supposed first to have handed over documents while he was working for the Nye Committee—that is, at some time before August 1935. This Committee had been set up under Senator Nye to investigate certain aspects of the trade in munitions of war and to enquire into alleged scandals.

It is clear that the Nye Committee were anxious to get the fullest possible publicity for their work, and in fact relied on such publicity as a means of getting further information. It also seems plain that it was one of the duties of Hiss as legal assistant to the Committee to receive journalists in his office and to make available to them any documents which had come before the Committee.

The deposition of a certain Mr. Green, an official of the State Department, who had been assigned by the Secretary of State, Mr. Cordell Hull, to act in liaison with the Committee, was read at the trial:

> For the great majority of the documents, running into thousands [he said], the procedure was as follows: The Nye

> Committee had a representative who was given office space in the Department close to my office. She asked for documents, which I obtained from the files for her. She combed those over and decided which ones would be of interest to the Committee and then had a stenographer from the Committee, who came up and sat in the department also, to make copies of the documents; or, if they were in secret code, paraphrases of them. Then these copies and paraphrases were submitted to me, and I authorized her to take them to the Nye Committee.
>
> The documents which went up to the Nye Committee were either copies, typewritten copies, of documents from our files, or paraphrases of documents from our files, not originals. . . . That was an invariable rule.

Mr. Green explained that he was responsible, throughout the life of the Committee, for knowing what papers they received and the procedure which was followed. He first met Alger Hiss some time in 1935. He said categorically that Hiss had never himself asked for any documents and that he had never got any documents. Mr. Green had never had any business dealings of any description with Hiss, though he did remember his being present at one Committee meeting. Mr. Green said that all the documents were supplied under his direction to representatives of the Committee; in a very few cases a special request would be made, either by Senator Nye himself or by the Committee's Secretary, Mr. Stephen Raushenbush. The Committee, said Mr. Green, had sent up a young woman who was a highly trained person in international law and with very profound knowledge of recent international relations who knew what documents, what information she was trying to find in the files, and she would ask him to make available to her documents relating to certain phases in their past international relations. He would make these documents available to her, getting them from the files, and she would look them over; she would pick the one that she thought would be of interest to the Committee and have it or them typed by a stenographer whom she brought with her, or paraphrased if they were in secret code, and obtain his approval before transmitting them to the Committee; and then she would take them to the Committee, copies and paraphrases of these documents. The Committee then published all but a very few of them. Mr. Green added that permission to receive documents was given in thousands of cases, and was refused in only about twenty cases in all, and that for reasons of international courtesy.

Mr. Green's evidence was not challenged and was plainly reliable. The Nye Committee was engaged in an important piece of public work, and it was natural that the State Department would help in every way possible by making documents available.

At the second trial this incident was referred to by Mr. Murphy in his opening statement. He said: "Chambers tested Hiss first when Hiss was counsel to the Nye Committee. . . . He asked him for some State Department papers, and he got them. Not too important, but it shows a willingness to give secret papers to a Communist espionage agent." Counsel in his opening statement will, of course, base himself on the evidence which he expects his client is going to give, which will have been put before him in the form of a proof. Mr. Murphy, it will be observed, represented this as a "test," and rightly emphasised that it had some importance; for if, in fact, Hiss had been willing to comply with such a request in a small matter, he could surely have been relied on in the future in more important matters.

When the time came for Chambers to give evidence, however, the incident no longer appeared as a test which he had put to Hiss. It had become something which Hiss volunteered to do. Chambers told of a conversation which he said took place at the 28th Street apartment, which Hiss occupied from the 9th June 1934 to the 19th April 1935. We are thus able roughly to fix the date. Chambers gave this account of what took place:

> Mr. Hiss told me that he had the opportunity of using his position in the Nye investigation to obtain confidential documents from the State Department dealing with some angle of the munitions investigation. He asked me whether or not I wished him to bring out these documents or to try to get them—I should have put one before the other—and I think

that would be—well, I answered that I would have to consult J. Peters.

Mr. Chambers added that he did consult J. Peters very shortly afterwards, and that as a result he told Hiss that they would like him to bring out documents. Hiss, according to Chambers, in fact did so. Pressed about the nature of the documents, all Chambers could say was that "they dealt with some phase of munitions traffic, as nearly as I can remember"—which adds little to our knowledge, since presumably all the documents which the Nye Committee received dealt with some phase of munitions traffic. Chambers said that he photographed the documents and then returned them. He remembered positively photographing them on the third floor of the house in P Street, Washington, which Hiss occupied between April 1935 and June 1936. Chambers was pressed in cross-examination to fix an exact date for the handing over of the documents, but this he was quite unable to do, beyond saying that it was somewhere about the middle of 1935, perhaps from May to July. It is not clear from his evidence whether documents were handed over on several occasions or only on one occasion.

Again, Chambers was pressed about the nature of the papers. His impression was that they were "original State papers with seals and signatures on them." That was his recollection, but he refused to be positive about it. He asserted that Hiss had said that he had procured the documents from Mr. Green in the name of the Nye Committee. When he had photographed the papers, Chambers said that he returned the originals to Hiss and gave the photographs to a man called Bill, who was a Soviet agent in the United States. He was challenged about this, because he admitted that he had stated at the first trial that he turned over the developed films to J. Peters—and J. Peters and Bill were two different individuals.

Hiss in his evidence in chief told how he first came to meet Chambers, whom he knew as George Crosley, in December 1934 or January 1935. Crosley claimed to be a free-lance journalist writing a series of articles on the Nye investigation. Hiss described how after any particular hearing regular members of the daily press would follow him to his office to ask more detailed questions. With the full approval of the Committee, he made available to them documents which the Committee had received. There was a definite attempt on the part of the Committee to publicise as much as possible the results of their hearings. "George Crosley" had asked to see some of the exhibits, and Hiss had shown them to him. These exhibits, Hiss added, which mounted to some thirty volumes, were later published in Government reports.

Such was the evidence in chief which Hiss gave, and I turned with interest to see how Mr. Murphy would deal with this aspect of the case in cross-examination. To my surprise, I found that he asked not one question designed to show that Hiss had handed over any secret or confidential documents from the Nye Committee to Chambers. Indeed, the only reference to the matter at all in Mr. Murphy's cross-examination is contained in the following questions:

> *Mr. Murphy:* Now in connection with the Nye Committee, there is no doubt, is there, that Mr. Green in the State Department was the man who was in charge of furnishing State Department documents to the Committee?
> *Mr. Hiss:* No doubt. He was the liaison officer with the Nye Committee.
> *Mr. Murphy:* And when you say that you did not receive any documents from him, or copies, you meant that you did not physically receive them from his hands, is that right?
> *Mr. Hiss:* It was not part of my function to obtain State Department documents.
> *Mr. Murphy:* But there is no doubt that the man who did receive them received them from Mr. Green or people working under him or for him?
> *Mr. Hiss:* That is right. It happened to be a girl, but otherwise you are quite correct.
> *Mr. Murphy:* But we are agreed that for practical purposes Mr. Green can be called the supplier of the documents to the Nye Committee?
> *Mr. Hiss:* He was in charge of it at that time.

This absence of any cross-examination is indeed remarkable. Chambers had made a perfectly definite allegation of treachery;

he had described the documents as confidential and had said that before agreeing to receive them he had to get the consent of J. Peters. Mr. Murphy himself, in his opening speech, had referred to them as "secret documents." Hiss, on the other hand, had said that these documents were available to any journalist and that, indeed, the Committee were anxious to publicise them. Mr. Green had said that the documents supplied to the Committee were not confidential.

Mr. Cross dealt with this matter in his closing speech on behalf of Alger Hiss. He briefly summarised the evidence and said it was "just one more fabrication that Chambers has added to his long string of lies to make out a plausible case against Alger Hiss." It is, of course, easy for anyone with the entire transcript before him, who has had weeks in which to analyse the evidence as a whole, to find fault with any speech which is made by Counsel more or less on the spur of the moment. My own opinion is that it would have been better if Mr. Cross had put greater emphasis on this particular matter and had dealt with it rather as a thing apart; for it is the first instance in which it was alleged that documents had been handed over by Hiss to Chambers and, to my mind, this incident far transcends in importance many of the other incidents in the case. If it is established that Chambers was lying in this particular matter, his evidence of the turning over of the other documents can only be accepted with great caution.

"God," said Chambers in his evidence, "is not only a god of justice but a god of mercy," and therein he spoke truly. He represented himself as being influenced by the latter godlike quality in withholding evidence of espionage. His explanation of his failure to reveal the facts of espionage before the House Committee and in the early sessions of the Grand Jury was that he was anxious not to cause unnecessary damage to Alger Hiss and his other friends. There would be nothing godlike in fabricating a case against an erstwhile friend by representing him as being guilty of treachery in handing over secret documents, if the truth turned out to be that that friend had done no more than supply copies of documents which were intended to be available to any and every journalist. Is this the true view? If it is, the consequences are indeed far-reaching. The reference to the "god of mercy" stands revealed as the most rank and revolting hypocrisy. But much more is involved, for where would a man who was capable of such conduct think fit to draw the line? If Chambers was concerned, as in his recent book he says he was, to establish a "life preserver" by obtaining some documents which on the face of them would incriminate Hiss, what steps might he not be prepared to take to accomplish his end?

The evidence relating to these documents is, to my mind, the most important evidence in the case—short of that relating to the handing over of the documents in or about February or March 1938, and it throws light, or may throw light, on the true facts relating to these later documents. What, in Mr. Murphy's words in his opening statement, started as being "a test for Hiss" may have become a test for Chambers. The contrast between Chambers' evidence on this topic and that of Hiss, and the absence of any challenge to the evidence of Hiss in his cross-examination by Mr. Murphy, is so striking that it would inevitably have impressed the jury if only it had not been allowed to become submerged by other less important aspects of the case.

The reader who has followed me thus far must decide for himself what effect this incident would have had on his appraisal of the evidence of Chambers.

CHAPTER XXIII

OF DONALD HISS

That the right to cross-examine is a double-edged weapon is a fact well known to any experienced Counsel, but it may not be so generally recognised by the public. It is one thing to cross-examine a witness whose evidence is in direct conflict with the evidence given by your own client when there is material on which to base the cross-examination; it is quite another thing to cross-examine a witness who has given direct and simple testimony, completely and utterly opposed to that of your own client, where there is no such material.

In such a case, if the witness is a witness of truth, any cross-examination is apt to emphasise the difference between the two testimonies; but if, on the other hand, there is no cross-examination at all, there is the risk that the jury will think that Counsel has really abandoned the attempt to establish the truth of his client's case. Faced with this difficulty, I have known leaders of great distinction at the Bar decide to leave the cross-examination of such a witness in the hands of the most junior member of the team; not out of cowardice, but because they hope that the jury may get the impression: "Well, this witness got off very easily, but he was only cross-examined by Mr. B; if only he had been cross-examined by the leader, Mr. A, how different would the result have been." Personally, when confronted with this dilemma, I have always thought the best line to take was to make the cross-examination as short as possible and try to create the impression that the conflict between the evidence of the witness and that of my own client was not really of any great importance.

This was the difficulty that faced Mr. Murphy when he came to cross-examine Donald Hiss. Mr. Murphy in his cross-examination was accustomed to use the broad sword rather than the rapier; he certainly did not lack courage in putting his case. Yet this was a matter which called for discretion rather than valour, and he showed that he did not lack discretion. He had none of the material which existed in the case of Alger Hiss on which he could base his questions. There was no question here of the giving or receiving of a rug or a car or of the subletting of an apartment, of making loans, or of trips made together. There was no question of a wife committed, at any rate at some time in her life, to Left-wing sympathies, or of the suggestion that she had at one time been a member of a Left-wing organisation. Chambers himself told the House Committee that Donald Hiss was married to the daughter of a Mr. Cotton who was in the State Department. "She was not a Communist and everybody was worried about her," said Chambers.

Yet, although there was no material of any sort or kind on which to cross-examine Donald Hiss, the conflict between his evidence and that of Whittaker Chambers was fundamental. As long ago as 1939, Chambers had committed himself to the proposition that Donald Hiss was a member of the underground group. We have only to look at Mr. Berle's notes[1] of their interview to see how Donald Hiss was described: "Philippine Adviser—Member of C.P. with Pressman and Witt—Labor Department. Asst. to Frances Perkins—Party wanted him there—to send him as arbitrator in Bridges trial—Brought along by brother." Chambers again mentioned Donald Hiss when he saw Mr. Ray Murphy[2] on the 20th March 1945: "Later adherents to

[1]Appendix I.

[2]Appendix II.

the Party included Donald Hiss, Henry Collins and a man named Post in the State Department." And in the notes[3] Mr. Murphy made of their interview eighteen months later there is this passage: "The heads of the various underground groups in Washington who met with Peters were the Hisses, Kramer (Krivitsky), Henry Collins, who was either Secretary or Treasurer of the Group, John Abt, Lee Pressman, Nat Perlow and Nat Witt. These men met regularly at special meetings. With the exception of Donald Hiss, who did not have an organization, they headed parallel organizations. . . . Peters praised the Hiss boys."

When Chambers gave evidence for the first time before the House Committee on the 3rd August 1948, he mentioned Donald Hiss as being a member of the apparatus operating in Washington, which used the apartment of Henry Collins in St. Matthew's Court as a kind of headquarters. In his second testimony in executive session on the 7th August, Chambers enlarged on this. He was asked when he first met Donald Hiss and replied: "Probably within the same week in which I met Alger Hiss." The reader will remember that Chambers first met Alger Hiss at or about the time when Alger Hiss became legal assistant to the Nye Committee, that is to say, in the spring of 1934. Chambers continued that his relationship with Donald Hiss was purely formal, that Donald Hiss knew him as Carl, that Chambers collected dues from him, and that he had once met his wife. When asked where he collected dues from Donald Hiss he said: "Probably in Alger's house. He frequently came there." Chambers went on to say: "Donald was much less intelligent than Alger. Much less sensitive than his brother. I had the impression he was interested in the social climb and the Communist Party was interested in having him climb. At one point I believe he was fairly friendly with James Roosevelt."

Later, when he was asked whether he had had any conversation with Donald Hiss which was out of the ordinary, Chambers replied:

> Yes; one I think I can recall. He was working in the Labor Department—I believe in the Immigration Section—and it

[3]Appendix III.

was the plan of the Communist Party to have him go to California, get himself sent by the Government to California, to work in the Bridges case.

At that moment he had an opportunity to go into the State Department as, I think, legal adviser to the Philippine Section, which had just been set up.

It was the opinion of the Party that he should do that and not the Bridges matter. It was his opinion that he should continue in the Bridges matter and there was a fairly sharp exchange, but he submitted to discipline and went to the State Department.

Immediately on reading the transcript of the testimony given by Chambers on the 3rd August 1948, Donald Hiss wrote to the Chairman of the Committee, asking for permission to appear before the Committee and give evidence under oath. He said that he was willing to answer any questions and forwarded a statement in which he said:

I have read the full transcript of the testimony of Mr. D. Whittaker Chambers given today before the House Committee on Un-American Activities. Among other things, Mr. Chambers said that he knew me as a member of the Communist Party, as one of an elite Communist group which regularly met in a certain apartment in Washington, and as the leader of a local Communist cell. With the exception of the facts, which he also stated, that I have an older brother named Alger Hiss, that I have been employed in the Departments of Labor and State and that, as an employee of a local law firm (other than the one he named) I assisted in rendering legal service to the Polish Supply Mission in connection with a loan granted in 1946 by the Export-Import Bank, I flatly deny every statement made by Mr. Chambers with respect to me.

I am not and never have been a member of the Communist Party or of any formal or informal organization affiliated with or fronting in any manner whatsoever for the Communist Party. In fact, the only organizations and clubs to which I have belonged are the local Y.M.C.A., the Miles River Yacht Club of Maryland, the old Washington Racquet Club, the

Harvard Law School Association, the American Society of International Law, and college fraternities and athletic clubs.

I have no recollection of ever having met any person by the name of D. Whittaker Chambers, nor do I recognize his photograph which I have seen in the public press. I am not and never have been in sympathy with the principles of the Communist Party. Any interested person could easily have discovered these facts by inquiry of any of the distinguished, respected and unquestionably loyal Americans with whom I have been intimately associated.

Donald Hiss appeared before the Committee on the 13th August 1948. He answered the questions put to him with complete frankness. He said that he had never in his life been to the apartment of Mr. Henry Collins, and that he had never met anybody of the name of Harold Ware, Charles Kramer or Krivitsky, Victor Perlo, Whittaker Chambers or Carl. He had seen a number of photographs of Chambers and said that, to the best of his knowledge and belief, he had never met him under any name. He had met Mr. Collins a number of years back, probably in 1933 or 1934, but he had seen him only infrequently and knew him only casually and had never had any political discussion with him. He had known Mr. Pressman and Mr. Abt when they were with the Agricultural Adjustment Administration in 1933 or 1934; he had been classmate with Mr. Witt in their first year at the Harvard Law School. He had never seen either Witt or Abt since 1935, and Pressman only on one occasion, apart from passing him in the street, at a social function at the Polish Embassy. He detailed the nature of his work in connection with the loan granted in 1946 by the Export-Import Bank to the Polish Supply Mission, when he acted under the instructions of the senior partner of his law firm.

Such was his evidence before the House Committee, and this was, of course, known to Mr. Murphy when the second trial began. Mr. Murphy must also have had in his mind the evidence given by Chambers of the meeting which he said took place at a movie house in the early part of 1937 between Alger Hiss and Colonel Bykov; for here, said Chambers, after Hiss had agreed to procure documents from the State Department, Colonel

Bykov asked him if his brother Donald could do the same. Hiss is supposed to have replied that he did not know whether his brother was yet sufficiently developed for such work. Colonel Bykov then said perhaps Alger Hiss could persuade Donald. It is just possible that Alger Hiss might have said this about his brother even though Donald was in no way allied to the Communist Party, but this seems extremely improbable.

It must, therefore, have been with considerable feelings of disquiet as to the line he would take in cross-examination that Mr. Murphy heard Donald Hiss called as a witness on the 16th December 1949. Donald Hiss began by outlining his career, the details of which, of course, could be established beyond controversy. He was born in 1906 and educated at Baltimore Friends' School, Johns Hopkins University and the Harvard Law School, from which he graduated in 1932. After serving as secretary to Mr. Justice Holmes, he transferred first to the Public Works Administration, then to the Interior Department. In 1936 he entered the Labour Department, where he worked in the Solicitor's office until 1938, when he went to the State Department. He explained that he had discussed the question of this last transfer with Mr. Sayre and Mr. Dickover, both of the State Department. He had been much interested in the post as outlined by them, but had told them that he would have to speak to Mr. Gerald Reilly, his superior in the Labour Department. He described how Mr. Reilly had asked him to postpone leaving for some months, and how the matter had finally been arranged between Mr. Reilly and Mr. Sayre. He started work in the State Department on the 1st February 1938. He had a serious illness in 1944 involving a collapse of the lung, and in 1945 joined a well-known legal firm, where he became a junior partner the following year.

Donald Hiss described how he had met Whittaker Chambers before the Grand Jury: "The door opened and in came this person who walked across the room, turned back and walked out with his eyes fixed at the ceiling." He had said then that he was certain it was Whittaker Chambers because he had seen a large number of his photographs ever since Chambers first publicly made his accusations in August 1948. He recalled what had taken place before the House Committee, and finally repeated the denial, which he had there made, that he had ever been a member of a Communist organisation.

This was the situation which confronted Mr. Murphy when he rose to cross-examine. Was he to put to Donald Hiss the various allegations that Chambers had made? Should he challenge him about the meetings at Henry Collins' apartment, or about the payment of the dues at his brother's house, or about his membership in a Communist group, or about his having submitted to "discipline" on the question of leaving the Department of Labour; or should he pass these matters over in discreet silence? Mr. Murphy chose the latter course, showing, in my opinion, a wise discretion. His examination consisted of only eleven questions, and I strongly suspect that he was greatly relieved when it was over. I set out the cross-examination in full. It was as follows:

Mr. Murphy: Mr. Hiss, I have only a few questions. One of the last things Mr. Cross asked you was whether or not you had worked on the Bridges case. There is no testimony about the Bridges case so far, but while we are on that subject I take it that you were at least familiar with the Bridges case; one of your superiors asked you about doing some work. Had you been in California? Isn't that so?

Mr. Donald Hiss: There is something along that line, sir.

Mr. Murphy: I think you had left California and had you been there you would have had to take some depositions or something?

Mr. Donald Hiss: That is correct, sir. I did not know that until I returned to Washington.

Mr. Murphy: And one of your superiors told you that?

Mr. Donald Hiss: Who made the investigation.

Mr. Murphy: When, Mr. Hiss, as far as you recall, was the first time you heard the name of Whittaker Chambers, prior to August 3, 1948? August 3 is the date Mr. Chambers testified in Congress.

Mr. Donald Hiss: I would put it at February or March 1948.

Mr. Murphy: And you heard the name, I think, from some friend of yours in a downtown law firm?

Mr. Donald Hiss: John Ferguson, precisely.

Mr. Murphy: And he told you he had heard it from somebody else who was at a party.

Mr. Donald Hiss: That is right, sir.

Mr. Murphy: And it was reported back to you that Mr. Chambers had said you were a Communist?

Mr. Donald Hiss: That is right, sir.

Mr. Murphy: And did you tell your brother of that incident?

Mr. Donald Hiss: I did not.

Mr. Murphy: Never told him at all.

Mr. Donald Hiss: No. We mentioned it after he heard also.

Mr. Murphy: I beg your pardon?

Mr. Donald Hiss: He had heard also and we mentioned and discussed the incident later on, but at the time I never told him.

Mr. Murphy: Well, I think he had come to you a short while before that, didn't he, and asked you or told you he might need a lawyer or something?

Mr. Donald Hiss: He did.

Mr. Murphy: That was even before?

Mr. Donald Hiss: That was in June of 1947, I should put it.

The reader must form his own conclusion on what is involved in this cross-examination, or perhaps I should say in this absence of cross-examination; for Mr. Murphy made no real attempt to establish the story which Whittaker Chambers had told in so far as it related to Donald Hiss; he asked no question about the payment of dues, which after all would have established the most conclusive proof that Donald Hiss had belonged to a Communist organisation, or, indeed, about any of the other allegations which Chambers had made.

I am at a loss to understand whether or not Mr. Murphy was persisting in maintaining the truth of the charges which Chambers had made against Donald Hiss. It is certainly true that there was no formal withdrawal of these charges, but it is equally true that he never referred to the matter of Donald Hiss in his closing speech. This, at any rate, seems clear, and must leave a most damaging impression of the truth of Chambers' evidence as a whole: that the allegations were demonstrated, so far as human testimony can demonstrate, to be entirely without foundation. There was, as it seems to me, no scope for explaining away the discrepancies as mere differences of recollection.

The categorical statement that Chambers had met Donald Hiss at Alger's house and had collected Communist dues from him is either true or false, and Mr. Murphy made no attempt to prove that it was true. I think anyone acquainted with this evidence must feel grave doubts about the reliability of the testimony of Chambers where it is not corroborated from other sources.

CHAPTER XXIV

OF WHITE, WADLEIGH AND OTHERS

There were two persons, apart from Alger Hiss, whom Chambers referred to as being the main sources of his information. One was Harry Dexter White, Assistant Secretary of the Treasury, and the other was Julian Wadleigh. White figures in the present case, because when the typewritten documents which Chambers testified had been given him by Hiss were at last produced, it was apparent on examination that one of them had not been typed on the typewriter belonging to Hiss. Chambers, when pressed about this, said that he thought it was a document he had obtained from White. He then asserted that White had given him many documents, some of them even in his own handwriting.

White was first mentioned by a Miss Elizabeth Bentley, who gave evidence before the House Committee on the 31st July 1948, three days before Chambers appeared before them. She described him as being a Communist, though she did not know whether he was a "card-carrying" Communist. She claimed that White gave information to one Silvermaster, who in his turn passed it on to her. White, she asserted, would help to get people of Communist sympathies into Government employment.

She said that she had heard from Silvermaster and one Ullmann that White realised that any information he relayed to her would find its way to the Communist Party. The evidence given by Miss Bentley was widely circulated in the press. On reading one of the reports, White is said to have exclaimed to newspaper correspondents: "This is fantastic—it's shocking." It must be observed that Miss Bentley did not suggest that she had ever met White. The evidence she gave about White was based on what Silvermaster had told her.

When Chambers was asked by the House Committee whether White was a Communist, he replied that he could not say positively that he was a registered member, but that he was certainly a fellow traveller so far within the fold that his not being a Communist would be a mistake on both sides. The Committee asked whether, when he himself left the Party, he had visited White to ask him to break away too. Chambers answered that he had used an easy phrasing; he had not asked White to leave the Communist Party but to break away from the Communist movement. He had parted with White in a very agitated frame of mind, which had led Chambers to think he had persuaded him to leave the movement. In view of Miss Bentley's testimony, Chambers feared he had been mistaken.

White himself appeared before the Committee on the 13th August. He asked leave to make the following statement:

> I voluntarily asked to come here before this Committee, and the Committee has been kind to grant my request. I have read in the newspapers charges that have been made against me by a Miss Elizabeth Bentley and a Mr. Whittaker Chambers. I am coming before you because I think it is important that the truth be made known to the Committee, and to the public, and I am prepared to answer to the best of my ability any questions that any member of the Committee may wish to ask.
>
> I should like to state at the start that I am not now and never have been a Communist, nor even close to becoming one; that I cannot recollect ever knowing either a Miss Bentley or a Mr. Whittaker Chambers, nor, judging from the pictures I have seen in the press, have I ever met them.

The press reported that the witnesses claim that I helped to obtain key posts for persons I knew were engaged in espionage work to help them in that work. That allegation is unqualifiedly false. There is and can be no basis of fact whatever for such a charge.

The principles in which I believe, and by which I live, make it impossible for me ever to do a disloyal act or anything against the interests of our country, and I have jotted down what my belief is for the Committee's information.

My creed is the American creed. I believe in freedom of religion, freedom of speech, freedom of thought, freedom of the press, freedom of criticism and freedom of movement. I believe in the goal of equality of opportunity, and the right of each individual to follow the calling of his or her own choice, and the right of every individual to an opportunity to develop his or her capacity to the fullest.

I believe in the right and duty of every citizen to work for, to expect and to obtain an increasing measure of political, economic and emotional security for all. I am opposed to discrimination in any form, whether on grounds of race, color, religions, political belief or economic status.

I believe in the freedom of choice of one's representatives in Government, untrammeled by machine guns, secret police or a police state.

I am opposed to arbitrary and unwarranted use of power or authority from whatever source or against any individual or group.

I believe in a government of law, not of men, where law is above any man, and not any man above law.

I consider these principles sacred. I regard them as the basic fabric of our American way of life, and I believe in them as living realities, and not as mere words on paper.

That is my creed. Those are the principles I have worked for. Together those are the principles that I have been prepared in the past to fight for, and am prepared to defend at any time with my life, if need be.

That is all I am going to say at this time. I am ready for any questions you may wish to ask.

A little background information is needed to understand the point of some of the questions that followed. For instance, one needs to know that Miss Bentley had said in her evidence that Silvermaster had photographic appliances in the basement of his house on 30th Street, where he and a man called Ullmann took photographs of secret documents, which Silvermaster then transmitted to Miss Bentley. Mr. White gave his evidence in the most forthright way. He said that he had known Silvermaster, and had known that Silvermaster had been accused of being a Communist and had therefore been in danger of losing his position on the Board of Economic Warfare. White said he thoroughly sympathised with the point of view that if there was the smallest question of a man being a Communist he ought not to hold a position which gave him access to confidential information. In such a case mere suspicion without any proof was enough. But, added White, if the case was one merely of suspicion and not of proof, there was no reason why he should not be employed in a position where he had no access to confidential information. Accordingly he had asked Herbert Gaston, Assistant Secretary of the Treasury and a member of the Loyalty Board, to look into the case and see what ought to be done.

White said that he had been in Silvermaster's basement for a party and had played ping-pong there. He knew Ullmann well and had seen some of his photographs and, indeed, had asked him to take photographs of his own children. He knew Lee Pressman well and had formed a high opinion of him. He was anxious to make it plain that Ullmann was his friend.

As I have said before, it is impossible to form a conclusive judgment merely from a transcript of the evidence, but—having made this point—I must add that I have seldom read the evidence of a witness who struck me so forcibly as being a witness of truth. At the time of the hearing White was recovering from a severe heart attack, and unhappily a few days afterwards he died from this complaint. It was not until after his death that Chambers alleged that he had handed over documents, and, without hearing from White, we shall never know the truth of this. Chambers, in his evidence, claimed to know White, but White, in his evidence, said that he had never heard of Whittaker Chambers, and when shown a photograph had no recollection of ever having seen him. He added that, whether or not he had met him, he was able to confirm "without any qualification, or hesitation, or shortness of memory or breath," that Chambers had never tried to persuade him to leave the Communist Party or Communist ring. Indeed, White had made it plain in his evidence that he had never been a Communist, or a fellow-traveller, or in sympathy with Communist doctrine. Chambers was specifically asked by the House Committee, on the 3rd August 1948, whether he had considered White as a source of information to the Communist cell, and he replied with a categorical "No," going on to say what he had already said to Adolf Berle in 1939, that in effect this was an "elite group" and that espionage was not involved in their activities.

In the information which Chambers supplied to Mr. Berle in September 1939, White's name was not mentioned, but in his statement to Mr. Murphy of the F.B.I. on the 20th March 1945, there is this cryptic sentence:

> Harry White of the Treasury was described as a member at large but rather timid. He put on as assistants in the Treasury Glasser, a member of the underground group, and an Adler or Odler, another Party member. The two Coe brothers, also Party members, were also put on by White.

White is referred to briefly in Chambers' second statement to Mr. Murphy of the 28th August 1946, though again it is emphasised that the "elite policy-making top-level group" did not exchange secret documents from the Government departments.

Chambers says in *Witness* that White used periodically to turn over to him handwritten memoranda covering documents or information which had come to his notice. One such memorandum[1] was contained in the envelope produced by Chambers on the 17th November 1948. Its contents were later made public. How odd that White, like Hiss, should have made the mistake of supplying incriminating documents written in his own handwriting. May it be that some thief passed on to Chambers documents he had stolen from White? I feel tolerably cer-

[1]See Appendix VI and page 147 *supra* for comment on this document.

tain that if White, the "timid" Communist, had been alive when the assertion was first made that he had handed over documents to Chambers, he would have been far from timid in his denial.

Long after White's death, which took place in August 1948, Chambers continued to state on oath that he had no evidence of espionage or of the handing over of documents. It will be remembered that the explanation Chambers gave for this statement was that he felt that God was a god of mercy, and he did not want to bring too great trouble on the individuals who had helped him in obtaining documents. It is obvious that after White was dead this excuse was no longer good for his documents. Chambers could have revealed the documents he had got from White at any time after the latter's death without doing him a direct injury. It may well be that he would have done grievous harm to White's memory—but equally he may have done this by his later evidence.

Wadleigh, I regret to say, though born in America, was educated in England, at Oxford and the London School of Economics. He returned to the United States in 1929 and joined the Government service the following year at the age of 26. He was transferred to the State Department in 1936 and worked in the Trade Agreements Section.

He decided in 1935 to collaborate with the Communist Party, but according to his testimony he never became a member of it. A friend introduced him to a man named Carpenter, whom he simply knew as Harold. He said that he used to take from his desk any papers he thought would be of interest and hand them to Carpenter at a prearranged meeting place. They would meet again next morning, when Carpenter would return the brief case to Wadleigh, who would replace the documents on his desk. Occasionally he handed documents to Chambers, whom he knew as Carl. This continued until Wadleigh left for Turkey on the 11th March 1938—a date of some importance in the present case, since it follows that Wadleigh could not have handed over those documents which came into existence only after he had left the country.

Wadleigh was quite certain that he had never handed over any documents which had been typed outside the State Department, but when he was confronted with one of the typewritten documents produced by Chambers, he said it was possible that he might have brought out the original State paper from which the typewritten copy had been made. After looking through the various documents, he was not prepared to say definitely that he had handed over the originals, but in the case of some of them—and those of course dated before the 11th March—he said it was possible.

He was cross-examined at great length about whether his conduct amounted to stealing the documents. I cannot think this matters. He was undoubtedly guilty of the most base and shocking treachery and seemed to have not the least feeling of shame or remorse for his conduct. His acquaintanceship with Hiss was slight, and no one has ever suggested that Hiss had any idea that he was turning over documents.

Wadleigh described two meetings with Chambers in about February or March 1939, after his return from Turkey. At their first meeting Chambers told him that he had left the Communist Party and was going to become a bourgeois, adding, "That is what you will have to do." The second meeting was about three weeks later. Wadleigh said that Chambers rang him up, sounding hysterical and perhaps desperate over the telephone. Chambers said, "Do you want me to starve?" and asked him to meet him in Jackson Place, which is right in front of the White House. Wadleigh thought he must be crazy to suggest such a public place, but he kept the appointment and gave Chambers a $20 bill. Wadleigh was quite definite that Chambers had never mentioned Alger Hiss to him, but he said that he had indicated that he had other sources in the State Department.

There was one other odd feature in Wadleigh's evidence. He described the introduction to Colonel Bykov, who was using the name of Sasha. Sasha expressed dissatisfaction with the quality of the documents which Wadleigh was bringing out and asked him to try to do better. Wadleigh said that the thing about Sasha that stood out in his memory was that the right sleeve of his coat hung loose and that he gave him his left hand when they shook hands. Bykov, alias Sasha, according to Chambers, had both arms intact.

I have called this chapter "Of White, Wadleigh and Others."

Having dealt with White and Wadleigh, it behoves me to say something about the others, but here I find myself in the difficulty of not knowing who they were. I have no doubt at all that there were others, some of whom were supplying secret documents to Communist agents, and possibly to Whittaker Chambers himself. Chambers asserts in *Witness* that there were, at an estimate, probably seventy-five underground Communists in the Ware group alone. A critical review of the evidence furnished by the documents leads me, anyway, to suppose that one of these sources was in the Far Eastern Division of the State Department.

CHAPTER XXV

THE SUPPOSED CONTROVERSY BETWEEN MR. JOHN FOSTER DULLES AND ALGER HISS

It is important to see whether there was any substantial controversy between the evidence of Hiss and that of Mr. John Foster Dulles. It is important for this reason, that in Mr. Dulles we have a witness of the most obvious and complete integrity, whose desire to hold the scales absolutely fairly cannot be doubted by anyone who reads his evidence. If, therefore, there were in reality any substantial controversy between the evidence of these two men, one would be bound to view the evidence of Hiss with considerable suspicion. On the other hand, between two busy men, each doing his best to recount conversations which had taken place a good many months before, it is almost inevitable that there will be differences of recollection. This matter was canvassed after the trial in the Court of Appeals, and it is interesting to note that in the careful judgment then delivered on the question as to whether it was permissible to call Mr. Dulles in rebuttal, the phrase was used "in so far as Mr. Dulles's testimony may be said to be contradictory." It is, I think, very doubtful whether there is any substantial controversy in the evidence of the two men, but in order that the reader may judge for himself whether this is so or not, I set out the relevant passages of the evidence of Hiss and of the evidence of Mr. Dulles, who was called in rebuttal after the close of the defendant's case.

There are undoubtedly differences on several matters of detail in the evidence of Hiss and Mr. Dulles, but none of these seems to be of any considerable importance. For what they are worth, they arise out of four conversations which took place between Mr. Dulles and Hiss, as follows:

(1) The first conversation during the voyage to England to attend the first meeting of the United Nations.
(2) The second conversation early in January 1947 consequent upon the receipt of a letter by Mr. Dulles from a Mr. Kohlberg.
(3) The third conversation in March 1948 consequent upon further allegations from Mr. Kohlberg.
(4) The fourth conversation in August 1948 after Chambers had given evidence before the House Committee.

I shall now deal in some detail with these four conversations, and shall then make some observations on the circumstances attending the resignation of Hiss from the presidency of the Carnegie Endowment.

(1) *The Conversation during the Voyage to England*

When Mr. Dulles and Hiss were fellow passengers on the ship taking them to England for the first meeting of the United Nations at the end of 1945, they undoubtedly had some conversation as to a possible opening for Hiss in the future if he decided to leave Government service. The presidency of the Carnegie Endowment for International Peace had become, or was shortly to become, vacant; and Mr. Dulles was one of the appointing trustees. His recollection was that he sounded Hiss to ascertain whether he contemplated leaving Government service, but that he did not mention any particular post either in the Carnegie Endowment or elsewhere. He admitted that he had had the possibility of Hiss becoming President of the Carnegie Endowment at the back of his mind, but he added that he was only one of about twenty trustees and had no authority from the other trustees in the matter of the appointment. He thought that he only mentioned this particular position to Hiss some four months later, in April or May 1946.

Hiss, on the other hand, deposed that Mr. Dulles actually mentioned this post to him as a possibility during their conversation on board the ship. In his evidence on the 20th December 1949, at the second trial, Hiss gave this account of what took place:

> We had a discussion on the trip to London for the first meeting of the United Nations General Assembly. [This was in December 1945.] Mr. Dulles was a delegate and I was the principal adviser to the American delegation. While we were going abroad on the ship, Mr. Dulles first asked me whether I would be interested in becoming President of the Carnegie Endowment. He was then Chairman of the Board of Trustees.

Mr. Dulles, in his evidence regarding this incident, said:

> My recollection is that I possibly asked Mr. Hiss as to whether he expected to stay on indefinitely in Government service or was thinking of getting out. I don't think I discussed at that time with him the presidency of the Carnegie Endowment, because I was only one of twenty or more trustees, and the trustees did not until their main meeting take up definitely the matter of seeking a president.

In cross-examination he was asked these questions:

> *Mr. Cross:* When you spoke to Mr. Hiss about whether or not he had thought about leaving the State Department, did you have in mind the possibility of his being considered for the Carnegie Foundation?
>
> *Mr. Dulles:* Yes, that was a possibility in the back of my mind.
>
> *Mr. Cross:* While no act or formal action had been taken in connection with your inquiry of Mr. Hiss, would you say whether or not you remembered whether or not the Carnegie Endowment was mentioned?
>
> *Mr. Dulles:* Well, one hesitates to be absolutely categorical

about conversations. It took place some time ago. I am quite clear in my own mind that I did not mention the Carnegie Endowment to Mr. Hiss at that time.

Mr. Cross: When did you first mention it to him?

Mr. Dulles: I would think it was after I had gotten back and had talked with some of the other trustees; that is probably around April or thereabouts of that year [1946].

Mr. Cross: Well, you did speak to him informally before the Board of Trustees took any formal action by way of appointing a committee, didn't you?

Mr. Dulles: Well, I can't remember, but I rather doubt it.

Mr. Cross: But did you prior to May tell Mr. Hiss that there was some consideration being given to the possibility of him, along with others?

Mr. Dulles: It is quite possible, yes.

The difference here seems almost microscopic. It may well have been that, as Mr. Dulles had this matter at the back of his mind, he did on board the ship refer to the Carnegie Endowment as being a possible opening for Hiss. On the other hand, Hiss may easily have confused a later conversation with this earlier one. But whatever the truth of this matter may be, it seems to me to be of no importance whatever. Hiss was, in fact, elected to the presidency of the Carnegie Endowment in December 1946, and he took up the appointment on the 1st February 1947.

(2) *The Conversation Early in January* 1947

Shortly after the election of Hiss was announced, Mr. Dulles had a communication from a man, whose name was ultimately revealed as Kohlberg, alleging that Hiss was or had been a Communist. This Mr. Kohlberg was the publisher of *Plain Talk*, a magazine at one time edited by Mr. Isaac Don Levine (who will be remembered as the individual who had taken Chambers to the interview with Mr. Berle in 1939). There was some discrepancy between the evidence of Hiss and that of Mr. Dulles as to the precise information which the latter passed on to Hiss about the disclosures then made by Mr. Kohlberg.

Hiss said that in December 1946 Mr. Dulles telephoned to

him saying that he (Dulles) had received information tending to show that Hiss was a Communist. It was not suggested that at this time the name of the informant was revealed. Hiss, at the trial, gave this account of their conversation:

> Some time in December 1946, after my election as President of the Carnegie Endowment had been announced in the press, Mr. Dulles called me on the telephone from New York and said, "What shall I say in answer to a letter from some man who claims you are a Communist?" I replied to him that I thought that subject had been laid to rest; did he know the background? He said that he had discussed the whole matter fully with Justice Byrnes, presumably in New York, but what he wanted to know was what would be an appropriate answer to the individual who had written to him. I said that I could only suggest that he ask for any possible basis for such a charge, any possible evidence or information, that that was what I had been inquiring for when I heard the charge before. Mr. Dulles said he thought that was a good idea, and that concluded the conversation.

Mr. Dulles's evidence, which conflicted with that of Hiss in several respects, was as follows:

> I received a letter . . . on the morning of January 2 and I immediately got in touch with the writer of the letter, who came down to see me that afternoon.
>
> I am quite—my recollection is quite clear that I did not discuss with Mr. Hiss about the letter until—the contents of the conversation which I then had with the gentleman until some days later on. . . .
>
> I had no discussion at all with Mr. Justice Byrnes about any possible Communist connections of Mr. Hiss. . . .
>
> I never wrote a letter to Mr. Kohlberg.

The difference, for what it is worth, amounts to this: Hiss would appear to have been wrong in stating that Mr. Dulles said he had discussed the matter with Mr. Justice Byrnes; he must have been wrong in saying that Mr. Dulles's object in telephoning him was to ask how he should reply to the letter; for, in fact, Mr. Dulles never answered the letter, and he had had an interview with Mr. Kohlberg before he said anything about it to Hiss. Mr. Dulles would, of course, in any case have communicated with Hiss about this, and he admitted that he did so a day or two after he saw Mr. Kohlberg. The discrepancy here seems to be of negligible importance, and as Mr. Dulles allowed the matter to rest, it seems a reasonable inference that he was not unduly disturbed by any disclosure which Mr. Kohlberg had then made to him.

(3) *The Conversation in March* 1948

However, Mr. Kohlberg returned to the charge and wrote two more letters to Mr. Dulles, who as a result arranged to see Hiss in March 1948, on the very day on which Hiss first gave evidence before the Grand Jury. Hiss gave the following account of their interview:

> In March 1948 I was asked to appear before the Grand Jury and did so briefly for about fifteen or twenty minutes.
>
> As soon as I had left the Grand Jury I went to see Mr. Dulles and told him of my appearance. As I recall it, he told me at the same time that he had been wanting to see me because he had had another report charging me with being a Communist. . . .
>
> On that occasion he told me that the first letter he had received in December 1946 he had replied to along the lines that I had suggested, and had received a reply from the man, whose name he then told me for the first time, a Mr. Kohlberg, who is the publisher of *Plain Talk*, a magazine; that Mr. Kohlberg had replied he had no facts, and the matter had thereupon been dropped. On this occasion in March 1948 Mr. Dulles said he had received another letter or another communication. We discussed it at some length. I told him of my testimony before the Grand Jury; I told him of the questions that had been asked me in May 1947, which I told him about previously but which had been reread that day; I told him of people about whom I had been interrogated, and I remember specifically telling him that from the time Mr. Byrnes had first spoken to me in March 1946, that the name of Mr. Pressman had figured. Mr. Byrnes had men-

tioned it to me; the F.B.I. had asked me about it when I went to see them in March of 1946; they had again asked me about it in May or June of 1947, and it was contained, of course, in my statement written on that day which had been read just before I saw Mr. Dulles, at the Grand Jury.

Mr. Dulles said that the last person who had written to him had mentioned Assistant Secretary Peurifoy of the State Department in a way that had led Mr. Dulles's correspondent to feel Mr. Peurifoy had some question about me. I urged Mr. Dulles to communicate directly with Mr. Peurifoy. . . .

He subsequently told me he had seen Mr. Peurifoy and talked to him, and Mr. Peurifoy said any such implication was a complete misunderstanding and he had said no such thing and had full confidence in me.

When cross-examined, Hiss said that his very definite recollection was that it was Mr. Dulles himself who had told him that Kohlberg was the name of the man who had written, and he repeated that he thought it was in March 1948.

Mr. Dulles's evidence was as follows:

Mr. Murphy: Now, will you tell us, Senator, what your conversation was with Mr. Hiss the day or the day after he testified before the Grand Jury in March 1948 and came to see you pursuant to your request?

Mr. Dulles: I told Mr. Hiss of a communication which I had recently received, and he mentioned to me the fact that he had just been before the Grand Jury.

Mr. Murphy: Now, by the way, that is a different communication than the Kohlberg communication, is that correct?

Mr. Dulles: About a year and a half later on. It was a coincidence, so far as I was concerned, that it was the day he testified before the Grand Jury, and I had not known that he was going to testify, that he told me that he had testified before the Grand Jury, and I asked him whether anything had come out there which had any bearing upon the subject matter of this communication which had been the primary reason that I had suggested that he see me.

He said that he had been asked before the Grand Jury of an acquaintanceship with a number of people, and that most of the people whose names had been put to him were people that he was not acquainted with; that the only person that was named that he did have an acquaintance with was a Mr. Pressman—a Lee Pressman, I think the name was—with whom I recall Mr. Hiss said he had been associated, I think, at the Harvard Law School, perhaps on the *Harvard Law Review*, and when they came to New York together they had collaborated for about a year, I think, in getting out a little magazine or bulletin dealing with the decisions of the courts in labor cases, which was a subject they were both particularly interested in.

I inquired further then as to the basis, if any, for the communications that I had received; and Mr. Hiss said that outside of the contact with Pressman, of which he had told me, he had not any contact with any persons whom he knew to be Communists, except perhaps that there were at the time when he was in the Department of Agriculture, there were some persons of rather Leftist tendencies who might be Communists whom he had met in a casual way but with whom he did not have any intimacy other than that which came from their being employed in the same department at the same time.

It is not clear from the evidence of Mr. Dulles whether or not he mentioned the name of Mr. Kohlberg at this interview in March 1948. He was not asked about Mr. Peurifoy.

Generally, on the conversation in March 1948, it is clear to my mind that there is no real controversy between the evidence of Mr. Dulles and that of Hiss.

(4) *The Conversation in August* 1948

We now come to the month of August 1948, when Chambers first came before the House Committee and revealed to an astonished world that Alger Hiss had been a member of a Communist group, whose function it was to obtain positions of power and influence in the Government in the interests of the Communists. That very night, August 3rd, Hiss said he telephoned Mr. Dulles, who was then Chairman of the Board of Trustees of the Carnegie Endowment. He said that he told Mr.

Dulles then that if these allegations were going to prove a source of embarrassment to the trustees he would be very ready to resign from the presidency *nunc pro tunc*. He added that he would obviously be very busy during the next weeks in answering the attacks made upon him, and he would be grateful if Mr. Dulles would take the responsibility of this decision off his shoulders.

Mr. Dulles could not recall this conversation at all. There is no doubt, however, that he did meet Hiss some time during August, and both he and Hiss put the date of this interview in the latter part of the month. Mr. Dulles gave his account of their conversation:

> I said to him that naturally what was coming out in the press with reference to the testimony being given before the Committee on Un-American Activities was very disturbing to the trustees of the Carnegie Endowment, and that some of them had communicated with me, but that I was confident that the trustees would not take any initiative in asking for his resignation or in embarrassing him in any way or seeming to pass a verdict upon him at a time when the matter was being considered by the Committee on Un-American Activities, and I was quite confident that the trustees would want to lean over backwards to avoid doing anything that might seem to be a prejudicial action or judgment on their part.
>
> I went on to say, however, that I felt that he, as President of the Endowment, had a certain responsibility to consider whether he was able to discharge the duties of the presidency in an organization which depended a great deal upon public good will and public confidence, and while the trustees were going to be very scrupulous, I thought, in their conduct toward him, that I thought he might want to consider his own responsibility to the Endowment as President.
>
> At that point, Mr. Hiss said that he had been considering the same aspect of the matter and that he had come to the conclusion that he had probably better resign, but that it would be questionable whether he ought to resign while the hearings were going on, because that might seem to be some admission on his part—and I quite agreed with him that any

action like his resignation ought not to take place while the hearings were going on. Mr. Hiss said he thought the hearings would be over in about two weeks and it would be his intention to resign some time during the month of September, at which time I would be away, but I wanted to clear the matter up before I left.

The evidence of Hiss with regard to this conversation was that he saw Mr. Dulles on about the 18th August 1948, that Mr. Dulles told him that some of the trustees were seriously concerned about the effect on the Endowment of the sensational publicity, and that the question of his resignation was discussed. Hiss said he told Mr. Dulles that he was thinking of submitting his resignation as soon as the hearings before the Committee were concluded. Mr. Dulles replied that he thought nothing should be done until the matter had been discussed with Mr. Marbury, Hiss's Counsel, who was at that time in Europe. Hiss elaborated this statement under cross-examination. He said that Mr. Dulles had told him that "he did not think I should resign while the hearings were going on nor without my Counsel being consulted and talking either to him [Dulles] or to some other representative member of the Board of Trustees." His Counsel, he said, did thereafter talk to Mr. John W. Davis, who became acting Chairman while Mr. Dulles was abroad. Hiss added that it was "in a sense understood that, subject to Counsel being consulted, I would resign some time in September, about the middle of September."

The Circumstances Attending the Resignation of Hiss from the Presidency of the Carnegie Endowment

Hiss, in fact, submitted his resignation in writing on the 12th December 1948, at a dinner meeting of the trustees, where he was asked questions about the testimony he had given to the House Committee. His resignation was not accepted, and he continued as President of the Endowment until May 1949, when his term came to an end. He then made it plain that he would not stand for re-election. I might add that not only did the trustees refuse to accept his resignation, but they also voted to continue his salary at the full rate. December 12th, moreover, was a date after the date on which Chambers had publicly repeated on the radio his allegation that Hiss was or had been a Communist; it was after the libel action had been started, and only three days before the Grand Jury preferred the indictment on which Hiss was ultimately convicted.

In my view, the trustees behaved with generosity in this matter; both they and Hiss were in a very difficult position. As Mr. Dulles rightly explained, the Carnegie Endowment depended a good deal upon public good will and confidence, yet it was surely right that they should "lean over backwards" rather than take any step which might seem prejudicial to Hiss. Hiss, too, was placed in an embarrassing position. He would have been wrong to take any step which might have appeared to the unthinking public almost as an admission of his guilt. His resignation, while the case was still pending, might well have been so regarded. It was, to my mind, eminently right and proper that before any decision was made Mr. Marbury, his Counsel, should have had a full discussion with Mr. John W. Davis, the acting Chairman.

I should not have dealt with this matter in such detail had not Mr. Murphy, in his closing speech for the Prosecution, referred to the delay in Hiss's tendering his resignation. After contrasting the action of Chambers in promptly resigning from *Time*, he said:

> Compare Mr. Hiss: Did he, as soon as his name was mentioned, say to the Carnegie people, "Here, I don't want to embarrass you at all. I will just disassociate myself with you"? He hung on to that $20,000. He hid behind the skirts of that almost public foundation.
>
> Mr. Dulles told you what happened. Mr. Dulles was in there fighting to get him out. But "I will do it a little later."
>
> Mr. Hiss was here, smiling all the time, charming, equivocating, a little fencing. Those, ladies and gentlemen, are the things that you have to remember in coming to the facts, to get the answer to the facts. You have to weigh those in your minds and judge for yourselves.

In my opinion, Mr. Murphy was in this matter unwittingly less than fair to Hiss. It was only when it had been established that the typewritten documents had been typed on a typewriter belonging to Hiss that the Grand Jury were prepared to find that there was even a prima facie case against him. I feel confident that had Mr. Murphy been acting for Hiss he would have been most anxious that Hiss should do nothing which might be interpreted as an admission of guilt.

Reviewing the whole controversy, in so far as there is a controversy, between the evidence of Hiss and that of Mr. Dulles, I am bound to say that there seems to me to be very little substance in it. Let me conclude the matter with a short extract from the cross-examination of Hiss:

> *Mr. Murphy:* Well, you did not tell Mr. Dulles in words or substance that after you got out of college law school you were thrown into association with people who were Communists?
> *Mr. Hiss:* Not in that form; definitely not.
> *Mr. Murphy:* If that is the form that Mr. Dulles remembers, you were referring not to that time but to some subsequent time when the charges were made, is that correct?
> *Mr. Hiss:* If that was the form that Mr. Dulles remembered, I would be quite sure that he had put together two periods of time which I had not put together in talking to him or in my mind.

Mr. Dulles, it will be observed, did not remember the question in that form. He remembered Hiss mentioning Pressman, and he remembered his saying that in the Department of Agriculture he had met persons of rather Leftist tendencies who might be Communists, "whom he had met in a casual way, but with whom he did not have any intimacy." I have considered in Chapter XI who these people were and what was the extent of the intimacy.

I have now dealt at, I fear, undue length with the supposed controversy between Mr. John Foster Dulles and Hiss, and for this reason: Two persons whom I have met, who were present during some part of the second trial, have told me that they were satisfied of the guilt of Hiss by reason of the evidence of Mr. Dulles; and I have met one other person who followed the reports of the trial who thought that Hiss was "probably guilty" because he had admitted to Mr. Dulles that he had been brought up "in a nest of Communists." Incidentally, he never made any such admission; but even if he had made that precise admission, it is astounding to me that anyone who has taken the trouble to follow the Hiss case should draw any conclusion adverse to Hiss from the evidence of Mr. Dulles. Accepting, as I most readily accept, every word of the evidence given by Mr. Dulles as accurate, I find nothing whatever which throws the smallest light upon either the guilt or innocence of Alger Hiss.

If the reader wants to satisfy himself on the critical question: "Did Hiss turn over secret documents in or about February and March 1938 to Chambers?" he must assuredly turn to other sources of evidence. Indeed, I find myself in agreement with the Court of Appeals in doubting whether there was any controversy between the evidence of Mr. Dulles and that of Hiss on any matter in the least relevant to this case.

CHAPTER XXVI

HEDE MASSING AND HENRIKAS RABINAVICIUS

I must now tell the strange story of Hede Massing. Mrs. Massing's evidence was rejected at the first trial, a fact which was apparently made the basis of virulent criticism of the judge's conduct. At the second trial, however, it was admitted, so far as I am aware, without any objection.

The substance of Mrs. Massing's evidence was that she had once met Alger Hiss in the late summer or early fall of 1935. She had not seen him again until the time of the trial. She deposed to a conversation which had taken place at the meeting in 1935, which would indicate that Hiss was at that time a member of the Communist Party. As I have repeatedly had occasion to point out, Hiss was charged with perjury, and the perjury with which he was charged fell under two heads—one, that he had denied handing over secret documents in or about February and March 1938, and two, that he had denied having met Chambers in and after 1937. It is obvious, therefore, that evidence of a conversation in 1935 could not have any direct bearing on the subject of the charge. The case against him was not that he had been a Communist or that he had had Communist connections in the year 1935.

Under the English system it would have been permissible to cross-examine Hiss and to ask him whether he had been a Communist in 1935, whether he had had a conversation with Mrs. Massing in that year, and whether he had not in the course of that conversation told her that which she alleged. It would not have been permissible to call her as a witness. The broad principle prevailing in English courts is that a witness may be cross-examined as to credit or credibility, but that the answer he gives must be accepted and cannot be contradicted by independent evidence, though documents may be put to the witness even if tending to contradict his answer. I believe a similar rule prevails in the courts of the United States. It is, however, the fact that Mrs. Massing gave her evidence as part of the case for the Prosecution before Hiss was called, and thereafter Hiss, when he came to give evidence, denied that there had been any such conversation. A Mr. Rabinavicius was also called by the Defence, and his evidence, to say the least of it, cast grave doubts upon the value of Mrs. Massing's testimony. I do not know how far this would have been allowed to go; if, for example, there had been another witness who had cast doubt on the evidence of Mr. Rabinavicius, would the Prosecution have been allowed to call him in rebuttal?

It is not for me to express any opinion as to whether the judge at the first trial was right in rejecting this evidence, or as to whether the judge at the second trial was right in admitting it; for I have no expert knowledge of the rules of evidence in America. It is, however, plain beyond argument that the evidence which Mrs. Massing gave would have been inadmissible in any English court. But since it was allowed, I must set out as simply as I can what it amounted to. I shall then deal with the testimony of Mr. Rabinavicius.

Mrs. Massing, or Hedwig Tune as she was then, was born in Vienna in the year 1900. She was married first to a Dr. Gerhart Eisler, also of Vienna, but she was unable to give the date, as she said she had a bad memory. In cross-examination she said it might have been in 1920 or it might have been in 1921; she could not remember, but it was in the summertime. Dr. Eisler was a Communist. When giving evidence before the Department of Justice in connection with her American naturalisation, she explained that in Germany (and she obviously intended the word Germany to include Austria) marriage at that time was a technicality which Liberals did not observe. However, her marriage, if marriage it was, to Dr. Eisler did not last long. It was terminated by divorce, but here again she was unable to give a date; she said that neither the marriage nor the divorce was significant to her. A Mr. Gumpertz arranged the divorce; indeed, he organised it—"he hired a lawyer and he had me divorced." She then married Mr. Gumpertz in 1926, but this marriage appears to have been brought to an end by divorce in or about 1932. Her third husband was a Mr. Paul Massing, from whom she was separated at the time of the trial. In her evidence at the second trial, in December 1949, she said that she had been married to him for eighteen years.

She had been affiliated with the Communist Party from about the year 1919. She applied for and obtained American citizenship in 1927, on taking an oath that she was not connected with any organisation opposed to organised government. From time to time since her naturalisation she had taken trips to Germany, Moscow and Paris, some of which had been paid for by the Russians. I mention these facts to show that there was little in her past activities to commend her as a reliable witness.

Mrs. Massing said that she met Alger Hiss in 1935 at the house of Noel Field in Washington. She had known the Fields intimately since 1934. On this occasion she said to Hiss: "I understand you are trying to get Noel Field away from my organisation into yours," and he said, "So you are this famous girl that is trying to get Noel Field away from me?" Mrs. Massing answered, "Yes," and he said, "Well, we will see who is going to win." She replied, "Well, you realize that you are competing with a woman," and either he or she then said, "Whoever is going to win, we are working for the same boss."

Mrs. Massing went on to describe how she had met Hiss fourteen years later, namely in December 1948. He had his lawyer, Mr. McLean, with him, and she was accompanied by a Mr. Ward, one of the F.B.I. agents. She told Hiss who she was, and reminded him that they had met at Noel Field's house, and that the purpose of that meeting had been to discuss the possibility of getting Field into her apparatus. Hiss, she said, was friendly and polite, but said he did not remember her.

Mr. Rabinavicius had served in various high posts in the Foreign Service of Lithuania. He left his native country when it was "gobbled up by the Bolsheviks," and obtained American naturalisation in 1929. He said that he had once met Mrs. Hede Massing in September 1949. He had called round with friends after dinner on a Mr. and Mrs. Lyons, and there they met Mrs. Massing. Mr. Lyons asked Mrs. Massing to tell the company how she met Alger Hiss. She replied that she had been a spy in the service of the Russian Government. Her main assignment was in Washington, and her job was to try to contact young men in the State Department. She said she was an attractive woman and was quite successful with one young man whom she referred to as Mr. X. (It seems clear that the Mr. X of this conversation was Noel Field.) She concealed from him the fact that she was a Communist and a spy, as that would have frightened him away. She tried to get him to join an organisation she was forming to fight fascism, and one day he said to her: "Why should I join some organisation that you are creating? We have such an organization right in the Department of State and it is headed by a man in the Department of State." "Who is it?" asked Mrs. Massing. "It is Alger Hiss," replied Mr. X. Mrs. Massing said that she asked Mr. X to introduce her to Mr. Hiss, and he arranged a meeting one evening at his house. She said to Mr. Hiss: "I am going to take this young man away from you." Mr. Rabinavicius remembered that there she broke off her story and turning to Mr. Lyons, said, "Gene, what did Alger Hiss say?" Mr. Lyons retorted: "I don't know what Mr. Hiss said, I wasn't there, you ought to know yourself." And she said that she had repeated this story so many times recently that she was beginning to get confused. She continued that Hiss had said, "You can't have that man," to which she replied, "Oh, but I am a woman, and I have a better chance than you."

Then Mrs. Massing said she returned to New York and reported to her Russian chief that she had met Alger Hiss and she described what then happened in the following way. "Alger

Hiss," said the Russian chief in a whisper, "you better keep away from him."

Mr. Rabinavicius said he had tried to ask Mrs. Massing some questions about her story. He said: "Did you ever meet Alger Hiss again after that evening?" She said she had not. He then asked her: "During your conversation with Hiss at Mr. X's apartment did he tell you or intimate to you that he was a Communist or an *apparatchik*?" (She had used this word herself in telling her story.) She answered: "No. He did not tell me. He did not have to tell me. I knew that he was." Mr. Rabinavicius asked: "How could you know that a man was a Communist or a spy if he did not intimate to you or tell you that he was?" "Oh," she said, "you don't understand those things. One *apparatchik* understands, realizes who is another *apparatchik*."

Mr. Rabinavicius pressed her; he told her: "This is a very serious accusation against an important official of the Government of the United States, a member of the staff of the State Department, to say that he is not only a Communist but an *apparatchik* working for a foreign power. Did your Russian boss tell you that he was an *apparatchik*?"

Mrs. Massing said that he did not need to; she became angry and said: "Look straight into my eyes and tell me that I am lying." Later in the evening she said: "You wait and see; I will write articles after this trial is over and I will have one that will be addressed to you. You will find yourself in one of my articles. And if I am permitted to testify, Hiss will be indicted or put in prison."

Mr. Rabinavicius never heard her use the words, "We are both working for the same boss." He said that about a week later he repeated this conversation to his friend Judge Ploscowe, who advised him to tell Hiss's lawyer, Mr. McLean.

It is a fact that Noel Field left the State Department to go to the League of Nations on the 1st July 1936 and that Alger Hiss did not join the State Department until the 1st September 1936, so that if Mr. Rabinavicius was right in recording Mrs. Massing's account of her conversation with Field, "We have such an organisation right in the Department of State and it is headed by a man in the Department of State," that man cannot have been Alger Hiss.

Hiss, in his evidence, said that he had never met Mrs. Massing until he met her on the 10th December 1948, in company with his lawyer Mr. McLean, who dictated a memorandum of the talk as soon as it was over. On this occasion Mrs. Massing told Hiss that she wanted to help him and that that was why she had asked for an interview. She said that she had met him once in 1934 or 1935 at a dinner party with the Fields and that there had been a discussion about world socialism. Hiss gave the somewhat chilling reply that he was sure he had never met her.

It may or may not be the fact that the evidence of Mrs. Massing was admissible; but even if it was, it seems to me to have been of little if any importance.

CHAPTER XXVII

OF THE TYPEWRITER

The history of the typewriter on which the incriminating documents were typed is obviously a matter of the greatest importance. There is, I think, no escape from this conclusion: either Hiss was guilty, or Chambers had at some time got access to the typewriter and had either himself, or by some agent, caused the forty-three typewritten documents produced at Baltimore to be typed on that machine. There is no positive evidence whatever that Chambers ever did any such thing. There was no witness who ever saw him or anybody who could have been his agent using that typewriter, and there is not even any evidence that Chambers or his agents had access to it. The most that can be said is that it is by no means impossible that Chambers, if he had been sufficiently wicked to try to manufacture proofs of the guilt of Hiss, could, without great difficulty, have got access to the typewriter.

I have already commented on the fact that it is extraordinary that Hiss should have been so reckless and so foolish as not utterly to have destroyed this typewriter. He must have been completely ignorant of the conspiratorial technique, and must, indeed, have been an utter fool. If he had stopped to think, he must have known—after all, he was a lawyer—that if the typewriter were traced, the incriminating documents, if indeed they had been typed by him or his wife, could be brought home to him. Yet I think there can be no possible doubt from the evidence that he did, in fact, give the typewriter away to a coloured servant who had for several years done odd jobs for him.

How different was the technique of Chambers. How much better versed was he in the elementary precautions which any sensible conspirator should take. He, too, had once possessed a typewriter, on which it is almost certain that he from time to time typed documents in connection with his Communist underground activities. Chambers was much wiser in his generation; he explained what he had done to get rid of his typewriter. He travelled to New York, taking it with him, and then deliberately left it on the overhead railway or a streetcar, he could not remember which, having first made sure that there was no identifying mark on it. Of course it disappeared from the picture. It was never heard of again, and indeed it seems to me that by this simple method he destroyed the evidence which the typewriter might have afforded almost as effectively as if he had disposed of it in the depths of the ocean.

But Hiss, the arch-conspirator, gave his typewriter away to a man called Catlett, the son of one Clidi Catlett, who had been for several years employed by the Hisses as a domestic servant. It was an ancient Woodstock, which had originally belonged to a Mr. Fansler, the father of Mrs. Hiss. Mrs. Hiss had it in her possession by the year 1933. She was not by any means an expert, at least she disclaimed being an expert, but she had in her college career taken a course in typewriting. Several documents which she had produced on that typewriter were given in evidence at the trial, and even though she may not have been very expert, it seems plain that her performance in the use of the typewriter was quite adequate. Even while the typewriter was in the possession of the Hisses, it had begun to show signs of age. Mrs. Hiss, in her evidence, said that when she gave it to the Catletts it was in poor condition and not very serviceable, and this is not remarkable, considering its age, for it had been owned by Mr. Fansler certainly before 1931 and probably much earlier. There was produced a letter dated the 30th January 1933, to one Tibbetts, which was undoubtedly typed by Mrs. Hiss on that typewriter. It therefore seems safe to say that the typewriter was in her possession before that date. She testified that this was so to the best of her knowledge and belief, and there seeems no reason whatever to doubt this statement at any rate. There was no evidence that I have found showing the date of the typewriter, or any evidence proving how long it had been in the possession of Mr. Fansler.

There is, I think, no doubt at all that the typewriter was given away by Mrs. Hiss to one of the Catlett boys, but there was considerable doubt as to the precise date on which it was given. This point assumes importance in view of the fact that the originals of the typed documents were dated in the first few months of 1938.

The Catlett family gave evidence about the gift of the typewriter. Perry Catlett was certain that it was given to him by Mrs. Hiss at or about the time that they moved to Volta Place; that is, about the 29th December 1937. But pressed as to the precise date, he frankly admitted that it might have been before, it might have been during or it might have been after the move. He was quite definite, however, that the gift of the typewriter was associated with the move to Volta Place. If any of us were asked in the year 1949 the exact date at which a not very valuable typewriter was given to us some twelve or thirteen years before, it is almost certain that we should have great difficulty in remembering.

Raymond Catlett, who was a year younger than Perry, said frankly that he could not recall the year in which it was given, but said that he thought he was about thirteen or fourteen years old at the time. As he was twenty-seven years old at the trial, this would put the date back to somewhere about 1936. He remembered that the gift was made in connection with one of the Hisses' moves, but was inclined to think that it was the move from P Street to 30th Street, which took place on about the 1st July 1936.

A Sergeant Roulhac, who lived with the Catletts and indeed had signed the lease of the premises in which they lived, gave some rather more definite evidence about it. He was called by the Prosecution in rebuttal and said that the Catletts moved into their new home on the 18th January 1938 and that he had not noticed the typewriter until some three months afterwards. That would put it round about the month of April 1938, and as he had been living there every day since January, he would probably have seen it when it first arrived. But of course, inevitably, in dealing with incidents such as this, the recollection of the most honest witness may be unreliable.

Mrs. Catlett, the mother of Perry and Raymond, knew nothing about the typewriter being in her house until one of the boys mentioned it to her. She said frankly that she had forgotten all about it.

I think anyone who reads the evidence of the Catletts with care and experience would draw the conclusion that they were trying to do the best they could to help. They were none of them educated people. They had that suspicion of Counsel which is not uncommon in persons in that position. They were confused, and of course it is quite easy for any clever Counsel to make such witnesses appear slightly ridiculous. But I do not think anyone would doubt, or in fact did doubt, that the typewriter was given by Mrs. Hiss to one of the Catletts some time in the first half of 1938, probably not later than about April 1938 if the evidence of Roulhac is to be taken as reliable.

There was one further piece of evidence which may be thought to throw some light upon the date of the gift and also upon the condition of the typewriter. Sergeant Roulhac said that the keys were stuck when he first saw it; and Perry Catlett said that he carried it to a shop and that the man there told him that it could not be fixed and that the Woodstock people were out of business at that time. Perry Catlett was interviewed by a representative of the Federal Bureau of Investigation on the 13th May 1949, and made a statement which he signed. He said that he had taken the typewriter to a shop at the corner of Connecticut and K Street and that there was a drugstore on the corner. He said he was told it could not be repaired. In his statement he said:

Shortly after I got the typewriter, I took it to a repair shop located at the northwest corner of K and Connecticut. I cannot remember exactly when I took the typewriter. I think it was in the warm weather. It may have been about a week after I got it, or it may have been a month or two. I would say it was not more than three or four months.

It is obviously incorrect to say that the Woodstock people were out of business, because in fact they had in the year 1938 premises in Washington. They rented the first floor of a building, No. 1528 K Street, and were in occupation from the 1st May until some time in September 1938. In September they moved to a corner building, where they occupied space on the second floor as from the 15th September 1938.

If, therefore, Perry Catlett took the typewriter to be repaired, and if he took it to premises in the corner building, he cannot have taken it before September 1938. The value of this check as to the date on which the typewriter was given obviously depends on the accuracy with which the length of time between its first receipt by the Catletts and its being taken round to the shop can be assessed, and this, like most other things in the case, was left vague. Indeed, perhaps it was inevitable that it should be vague, since the witnesses were trying to recall events which took place some twelve years before the date of their testimony.

It remains to recount the evidence which Mr. and Mrs. Hiss gave on this matter. Hiss said that the Woodstock typewriter had been given to his wife by Mr. Fansler when he retired from the insurance business in the early thirties. He did not remember how they had disposed of it, but he remembered that in the fall of 1937 they had bought a portable. His recollection was that they had had two typewriters in the fall of 1937 for a period of some two months before they moved from 30th Street.

Mrs. Hiss remembered that in the fall of 1937 they had got a portable typewriter for Timmy, and indeed a document was produced comprising a list of Greek mythological characters which Timmy had typed on it. She said that they had disposed of the Woodstock when they moved from 30th Street to Volta

Place in December 1937, and that, she added, would have been about three or four months after they had acquired the portable. She admitted that she had originally thought that it had been given away as junk or to the Salvation Army and that this was what she had told the Grand Jury when she was first asked about it. She explained this mistake in her evidence by saying that in fact they had given the Salvation Army the portable which they had acquired in the fall of 1937, but that this had been later on, when they moved out of Volta Place in October 1943. She said that she had got the histories of these two typewriters mixed up.

The subsequent history of the typewriter, after it had been given to the Catletts, can be traced. When the Catletts first got it, it was kept in a sort of junk room which they had, and for some time it seems to have been in what they were pleased to call the den. It must have received pretty rough treatment in that household. The den was a vacant room where they used to have parties, dances and the like. They used to have these parties more often than once a month, and they were very crowded. The entry to the den was by an outside door from the basement. Raymond Catlett said that he used to play with the typewriter from time to time and that his brother Perry used to type on it. Sergeant Roulhac said that Perry used to bang on it sometimes, so did his girl friend, and that sometimes he (Sergeant Roulhac) used to hit it too.

After some months of this rather severe treatment it was given to Burnetta Catlett, who worked for a Dr. Easter. When Dr. Easter died, the typewriter was left by Burnetta at his house, and a Mr. Vernon Marlow took it from there. Then when Vernon Marlow was leaving his house in 48th Place in Washington, he got a man called Ira Lockey to do the moving for him, and Mrs. Marlow handed over the typewriter to him in part payment of the hauling job which Lockey had done for her. By this time the reader will not be surprised to hear that it was in pretty bad condition, and Lockey gave it to his daughter to type on because she was taking typing. She kept it for a time and tried to type on it, but no one bothered much about it. Then Lockey's boy got hold of it for his little girl and, as he said, "that is just where it stayed because no one ever used it—it was in such bad condition."

The last stage of all was when Mr. McLean, Counsel for the Defendant, made his researches to try to trace it. He got hold of the Catletts and traced it to Burnetta and Dr. Easter, from Dr. Easter to Vernon Marlow, and from Marlow to Lockey, from whom he bought it for the sum of $40. I would add this—and it is a remarkable testimony to the durability and qualities of Woodstock typewriters—at the trial an F.B.I. agent was called and was asked to type some document in the presence of the judge and jury on that selfsame typewriter, and he managed to do so.

Let us analyse for a moment the relevance of this matter. The incriminating documents were all dated in the beginning of 1938. If the typewritten copies were made from those very documents, it is inevitable that they must have been made contemporaneously with the documents. Hiss could only have brought out those documents for a very short time. They must have been returned to the proper custody the next morning. But of course if they had been photographed, and many documents at this very time were being photographed, it is clear that the typewritten copies could have been made from the photographs, which would give much more time in which to produce them. One can hardly imagine that any such wicked scheme can have been concocted; and the jury negatived any such scheme by their verdict. I suppose that some person might exist who would regard such a scheme as being not wicked, but merely clever. If such a man had wanted to manufacture evidence, he would certainly have said to himself: "Photographs of documents prove nothing as to their origin. If I make typed copies of the photographs which I have got, on a typewriter which belongs to the man against whom I desire to have a 'life preserver,' I shall almost certainly be able to convince the jury that he typed the documents."

It certainly would not have been difficult to get access to the typewriter once it had left the house which Hiss occupied and was in the possession of some of his coloured servants. Perhaps it might have been possible to get access to it even whilst it remained in the possession of Hiss, for the Hisses had no resident servant. If anyone knew when he was away, it might not have been difficult to enter his house. But this is mere speculation. It is right to say, and I have already said it, that there is no positive evidence which enables one to say that, whatever might have been done, Chambers ever did, in fact, have access to the typewriter.

The highest the case can be put against Chambers is therefore as follows:

(1) He realised that documents typed on a particular typewriter could be identified, and for this reason had got rid of his own typewriter in such a way that it could not be traced.
(2) Admittedly he desired to establish a "life preserver" by getting or at least retaining documents which would incriminate Hiss.
(3) He may possibly have had opportunities of getting access to the typewriter, either before or after its gift to the Catletts.

It only remains for me to add the line which Mr. Murphy took about this matter in his closing speech. His case was not that Hiss was unaware of how revealing the typewriter would be, or that he did not know that typewritten documents could be traced to a particular typewriter. Far from it; his case was that Hiss knew that the typewriter was an incriminating instrument and was determined to get rid of it in such a way that it could never be traced to him, and with this object in view he gave it to the Catletts.

With respect to Mr. Murphy, this seems to me a fanciful suggestion. If Hiss had wanted to dispose of the typewriter in such a way as to make certain it could not be traced to him, surely he would not have given it to the servant who worked for him.

CHAPTER XXVIII

OF THE LIFE PRESERVER

One of the questions which was forcibly presented to the minds of the jury was this—"What possible motive could Chambers have had for falsely asserting that Hiss had turned over to him confidential documents?"

It frequently happens in a criminal trial that the motive which operated on the mind of the criminal is never revealed. Yet we know now a little more than the jury knew, for we have had the advantage of reading *Witness*, in which Chambers tells us of the steps which he thought were essential to his break with the Communist Party. He thus lists them: (1) a weapon; (2) a hiding place; (3) an automobile; (4) an identity; (5) "a life preserver in the form of copies of official documents stolen by the apparatus which, should the Party move against my life, I might have an outside chance of using as a dissuader."

We need not concern ourselves with steps (1) and (2); as to step (3), we have seen how Chambers alleged that he obtained a loan of $400 from Hiss by pretending that he wanted a car to assist him in his work for the Communist Party, whilst in reality he wanted it for a contrary purpose. We have seen how he satisfied his fourth requirement by obtaining employment in the Government service. He took his oath of office on the 18th October 1937—at a time when he had become, so he says, a God-fearing man, and we recall the melancholy fact that, notwithstanding this auspicious change in his religious outlook, he had not scrupled to tell the most dreadful lies to secure that position.

Let us consider this remarkable admission that he wanted a life preserver in the form of copies of official documents. What good would official documents be unless they could be brought home to some particular individual? How unsatisfactory would mere photographs have proved—such documents might have been stolen by any petty thief; and the number of such thieves, according to Chambers, was legion. Of course, if he had documents in the handwriting of either Hiss or White, he might conceivably have been able to exert some pressure, though I confess it seems to me it would have been far easier to exert pressure on Hiss or White than on some potential Communist murderer. He might perhaps have exercised pressure on Hiss to induce him to use his authority to call off the Communist murder gang; indeed, if this was not the suggestion, I entirely fail to understand how "official documents" could act as a life preserver.

There was one other fact of which Chambers, by his own admission at the trial, was acutely aware: namely, that it is not difficult to identify documents as having been typed on a particular typewriter. He would not otherwise have taken such great care in the disposal of his own typewriter by leaving it in some public-service vehicle, after seeing of course that it had no identification mark on it which would have enabled it to be traced to him.

Chambers continued, so he said, to call at Hiss's house during the first few months of the year 1938. Was he then still a member of the Communist Party? His statements to Mr. Berle and to Mr. Ray Murphy were plain and emphatic that he had left the Party at the end of 1937. It was only after the documents had come into the case that his break was definitely stated to have been in April 1938. Although Chambers asserted that he continued to collect from Hiss his ration of stolen documents, he no longer passed the documents, or at any rate all of them, on to the Communists. This is self-evident, for he kept them, or some of them, himself. Why else should he have kept these documents, which he had taken the trouble to collect—unless it was that he wanted them as a "life preserver"? Was it not fortunate for Chambers that amongst the papers he had thus collected, and kept, were some in the handwriting of Hiss and of White, and others typed on the typewriter belonging to Hiss? How much more efficient as a "life preserver" would such documents be than those others which he also preserved, which were only photographs.

There was, as I have said, no evidence before the jury that Chambers ever had access to the Hisses' typewriter; but at least this must be admitted—if he had had access to it, he would have had a much better "life preserver" if he had been able to transform documents which were mere photographs into documents which were typed out on the typewriter belonging to Hiss. If such an opportunity had presented itself, would it have been neglected? Was there such an opportunity? This seems to me to be the real kernel of the case, for if the documents were typed by Mrs. Hiss, I cannot imagine that she could have done it without the knowledge and approval of her husband; and if it was done with his knowledge and approval, then he must have been guilty of the offence with which he was charged.

When Hiss was convicted, he made this remark: "I am confident that in the future the full facts of how Whittaker Chambers was able to carry out forgery by typewriter will be disclosed." If in fact Chambers, in some way unrevealed at present, had got access to that typewriter and had typed out photographed documents, which he was thus able to plant on Hiss, it would have been a wicked and dastardly act. But if a man believes that he is fighting for his life, and that that life can be preserved only in a certain way, he may be willing to take desperate steps. Such a course, amounting to a kind of forgery by typewriter, would indeed be hazardous. If things had gone wrong, as they might so easily have, there might well have been a charge of conspiracy to defeat the ends of justice. Accused and convicted of such a crime, he would undoubtedly have deserved and received a long sentence.

Any prudent man would have hesitated before he brought before a jury such fraudulent and incriminating documents. Chambers describes in *Witness* how he contemplated suicide before he decided to produce the documents, and how, having produced them, but before testifying on their contents, he actually tried to encompass that crime. But of this the jury knew nothing. They knew that it was not for Hiss to establish that Chambers did, in fact, have the opportunity of access to the typewriter which belonged, or had belonged, to Mrs. Hiss; nor yet was it for him to prove that Chambers took advantage of it, if indeed such an opportunity presented itself. They knew nothing of the "life preserver" theory. They had, however, to be satisfied of the guilt of Hiss; and, to my mind, to be so satisfied they must have negatived that opportunity, or negatived the fact that advantage was taken of it.

It is most certainly not for me to say that they were wrong; yet I could wish that they had considered the all-important typewritten documents in the context of the other documents. What view would they have taken if they had come to the conclusion that the Nye Committee documents, said to have been the first secret documents which Hiss handed over to Chambers, were not in fact secret at all? Would they have come to a different conclusion on the four documents in the handwriting of Hiss, if a careful analysis of these had been presented to them by the judge? What would have been their opinion of the photographed documents had a similar analysis been prepared for them? If they had believed that the Nye Committee documents were not confidential, that the four documents in the handwriting of Hiss had been stolen from him, and that some of the photographed documents could not have come from him, would they still have been satisfied that the case was proved in regard to the typewritten documents? I make no assertion about this, and I express no opinion. I merely state as a fact that in a corresponding trial in England these points would have been dealt with by the judge in his charge to the jury.

CHAPTER XXIX
THE FOUR HANDWRITTEN DOCUMENTS

Four documents were produced in the handwriting of Alger Hiss. They were rough notes derived from State Department documents which were also produced. The State Department documents bear the following dates: the 28th January 1938; the 2nd March 1938; the 3rd March 1938; and the 11th March 1938.

In order to understand the significance of these documents, a few facts must be appreciated. In 1938 there were being employed various lettered codes—A, B, C and D, the D code being the most confidential, and the farther back one went in the alphabet, the less confidential was the code. If a telegram contained something which had appeared in a newspaper, that part was put into a code called the gray code, so that the secrecy of the confidential codes might be protected. It is obvious that no code would long remain secret if it was used to transmit passages which had appeared in the press.

Chambers' story about these handwritten documents was as follows: "From time to time Hiss also gave me small handwritten notes. These notes were about documents which had passed under his eyes quickly, and which for some reason or other he was unable to bring out, but which he thought were of some importance. I would either turn over these documents directly to Colonel Bykov, or would have them photographed and then turn over the photographs."

The explanation which Hiss gave about the documents was this. Incoming despatches (and all the four handwritten documents were derived from incoming despatches) were sent to his desk by his assistants, Miss Newcomb and Miss Lincoln, so that he could decide which needed to be brought to the attention of Mr. Sayre. Sometimes he would simply mark a document to indicate that it should go to Mr. Sayre, and sometimes he would mark it in such a way as to indicate that it need not go to him. But on many occasions Hiss would report orally to Mr. Sayre on the significant portions of cablegrams or despatches. Hiss lunched with Mr. Sayre about twice a week at Harvey's Restaurant, and though he admitted quite frankly that he had no precise recollection of the particular documents which are now in question, he suggested that it was quite probable that he would have made memoranda in regard to certain documents which he wanted to discuss at lunch. Incoming telegrams used to come from all over the world, sometimes as many as two hundred a day. Mr. Sayre could not possibly have read all these documents, and he used frequently to impress upon Hiss the necessity of giving him only material which he ought to see. Therefore Hiss had adopted, so he said, the following method. When he read through a thick file of incoming telegrams which had accumulated over a day or a night, he would be on the lookout for matters which ought to be brought to the attention of Mr. Sayre. If the entire document had not got to go to Mr. Sayre, Hiss would make notes on slips of paper which he would put into the file at the appropriate place as he turned over the pages. He would make these notes as briefly and as quickly as possible. When he had finished reading the file, he would look through to see if he had picked out too many documents and whether the rough notes he had made were adequate. If the notes were not very comprehensible to Hiss himself, then he would expand them on the same piece of paper so that he would have the matter more clearly in mind when he came to see Mr. Sayre.

This would, of course, account for the remarkable fact that in two of these four documents (namely the second and third) the top part is written by Hiss in a blue crayon and the bottom part by him with a lead pencil; and in another, No. 4, lead pencil has been used by Hiss to make plain certain obscurities in the blue pencil he had previously used. After he had made his report to Mr. Sayre, the notes which he had prepared to help him would be thrown away.

Two of the four handwritten documents (Nos. 1 and 3) had been written on common "scratch pad" paper; that is to say, the sort of paper which might be found on any desk in any office for the purpose of making rough notes; whilst the other two (Nos. 2 and 4) were probably written on a small piece of paper which had at one time had on it a printed letterhead "Department of State Assistant Secretary," but this heading had been torn off.

All the papers had been creased in such a way as to indicate they had been folded, as would be natural and probable if they had been put into a man's coat pocket. In the case of Nos. 1 and 3 the fold was roughly in the middle of the paper; in the case of Nos. 2 and 4 the fold would have been roughly in the middle of the paper if the printed letterhead had not been torn off—but owing to the tearing off, the fold no longer appeared in the middle, as the distance from the fold to what had now become the top was less than the distance of the fold to the bottom. It seems reasonable, therefore, to draw the inference that the letterhead had been torn off after the paper had been folded. None of them had been crumpled up.

The problem can be thus stated. Are these four handwritten documents more like documents which were prepared for the express purpose of giving information to Chambers, or are they more like documents which were produced by Hiss to help him make his report to Mr. Sayre, thereafter to be discarded by some means such as being thrown into the wastepaper basket? In the latter case it is obvious that they might have been stolen by some thief.

This is one of the most critical issues in the case. It is to be regretted that it did not receive far closer attention. Nine tenths of the evidence tendered was addressed to the question whether

Hiss had in the past had Communist affiliations; but he was not charged with having had Communist affiliations; he was charged with perjury in denying that he had handed over documents.

Here we come to consider the "immutable witnesses," if I may borrow the impressive phrase of Mr. Murphy in his closing speech for the Government. I propose to consider each of these documents, to trace its origin and history, and, having done so, to revert to a consideration of the conclusions which can be drawn from these handwritten documents.

The First Document, dated the 28th January 1938

The background necessary to the understanding of the first of the handwritten notes was given by Hiss in his evidence. Under the treaty by which American recognition was accorded to Soviet Russia (which was concluded somewhere about the end of 1933), there was a provision that any American citizen arrested by the Russians should have the right to be interviewed promptly by the American diplomatic or consular officials. The Rubens, or Robinsons, who had been arrested by the Russians, were travelling on American passports, and there was every reason to believe that they were Americans. Yet the Russian officials for weeks would not allow any American representatives to see them. This was the first time that this question had arisen, and Secretary Hull was pressing for a prompt opportunity for his officials to interview these persons. The American representative in Moscow was Mr. Loy Henderson. At the very end of January 1938 an opportunity for an interview was afforded, and Mr. Henderson made an official report dealing with the interview on or about the 10th February 1938.

Mr. Sayre, in his evidence, had no recollection of the details of the matter beyond the fact that at the end of January 1938 the Robinson-Rubens case was being considered by the State Department. It was also receiving a certain amount of attention in the press. On the 25th January 1938, there was an article in the New York *Times* under the heading: "Long wait foreseen in Mrs. Ruben's case. American officials in Moscow unlikely to see prisoner until inquiry ends." On the following day another article appeared headed: "United States presses right to see Mrs. Rubens. Hull orders Moscow Embassy to insist on an interview with woman in prison. Cites Recognition Pact. State Department rejects any interpretation that would add to delay." On the 27th January a third article appeared entitled: "United States awaits reply on Rubens demand."

On the 28th January Henderson sent the following cablegram to the State Department:

MOSCOW
DATED JANUARY 28 1938
REC'D 6:13 A.M.

SECRETARY OF STATE
WASHINGTON, D.C.
30, JANUARY 28, 11 A.M.

HAVE RECEIVED FOLLOWING TELEGRAM FROM MARY MARTIN, WIDOW OF HUGH MARTIN, FORMERLY EMPLOYED FOR SPECIAL WORK BY LEGATION AT RIGA.

(GRAY) "REMEMBER WELL RUBENS WHILE WORKING FOR HUGH, BE STRICT IF NEEDED, WRITE LIBRARY CONGRESS, LAW DIVISION.

"SIGNED MARY MARTIN." (END GRAY)

HENDERSON.

The document which Chambers produced, which was written in pencil and was by no means easy to decipher, reads as follows:

M.28.

Tel. from Mary Martin widow/Hugh Martin formerly employed for special work by Legation at Riga.

Remember well Rubens while working for Hugh, be strict if needed, write Lib. Cong., Law Div.

It will be observed that the pencil document omits the signatures, and that the date and place of despatch are somewhat cryptically referred to as "M.28," which signified "Moscow, 28th January."

But there are more important considerations which arise from an examination of this document. In the first place, it records the fact that Henderson had received a telegram from Mary

Martin, who would presumably have had no access to State Department ciphers and would therefore have sent her message either *en clair* or in a commercial code. In either case, the Russians would presumably already have had it in their possession and would therefore have gained nothing by its repetition. The second fact which stands out is that the important part of the telegram was sent in "gray"; that is to say, the code that was used to protect the secret codes. It seems quite obvious, therefore, that had the Russians wanted this information they could have got it from two sources; from the cable which Mary Martin sent to Henderson, and from the telegram in the gray code which Henderson sent to his Secretary of State. To pass such a document to a Russian spy in Washington would indeed have been "sending coals to Newcastle." Yet it was a matter which was of interest to Mr. Sayre and which was likely to form —and indeed already had formed—the subject of press agitation. Questioned in cross-examination as to whether he had ever seen either the telegram from Henderson or the pencil copy made by Hiss, Mr. Sayre simply said that he could not testify that he had seen them or that he had not seen them, as he had no specific recollection. Indeed, it is hardly conceivable that after an interval of ten years he would remember whether he had seen them or not.

There was an interesting sequel to this story. When at the beginning of September 1939 Chambers decided to reveal to Mr. Berle certain parts of the information he had, he referred to this matter. I quote the relevant part of Mr. Berle's notes of their conversation:

> *Note*—When Loy Henderson interviewed Mrs. Rubens his report immediately went back to Moscow. Who sent it? —Such came from Washington.

Assuming Chambers' evidence on this point to be correct, it follows that there must have been someone, presumably in the State Department, who sent to Moscow the official account of the interview with Mrs. Rubens. Who that person was remains a mystery. Hiss said in his direct evidence that he knew nothing about it, and he was not challenged in cross-examination. Chambers was not cross-examined as to the source of his information, nor how he came to know that the report "came from Washington." Thus the matter is left in complete mystery, but it is perhaps a pointer to the fact that the Russians had more sources of information in the State Department than have yet been revealed.

The Second Document, dated the 2nd March 1938

This was a telegram received from Paris, signed by Mr. Wilson, the American representative. It was sent in two sections, both despatched on the 2nd March, the second part being received at 3:17 P.M. and the first at 4:57 P.M. I set it out in full.

PARIS
DATED MARCH 2, 1938
REC'D 4:57 P.M.

SECRETARY OF STATE,
WASHINGTON,
324, MARCH 2, 5 P.M. (SECTION ONE)

THE CHIEF OF THE FAR EASTERN DIVISION OF THE FOREIGN OFFICE SAID TO ME TODAY THAT AFFAIRS IN CHINA HAVE REACHED A RELATIVELY "STATIC" STAGE. THE IMMEDIATE PREOCCUPATION OF THE FRENCH IS THE QUESTION OF THE CHINESE CUSTOMS. THE BRITISH AMBASSADOR IN TOKYO PRESENTED YESTERDAY OR WILL PRESENT TODAY A REQUEST THAT CUSTOMS REVENUES PLEDGED FOR THE SERVICE OF FOREIGN LOANS BE DEPOSITED IN A BRITISH BANK AT SHANGHAI OR IF THE JAPANESE INSIST UPON THE DEPOSIT IN THE YOKOHAMA SPECIE BANK OF THE REVENUES PLEDGED FOR JAPANESE LOANS THEN AT LEAST THE REVENUES EARMARKED FOR OTHER FOREIGN LOANS SHOULD BE PLACED IN THE BRITISH BANK. THE FOREIGN OFFICE HERE FEELS THAT THE JAPANESE WILL INSIST UPON THE DEPOSIT OF ALL CUSTOMS RECEIPTS IN THE JAPANESE BANK, BUT IS HOPEFUL THAT AN ARRANGEMENT CAN BE WORKED OUT TO CONTROL SATISFACTORILY THE DISBURSEMENT OF THESE FUNDS.

THE CHINESE ARE STILL GETTING A FEW AIRPLANES FROM FRANCE VIA THE INDO-CHINA ROUTE IN FULFILLMENT OF ORDERS "PLACED BEFORE THE OUTBREAK OF HOSTILITIES." (I have the impression that this phase is interpreted with some elasticity.) IN THIS CONNECTION THE NAVAL ATTACHÉ IS CONFI-

DENTIALLY INFORMED THAT AN ORDER WAS RECENTLY PLACED FOR CHINA FOR THIRTY POTEZ-63 PLANES, A LATEST TYPE FRENCH LIGHT BOMBER-PURSUIT PLANE.

HOPPENOT SAID THAT THE RUSSIANS ARE STEADILY INCREASING THEIR SHIPMENTS OF AIRPLANES AND WAR MATERIAL TO CHINA. HOW THIS IS BEING FINANCED IS A PUZZLE TO THE FRENCH. SUN-FO, THE SON OF SUN YAT SEN AND PRESIDENT OF THE CHINESE LEGISLATIVE YUAN, HAS BEEN IN RUSSIA FOR TWO MONTHS ARRANGING IT. IT IS BELIEVED THAT HIS VISIT HAS HAD TO DO WITH FINANCING AND ACCELERATING RUSSIAN SHIPMENTS OF WAR SUPPLIES TO CHINA.

WILSON.

PARIS
DATED MARCH 2, 1938
REC'D 3:17 P.M.

SECRETARY OF STATE,
WASHINGTON.

324, MARCH 2, 5 P.M. (SECTION TWO)

SUN FO IS DUE IN PARIS NEXT WEEK BUT THE ONLY INFORMATION THE FRENCH GOVERNMENT HAS RECEIVED REGARDING HIS VISIT HERE IS THAT IT IS OF A PERSONAL NATURE TO GET IN TOUCH WITH OLD FRIENDS, ET CETERA.

APART FROM SHIPMENTS OF SUPPLIES TO CHINA THE FOREIGN OFFICE IS CONVINCED THAT THE SOVIET GOVERNMENT WILL CONTINUE TO REFRAIN FROM TAKING ANY MORE DIRECT OR AGGRESSIVE INTEREST IN THE CHINO–JAPANESE CONFLICT. ON THE OTHER HAND, THE FRENCH AMBASSADOR IN TOKYO HAS REPORTED THAT WITHOUT ANY TANGIBLE PROOF HE NEVERTHELESS HAS THE "FEELING" THAT THE JAPANESE MAY BE PREPARING FOR A MOVE AGAINST THE RUSSIAN MARITIME PROVINCES. MY INFORMANT SAID THAT ALTHOUGH HE DID NOT HIMSELF SHARE THIS FEELING HE KNEW THAT IT EXISTED ON THE PART OF OTHER COMPETENT OBSERVERS OF THE FAR EAST WHO REASON AS FOLLOWS: THE JAPANESE ARMY CHIEFS REALIZE THAT TODAY THE JAPANESE PEOPLE ARE WORKED UP TO A PITCH WHERE THEY WILL ACCEPT ANY SACRIFICE IN PROSECUTION OF WAR; THAT IF THIS PATRIOTIC FERVOR IS ALLOWED TO SUBSIDE IT WILL BE EXTREMELY DIFFICULT TO WHIP IT UP AGAIN; AND THAT THERE-

FORE ADVANTAGE SHOULD BE TAKEN OF THIS SITUATION TO STRIKE AGAINST RUSSIA. FURTHERMORE THESE MILITARY CHIEFS ARE CONVINCED THAT THEY WILL BE ABLE TO WAGE A SUCCESSFUL WAR AGAINST RUSSIA WHILE HOLDING THE CHINESE IN CHECK ON THEIR FLANK WITH LITTLE DIFFICULTY. MY INFORMANT ADDED THAT THIS WAS ALSO THE VIEW OF MANY FRENCH MILITARY OFFICERS.

REFERRING TO THE RECALL, GENERAL MATSUI, MY INFORMANT SAID THAT IT WAS POSSIBLE THAT THE REAL REASON FOR HIS RETURN TO JAPAN WAS TO BE PREPARED TO HEAD A MILITARY COUP IN CASE THE NATIONAL MOBILIZATION BILL SHOULD BE DEFEATED BY THE CIVILIAN OPPOSITION OF THE ARMY. MATSUI IS JUST THE PERSON HE SAID TO HEAD A MOVEMENT OF THIS SORT. (END MESSAGE)

WILSON.

This document had a wide circulation in the Department of State, having been sent to no fewer than fifteen departments, one of which was the Far Eastern Division and another the European Division. These facts were given in evidence by Mr. Anderson. The subject matter of the telegram was of interest to Mr. Sayre because it dealt with neutrality. Hiss explained that Mr. Sayre's interest in neutrality was "more than a passing interest. It was a part of his actual responsibility in an over-all sense. He was frequently consulted by Judge Moore, the Counselor, who came into his office and to whose office he went for the specific purpose of Judge Moore getting Mr. Sayre's advice, and I think the Secretary, though I am not sure. I remember distinctly seeing Mr. Moore come to see Mr. Sayre and seeing Mr. Sayre go down and talk to Judge Moore."

I shall now set out the second of the handwritten documents, which reads as follows:

30 Potez-63
A latest type
light b p

About March 2 U.S. embassy in Paris cabled that although France was permitting shipment of military supplies to China via Indo-China only to fill existing orders, it was understood that this restriction was being liberally construed. For instance the Military Attaché had learned that China had recently placed an order in France for 30 Potez-63 planes, one of the latest French types, a light bomber-pursuit.

There are two striking features about this document. In the first place, part of it was written in crayon and part in pencil. The words at the top—"30 Potez-63 A latest type light b p"—were in blue crayon, the rest being in ordinary lead pencil. This may be thought to have a considerable bearing on the explanation given by Hiss: that he used to go through a file of telegrams, make very rough notes of those matters which he ought to bring to the attention of Mr. Sayre, then afterwards go through the notes and expand them if they were too obscure. It may be thought (bearing in mind the fact that Mr. Sayre was interested in this matter from the point of view of neutrality) that the blue crayon notes at the top would correspond with what Hiss would have jotted down on going through a large file of papers, and that the part in lead pencil would correspond with the more elaborate note required to make his first note intelligible even to himself.

The second remarkable feature of this document lies not so much in what it says but in what it does not say. For I should have thought that the second section of the telegram would have been very much more interesting to the Russians than the first. That passage, for instance, that the military chiefs of Japan were confident that they could wage a successful war on Russia whilst holding the Chinese in check on their flank is surely the sort of information the Russians would have wanted. So also is the part which says that the Japanese people were worked up to such a pitch that they would be prepared to accept any sacrifice, but that patriotic fervour, once allowed to subside, would be difficult to re-create. The pencil note makes no reference whatever to Section Two of the telegram, and merely states the French position about military supplies to China and the thirty Potez-63 planes.

The Third Document, dated the 3rd March 1938

The background necessary to the understanding of this document is this. Under the London Naval Treaty of 1936 the rate at which ships of war should be built was laid down; but there was a provision known as the escalation clause, which provided that if any signatory of the treaty exceeded certain specified limits, all the other signatories were entitled to "escalate"—that is, to increase their building. In the early part of 1938 there were persistent reports that Japan was building larger battleships than she was allowed. Formal enquiries were made, but the Japanese refused to give any information. Accordingly, the British and French Governments, in conjunction with the United States Government, had to consider whether or not they were entitled to use the escalation clause. On the 3rd March Mr. Herschel Johnson, the United States representative in London, sent his Secretary of State the following telegram:

LONDON
DATED MARCH 3, 1938
REC'D 3:55 P.M.

SECRETARY OF STATE,
WASHINGTON.
179, MARCH 3, 7 P.M.
MY 174, MARCH 1, 10 P.M.

ONE. THE NAVAL ATTACHÉ INFORMS ME THAT IN SUBSEQUENT PRIVATE TALK LORD CHATFIELD SAID IN HIS OPINION IT WAS IMPORTANT "TO GET ON" WITH THE CONVERSATIONS ON QUESTION OF ESCALATION AND MENTIONED THAT HE WAS GOING TO GIBRALTAR NEXT WEEK TO WATCH THE MANEUVERS OF THE FLEET. HE ADDED THAT WHETHER IT WAS DECIDED TO ESCALATE OR NOT, HE WOULD NOT (REPEAT NOT) CHANGE HIS PLANS FOR CRUISERS THIS YEAR AND THAT IN ANY CASE THE NEW BATTLESHIPS WOULD NOT (REPEAT NOT) BE LAID DOWN BEFORE THE END OF THE CURRENT YEAR.

TWO. THE FOREIGN OFFICE HAS INTIMATED INFORMALLY THAT THEY VERY MUCH DESIRE TO HAVE A FURTHER INFORMAL CONFERENCE BEFORE NEXT WEDNESDAY, WHEN LORD CHATFIELD LEAVES, IF IT COULD BE FOUND PRACTICABLE. THEY REALIZE APPARENTLY THAT THERE WOULD BE NO POINT IN HAVING A CONFERENCE BEFORE THERE HAS BEEN SOME EXPRESSION OF AMERICAN VIEWS. LORD CHATFIELD AT THE MEETING ON MARCH 1 WAS OBVIOUSLY PREPARED FOR A FULL DISCUSSION AND GAVE AN

UNMISTAKABLE IMPRESSION OF DISSATISFACTION AT THE WAY THE MEETING DEVELOPED.

JOHNSON.

The document in the handwriting of Hiss, which Chambers produced, reads:

3
Chatfield N.A.

whether decided escalate or not would not change plans for cruisers this year and in any case new battleships would not be laid down before end of current year.

March 3. Johnson U.S. Chargé at London cabled that Lord Chatfield had told the Naval Attaché that whether escalation was eventually decided on or not he would not change his plans for cruisers this year and in any case new battleships would not be laid down before the end of the current year.

The first half of this document was written in blue crayon, and the second half in lead pencil. The top part, namely that written in blue crayon, is very difficult to decipher. The number "3" looks more like an *R*, though doubtless it stands for the date of the 3rd March. The words "Chatfield N.A." might lead one to suppose that Chatfield was the name of the Naval Attaché.

Mr. Murphy suggested that the top part in itself would have been sufficient to enable Hiss to call Mr. Sayre's attention to the matter, but Hiss replied that this was not so, "particularly if I found it difficult to read while standing up in front of him." Moreover, it not infrequently happened that Hiss had to report to Mr. Sayre a day or two after he had made his notations on a large number of telegrams. Mr. Murphy's suggestion still gives rise to the question—even if the purpose of this document was to furnish information to the Russians, why was it necessary to write it out twice?

The Fourth Document, dated the 11th March 1938

This related to the application, or non-application, of the Neutrality Act to the Sino-Japanese conflict. Although it was for the President to make a decision on this, he relied largely on the advice of Secretary Hull and Judge Moore, both of whom, as I have already said, used to consult Mr. Sayre on questions of neutrality. It was therefore a matter in which Mr. Sayre was interested. The original document, which I now set out, was addressed to the Secretary of State, Washington, by Mr. Gauss, the American representative in Shanghai. Part of it was sent in the "gray" code and part *en clair*.

GRAY AND PLAIN
SHANGHAI VIA N.R.
DATED MARCH 11 1938
REC'D 8 A.M.

SECRETARY OF STATE,
WASHINGTON.
378, MARCH 11, 11 A.M.
MY 365, MARCH 5, 2 P.M.

FAIRLY HEAVY FIGHTING IS REPORTED IN THE IMMEDIATE VICINITY OF LINYI SOUTHEAST SHANTUNG. LITTLE ACTIVITY ON THE TSINING OR SOUTHERN TSINPU FRONTS. MILITARY OBSERVERS ESTIMATE JAPANESE REINFORCEMENTS TOTALING APPROXIMATELY 70,000 MEN WITH CONSIDERABLE QUANTITIES OF HEAVY ARTILLERY HAVE BEEN LANDED AT WOOSUNG DURING THE PAST TWO WEEKS. OVER FIFTY PER CENT OF THESE REINFORCEMENTS ARE BELIEVED TO BE DESTINED FOR THE SOUTHERN TSINPU FRONT THE BALANCE BEING DISTRIBUTED BETWEEN WUHU, HANGCHOW AND ALONG LINES OF COMMUNICATION.

MR. M. TANI, JAPANESE MINISTER AT LARGE WHO RECENTLY ARRIVED IN SHANGHAI, INFORMED JAPANESE PRESS REPRESENTATIVES THAT HE HAD BEEN PLACED IN CHARGE OF ALL JAPANESE DIPLOMATIC ORGANS IN CENTRAL AND NORTH CHINA AND WOULD COMMUTE FREQUENTLY BETWEEN SHANGHAI AND PEIPING. HE IS ALSO REPORTED TO HAVE STATED THAT JAPANESE INTEND TO RESPECT FULLY FOREIGN RIGHTS AND INTERESTS IN CHINA AND WITH REFERENCE TO ANGLO-JAPANESE RELATIONS THAT "THERE CAN BE NO FRICTION BETWEEN JAPAN AND BRITAIN UNLESS JAPAN INFRINGES BRITISH TRADE INTERESTS AND VESTED RIGHTS IN THE ORIENT. THIS HAS ESPECIALLY BEEN MADE TRUE BY THE REPLACEMENT OF EDEN DIPLOMACY BY CHAMBERLAIN DIPLO-

MACY OR IN OTHER WORDS THE REPLACEMENT OF IDEALISM BY REALISM. JAPAN MUST PAY CAREFUL ATTENTION TO THIS POINT SO AS NOT TO VIOLATE BRITAIN'S RIGHTS AND INTERESTS."

GENERAL CHOU FENG CHI, FORMERLY ACTING PROVINCIAL CHAIRMAN OF CHEKIANG, WAS ASSASSINATED HERE ON MARCH 7TH. HIS ASSASSINATION IS REPORTED TO HAVE BEEN CONNECTED WITH OVERTURES MADE TO HIM BY THE JAPANESE TO BECOME MINISTER OF WAR IN THE CENTRAL CHINA GOVERNMENT WHICH THE JAPANESE ARE SEEKING TO ESTABLISH.

REPEATED TO HANKOW AND PEIPING.

GAUSS.

The corresponding note in Hiss's handwriting reads:

> Mar 11 Gauss U.S. consul at Shanghai cabled that military observers estimated that over 70,000 reinforcements with considerable quantities of heavy artillery have landed at Woosung during past 2 weeks. Over 50% believed destined for the southern Tsinpu front, the rest to be distributed between Wuhu, Hangchow and along the lines of communication.

This document is a combination of blue chalk and ordinary lead pencil. It looks as though Hiss had made a quick note in blue crayon and then gone over the parts that were difficult to read in pencil. He explained the matter in this way: "I remember that having been through a file and making—having made notes, if I were interrupted, didn't get back to the file until the next day, my notes would be cold to me, just the way a stenographer sometimes can't read back their own shorthand after a short period of absence; and I would have to go back to the original again to be sure that I did have the details in mind. I think the lead pencil overtops the blue, and I put the lead pencil in places above the blue."

Such, then, were the four famous handwritten notes. They were undoubtedly in the handwriting of Hiss. Were they written by him for the purpose of giving information to Chambers which he could pass on to his Communist masters, or were they written to enable Hiss to give an account to Mr. Sayre of matters in which Mr. Sayre was interested? Were they handed by Hiss to Chambers? Or were they stolen from Hiss after they had served their purpose?

In the first place, I feel bound to point out that it seems to me a most extraordinary thing that a man engaging in such infamous conduct as that attributed to Hiss should have been such a fool as to hand over documents in his own handwriting. I confess I think it odd, too, that he should have handed over documents typed on his own typewriter; but I suppose it is possible, though I should have thought unlikely, that he might not have realised that a typewriter would reveal its own special peculiarities. Whatever may be the extent of knowledge of Hiss as to typewriters, he must have known that notes written by him in his own handwriting would give him away. In the course of a long life in the law I have often thought that as a general rule the wicked people are not foolish, and the foolish people are not wicked. This is a case in which, at one and the same time, a man is being very wicked and very foolish. For he makes extracts from documents in his own handwriting, and hands them over to a spy on whose reliability he has no adequate ground for reposing much trust and confidence.

Apart from this general consideration, there is the odd fact that these documents are written in different-coloured crayons. Why, if Hiss was preparing a document to give information to the Communists, should he use different-coloured crayons? This fact would seem to be more consistent with his own explanation —that on going through a file he made very rough notes, and thereafter, having finished the file, went back over those rough notes to see if they were too many in number and were reasonably intelligible to him. If some interval of time elapsed between going through the file and reading over the notes he had made, it is easy to understand that it would have been necessary to perfect the notes.

The next consideration that arises is: Why was it that these notes, which do not seem to deal with particularly secret or important matters, fall into the category of documents which Hiss could not bring out? The subjects they deal with were, of course, secret or confidential, but when one considers the importance of some of the documents which, according to Chambers, Hiss did succeed in bringing out, it is a matter for surprise that he could not bring out these four.

Moreover, if it be remembered that, according to Chambers' story, Hiss had been asked particularly to bring out documents relating to, amongst other places, the Far East, it is surely strange that the notes do not incorporate those parts of some of the original telegrams which would presumably have been of much greater interest to the Russians than the copied parts.

I do not myself think it especially significant that the documents had been folded. They might equally well have been folded if Hiss had put them in his pocket to take to a lunch with Mr. Sayre, as if Chambers had put them in his pocket on receiving them from Hiss. Nor do I think any inference can be drawn from the fact that the letterheading had in two cases apparently been torn off. For that might equally well have been done by Hiss on giving them to Chambers, or by a thief on picking them out from some such receptacle as a wastepaper basket. There is the fact that the notes had merely been folded and not crumpled, and it is undoubtedly a point, though not, I think, of great weight, that had Hiss disposed of them by putting them into a wastepaper basket, it might have been expected that the documents would have been found in a crumpled condition. On the other hand, if he had put them in some outgoing tray after they had served their purpose and they had been picked up by a thief from that tray, it would be unlikely that they would have been crumpled up. A point of greater importance is, I think, the fact that neither Mr. Sayre nor Miss Lincoln could recall ever having seen documents like these on other occasions.

I have dealt with the issue of the four handwritten documents at some length because I think it impossible to overestimate their importance. If Chambers was wicked enough to have arranged for the stealing of these documents, and thereafter to have alleged that they had been given to him by Hiss, great suspicion must be cast also upon his story relating to the typewritten documents which had undoubtedly been typed on the typewriter belonging to Mrs. Hiss. There is no evidence that Chambers or anyone acting on his behalf ever in fact had access to this typewriter. The most that can be said is that Chambers knew well that documents could be traced to a particular typewriter. This is obvious from the way in which he took care to dispose of his own typewriter. It is, I think, fair to say that there would have been ample opportunity for a clever and unscrupulous man to have got access to that typewriter, and it is plain that there was at least one thief in the State Department who, without the knowledge of Hiss, was stealing documents and handing them over to Chambers. If such a thief had stolen documents and had had them photographed, it would have been possible to have had the contents of the documents so photographed typed on any particular typewriter at any time afterwards. This may seem to the reader a fanciful hypothesis. If, however, he forms the view that the handwritten documents were never in fact given to Chambers by Hiss but were stolen from him, Chambers' story about the other documents must be looked at with great suspicion.

There is this further fact of great significance. At the time these documents were being handed over by Hiss—if indeed they were—Chambers had made up his mind to break with the Communist Party. His first step of obtaining a job with the Government had been taken in October 1937; the purchase of a car in November was the second step; and Chambers has said that he intended to build up what he called a "life preserver" for himself by obtaining documents which would incriminate Hiss. It is in the light of these circumstances that we must consider the facts relating to the other documents.

Finally, in considering the handwritten documents, the reader may like to be reminded of the documents in the handwriting of Harry Dexter White, which I have earlier discussed.[1] If he thinks that these latter documents were more likely to have been stolen from White than handed over by him, he may find it more difficult to accept Chambers' story that the four handwritten documents were handed to him by Hiss.

[1]See page 147 and Appendix VI.

CHAPTER XXX

THE PHOTOGRAPHED DOCUMENTS

The two rolls of developed microfilm were the documents which Chambers had hidden in a hollowed-out pumpkin on his farm. He delivered them to the agents of the House Committee on the 2nd December 1948. They consisted of fifty-eight frames, each frame being a copy of a page of a State Department document. For convenience of reference at the trial, enlargements were made so that the pages could be put together, and thus complete documents were made up. They were referred to as Government Baltimore Exhibits Nos. 48, 50, 51, 52, 53, 54 and 55. There was no exhibit in this category marked 49.

It could be proved, and was not disputed, that all the documents had been photographed at the same time; and as the latest, No. 55, was dated the 13th January 1938, it followed that none of them could have been photographed before then.

Five of the documents (Nos. 48 and 50–53) refer to certain negotiations for trade agreements with Germany and are therefore in some sense interrelated. With the exception of No. 53, there can be no doubt that the originals were all in Mr. Sayre's office, and were therefore available to Hiss if he had been minded to make use of them.

Let me remind the reader that when a document is typed, it is usual at the same time to make carbon copies; the number of copies that can be made in a single typing operation depends, of course, on various factors, such as the quality and thickness of paper and carbons and the nature of the typewriter; but given favourable conditions, as many as twelve could be made, though each successive copy would tend to be progressively less clear than the top copy. I must make it plain that it was not the fact, and indeed it was never suggested, that any of these documents had been typed on the Hiss typewriter; although it was a peculiar feature of the case that some parts had apparently been specially typed.

The first, Exhibit No. 48, is in the original a two-page memorandum, dated the 8th January 1938, and addressed to Mr. Sayre. It is typed on the letterhead of the Trade Agreements Section and is signed by Mr. Hawkins, the head of that section. I have before me on my table a photograph of the original document, State Exhibit No. 48, and Baltimore Exhibit No. 48, which is the enlargement of the microfilm. The original bears a stamp showing that it was received in Mr. Sayre's office on the 11th January 1938; the three days' delay is presumably accounted for by the fact that a week end intervened. It begins, apart from the letterhead and the date, as follows:

> A-S
> Mr. Sayre:
> I am returning the German aide-memoire which you sent me on November 23 together with a memorandum by Mr. Darlington.

It ends with this paragraph:

> Since the subject is of such outstanding importance, I believe it would be desirable for it to be further discussed with the interested Divisions. I believe that you will wish, therefore, to send the file next to Eu, since it has not yet been seen by that Division, and then back to EA for consideration of our comment.

The original is signed "Harry C. Hawkins" in ink, with his name typed in underneath. On the original, too, the words in the top left-hand corner, "A-S Mr. Sayre," have been ticked through in ink, presumably to show that he had read it; and in the last paragraph the letter *s* in the word "Divisions" is added in ink. Baltimore No. 48 has not got this correction, and was therefore presumably a photograph not of the original which went to Mr. Sayre, but of a carbon copy, as such an alteration must have been made by or on behalf of the sender. If this is a correct assumption, it becomes important to consider not only whether the original was in Mr. Sayre's office, but whether there was ever a carbon copy of the original in his office. Mr. Harry C. Hawkins, who was called for the defendant, gave evidence as follows:

> *Mr. Cross:* Now will you tell us what the practice of your Department was at that time with reference to whether or not any duplicate or carbon of this memorandum, which is January 8, 1938, would have been sent along to Mr. Sayre?
> *Mr. Hawkins:* It was not the practice to send along duplicates with action documents of this kind.

He went on to explain that carbon copies would have been kept in the Trade Agreements Section in his outer office, and that probably copies would have been sent to Mr. Darlington and would have been available to anyone in his Department. They would have been kept in a separate folder and would have remained indefinitely in the Division's files. Mr. Darlington's copies would have been kept in the same way in his office.

There may therefore be ground for supposing that the document which was photographed came from the Trade Agreements Section and not from Mr. Sayre's office, in which Hiss was working.

The second document, No. 50, also came from the Trade Agreements Section. It is dated the 31st December 1937 and is addressed to Mr. Hawkins, the head of that section, by his assistant, Mr. Darlington. It is indeed one of the documents referred to in No. 48, and was undoubtedly sent by Mr. Hawkins to Mr. Sayre with that document. There is this odd feature about it: that whereas the last fifteen pages are photographs of the original carbon copies and are therefore exact replicas of the original, the first page is not a carbon copy of the document as originally typed, but is a photograph of another typing of that page. This was pointed out by the Government's expert. Even if a carbon copy had accompanied the original from Mr. Darlington to Mr. Hawkins, and from Mr. Hawkins to Mr. Sayre, yet the document photographed, so far as page one is concerned, was not a carbon copy, and there is no reason to suppose that that page which was the subject of the photograph had ever reached Mr. Sayre's office. The document photographed might have been the copy retained on the working file of the Trade Agreements Section.

The third document, No. 51, is an official file carbon copy on blue paper of a four-page memorandum which it was proposed should be sent to the German Government. It was prepared by Mr. Darlington on the 31st December 1937 and was initialled both by him and by Mr. Hawkins. It is referred to in Exhibit No. 50 as being attached thereto. It undoubtedly went together with that document from Mr. Darlington to Mr. Hawkins, and with Exhibit No. 48 from Mr. Hawkins to Mr. Sayre.

Exhibit No. 51 was a document which could not have been sent without Mr. Sayre's approval, and under such circumstances it was the practice to send to his office both the original and a number of exact carbon copies typed at the same time as the original. In fact, it was decided that this proposal should not be sent to the German Government. The normal procedure on such an occasion would have been to destroy the original and to have an exact carbon copy on blue paper sent to the files as the permanent record copy. The photograph reproduces the text of this document (the proposal for the German Government), but all four pages are carbon copies of a typing run different from that which produced the original. It is most unlikely that the carbon copies which accompanied the original to Mr. Sayre's office would have been other than carbon copies made in the same typing run as the original.

This lends some force to the suggestion that there are grounds for supposing that Exhibits 48, 50 and 51 were not photographs of the documents which went to Mr. Sayre's office, but were photographs of documents which remained on the files of the Trade Agreements Section.

The fourth document in this series, No. 52, is an *aide-mémoire* in German, which was handed to the Under-Secretary of State by the German Ambassador in the latter part of October 1937. As there is no file number reproduced on the photograph, it is certain that it is a photograph either of the original document before the file number was typed on it, or of an exact carbon copy; and it becomes necessary to consider what was the practice about putting on file numbers. When a document in a foreign language was delivered by an embassy to the State Department, it would normally be accompanied by an exact carbon copy. The departmental practice was that any such document would be sent promptly to the Division of Communications and Records, who would have it translated and would put a file number both on the original and on the translation. They would not put this file number on the copies. It is certain that the file number had been placed upon the original before the end of November, and as the photograph cannot have been taken before the 13th January 1938 (which is the date of Exhibit No. 55), it follows that the photograph cannot have been of the original, but must have been a photograph of a carbon copy. It is clear from the text of Exhibit 48 that the original was sent from Mr. Hawkins to Mr. Sayre on the 23rd November, for Exhibit 48 contains the following sentence: "I am returning the German *aide-mémoire* which you sent me on November 23." Again, it is probable that a carbon copy of Exhibit 52 remained in the working file of the Trade Agreements Section.

The fifth of the photographed documents, No. 53, is an *aide-mémoire* dated the 21st July 1937, from the United States Government to the German Ambassador. It is referred to by Mr. Darlington in his memorandum of the 31st December 1937 (Exhibit 50). There is no evidence that it was ever in Mr. Sayre's office. It is said that it probably remained in the files of the Trade Agreements Section until such time in January 1938 as the microfilm was made.

The last of the photographed documents, Exhibits 54 and 55, undoubtedly were at one time in the possession of Mr. Sayre's office, and therefore of Hiss. They are photographs of stencilled information copies of three incoming cables, and were in fact initialled by Hiss himself. It is therefore possible that Hiss turned them over; but, on the other hand, if a person is engaged in a nefarious plot to deliver over documents to be photographed, it seems odd that he should first of all initial them to prove that he had had them in his possession. It was argued that it is more probable that they were stolen from Mr. Sayre's office.

In conclusion, there are undoubtedly odd features about these documents. Various pages were specially typed, but they were not typed on the Hiss typewriter. No one has given any explanation of why these pages were retyped. There seems to be no basis for asserting that those documents with the special typing ever reached Mr. Sayre's office; there is definite ground for supposing that Exhibit 53 was never in Mr. Sayre's office. All these documents could have come from the Trade Agreements Section where Wadleigh, who was undoubtedly turning over documents to Chambers, was employed. If it be the fact that they came from Wadleigh and not from Hiss at all, it follows that for some reason or other Chambers was trying to put on Hiss the responsibility for stealing papers which had been stolen by Wadleigh.

CHAPTER XXXI

THE TYPEWRITTEN DOCUMENTS

These documents were all, with one exception, typed out on the typewriter belonging to Mrs. Hiss. They must have been typed:

(a) *By Hiss or his wife.* I cannot think that they can have been typed by Mrs. Hiss without Hiss knowing all about it. If they were typed by Hiss or his wife (the wife is much the more likely of the two), I cannot think of any legitimate purpose for which this would have been done; the obvious and the only reason must, in my view, have been to give information to the Communists.

(b) *By some other person.* If they were typed by some other person, the object must have been to fabricate a case against Hiss; for if such another person had merely wanted to supply information to the Communists, he would not have sought out any particular typewriter. It is, of course, possible that he had a double purpose in mind—one being to incriminate Hiss, and the other being to supply information to the Communists. I think it a reasonable assumption that if these documents were typed by some other person, he was a Communist agent —either Chambers himself or some confederate.

It is impossible to fix the date on which the typewritten documents came into existence. Whoever produced them must have had before him at the time the typing was done either the original State papers or photographs of them; and if the latter, the typist would of course have had an almost unlimited time in which to do his work.

On the whole, from a comparison of the typed documents with the sources—be they originals or photographs of the originals—from which they came, I draw the conclusion that the person responsible for the typing had considerable intelligence. My reason for this is that the documents are sometimes mere summaries of a large number of original documents, so that the typist had to select which parts he should reproduce and which he should leave out. It is a fact that the typewritten documents omit certain statements which might have been of interest to the Communists, and include others which would appear less interesting. But, on the whole, I think that the summaries were intelligently made, and that as a rule they picked out the salient points.

Anyone looking at some of the typewritten documents would be impressed by the labour involved. One, for instance, appears to be a full copy of a state paper dealing with the "Economic Development of Manchukuo." It runs to many pages and contains columns of figures setting out the shareholdings in a new company. I should have thought—if only to save the labour of copying—that it would have been arranged to have such a document photographed.

Mr. Feehan, a member of the F.B.I. who was specially skilled and experienced in all matters relating to typewriters, gave convincing testimony to show that all these documents, with one exception, had been typed on the Hiss typewriter. He was not asked one single question tending to show that there were any peculiarities in the typewriting which might throw light on the identity of the typist. Mr. Murphy raised this matter for the first time in his closing speech. I feel that if a case on these lines were to be constructed at all, it should have been made by his experts at a time when the Counsel for the Defence could have dealt with it. I do not think, in any case, that the point was by any means convincing.

There was, as I have said, one exception to the general statement that all these documents had been typed on the Hiss typewriter. This was Exhibit No. 10, which is a counterpart of a report prepared by the Military Intelligence Division of the War Department. It would appear that this document went only to the Far Eastern office of the State Department and thereafter to the filing office. It never went to the Treasury or to Mr. Sayre's office, but somehow or other it got mixed up with the papers typed on the Hiss typewriter.

Chambers' explanation was confused. He said at first that he got it from Hiss; then that it came from White, who was in the Treasury; and finally he came back to his original story, that it was given him by Hiss. I strongly suspect that there was a third source in the Far Eastern Division, and that it was through him that Exhibit No. 10 came to Chambers. Chambers alleged that Hiss of Mr. Sayre's office, White of the Treasury and Wadleigh of the Trade Agreements Section were his suppliers; but it seems certain that the original of this document never found its way to any of these three sources.

It remains to consider whether the documents themselves lead us to any clear conclusion. Hiss had access to all, or nearly all, of the originals from which the typed copies or summaries were made, but so, too, did a large number of other people—in the somewhat lax conditions prevailing in 1938. One of the documents—a cable to the Secretary of State from the American Ambassador in Paris—which had been sent in the most secret code and was marked "Strictly confidential to the Secretary," was sent to no less than eleven offices within the State Department. If this was the extent of circulation given to the most secret documents, it as a fair assumption that less secret documents were even more widely circulated.

One document (Baltimore No. 13), which was typed on the Hiss typewriter, calls for particular attention. It is as follows:

> February 9, 1938
>
> Yokohama reports that Mr. Aikawa is scheduled to sail from Japan on the M.S. Shichibu Maru February 24 for the United States. According to a newspaper item in the Japan Advertiser Mr. Aikawa hopes to raise $300,000,000 in the United States.

Another Japanese newspaper item states that the success of Mr. Aikawa's efforts in the United States depends upon Mr. Aikawa's ability and upon the attitude of the American government toward his venture.

FE: Jones: NN

This is an exact copy of a document, Government Exhibit No. 13, which bears the letterhead of the Division of Far Eastern Affairs. There is no evidence to show that this document ever got outside the Far Eastern Division. The most that can be said is that it may have been attached to other papers circulated from the Far Eastern Division.

All this matter was fully canvassed at the trial, and I shall not burden the reader with a consideration of the evidence.

When at the close of the second trial the jury announced their verdict of guilty and Hiss was allowed to make a statement, he said: "Time will show how the documents came to be typed." Time has not yet shown.

Chambers has given a possible explanation of how some of the documents were typed and some photographed. Those that were typed were typed on the Hisses' typewriter. The real strength of the case against Hiss lay in the fact that he had had access to all, or nearly all, of the original documents; and it seems certain that it was this which made the jury decide against him.

It would, however, be wrong to consider the typewritten documents in isolation. If the jury had come to the conclusions:

(*a*) that the Nye Committee documents were not secret at all, and that the attempt to make out that Hiss was guilty of any treachery in regard to them was baseless;

and

(*b*) that the handwritten documents had been stolen from him and were also being used to construct a false case against him,

would they, then, have been satisfied—for to convict him they had to be satisfied and not merely suspicious—that he or his wife had typed out these documents?

CHAPTER XXXII

THE CLOSING SPEECHES

It was on the 19th January 1950 that Mr. Cross rose to make his concluding speech on behalf of his client Alger Hiss.

Two months had elapsed since Mr. Murphy—on the 17th November 1949—had risen to open the case for the Prosecution.

Mr. Cross had lived with the case for the last two months. He cannot have had any illusions about the difficulty of his task.

There is always a risk in these very long cases that the interest of a jury may begin to flag. They long to get their task over and to get back to their own interests and their own concerns.

It would not have been wise for Mr. Cross, with this consideration in mind, to attempt a review of the evidence.

He had to be—like the writer of this book—selective, and his problem—like mine—was to know what to select.

He had not called any of those men whose names had run through the case like a kind of leitmotif—Pressman, Witt, Abt, Kramer, and Collins.

His task would have been easier if he could have called Pressman to tell the jury that which, long after the trial was over, he had—on second thoughts—told the House Committee—that he had been a member of a Communist study group and that Alger Hiss was not a member of that group.

The jury knew nothing about this: all they knew was that these names had been mentioned and not one of them had been called—not even Collins, the friend of Alger Hiss since boyhood.

Mr. Cross, who plainly has a clear and logical mind, would of course have realised that these considerations did not bear directly on the guilt of his client—but to an untrained mind they might so easily create an unfavourable atmosphere.

The jury might have applied to Alger Hiss Molière's question: "*Que diable allait-il faire dans cette galère?*"

Then, too, Mr. Cross had decided not to bring in the evidence about the collection of dues, and I confess—with my limited knowledge of the case—that I find this surprising.

In the evidence Chambers had given before the House Committee on this question he had been so self-contradictory that there was here magnificent material for cross-examination—and Mr. Cross must have been puzzled as to why it was that an advocate so skilled and so experienced as Mr. Murphy had made no reference to it.

Here, after all, was the conclusive test: the rug, the car, the subletting, the loan—all of which Mr. Murphy had developed during the case at such length and with such persistency—did not prove Communist association half so effectively as the payment of dues.

Moreover, there was the strange case of Donald Hiss. Chambers had said that he had collected dues from Donald Hiss—yet Mr. Murphy had not challenged the assertion of Donald Hiss that he had never been directly or indirectly associated with any Communist organisation.

Then there was the question of the handing over of the Nye Committee documents. Mr. Murphy had mentioned that matter in his opening speech—and as the case went on had to all intents and purposes abandoned it.

Now if Chambers had been lying in that matter, he had been lying with the object of building up a false case of espionage against Alger Hiss—and if he was concerned to build up a false case based upon the events of 1935, might he not equally have been concerned to build up a false case based upon the events of 1938?

Of course Mr. Cross had not the advantage which we have today of reading *Witness*. He did not know that Chambers was anxious to construct a "life preserver."

If only he had known that—how far more significant would certain other things have then appeared.

Chambers, for example, had never mentioned the supposed loan of $400 in his evidence before the House Committee or, indeed, until the first trial; and by this time he could have found out from the F.B.I. that Hiss had withdrawn $400 at or about the relevant time—for the F.B.I. had obtained a copy of the account on the 31st January 1949.

The attempt to identify the rug which had decorated the P Street house (which Hiss had left in June 1936) with one of the rugs despatched in January 1937 would have assumed a new significance—so also would the endeavour to construct a link between Hiss and the Communists by bringing about a direct transaction between him and the Cherner Motor Company and Rosen.

Mr. Cross had of course the handwritten documents, written in different-coloured chalks and omitting so much that would have been of real interest to the Communists in favour of much that must have been of less interest.

He had material, too, in reference to the documents which had been photographed—there was, for example, that alteration by the insertion of the letter *s*.

Of course he must have realised that his difficulty lay in regard to the typewritten documents.

There was, of course, the reflection that it was passing strange that when two conspirators had developed a technique of photography, one of them should have started to type documents out so as to make the source from which they came so clearly identifiable.

There was the odd fact relating to that document known as Baltimore 10. How had that got into the bunch of typewritten documents? Mr. Cross had succeeded in demonstrating that that had not been typed on the Hiss typewriter—that it had been typed on Government bond paper with a Government watermark on it, and that the original from which it came had gone—and gone only—to the Far Eastern Division of the State Department.

Yet Mr. Cross must have been acutely aware that all the other typed documents had been typed on the Hiss typewriter and that he had not succeeded in proving that Chambers ever got access to that typewriter on which those documents had been indubitably typed. The most he could hope to show was that Hiss had not had access to all the originals from which the summaries had been compiled—or, at any rate, that there was not sufficient evidence to show that he had had access to all of them.

It could hardly have been, therefore, a case in which Mr. Cross could hope that his client would receive an acquittal which would completely rehabilitate him in the eyes of his erstwhile friends and associates—but it might well have been a case in which the equivalent of a Scottish verdict of "not proven" would have been returned.

That verdict may be—and I think is—illogical, but it may exactly express the mind of a jury who are far from satisfied that the defendant has established his innocence, but equally not satisfied that the Prosecution have established his guilt.

In any case, it was surely not unlikely that this jury—like the previous jury—would find themselves unable to agree on a verdict.

Then, of course, there was the evidence of Drs. Binger and Murray, distinguished in the sciences of psychology, psychiatry and psychoanalysis. It is impossible for me to express any opinion as to the weight which an American jury would be likely to attach to this sort of evidence—for in England any such evidence would be plainly inadmissible.

Mr. Cross must have known, too, that Mr. Murphy had the last effective word—for the judge would probably decide to make no comment on the evidence which had been spread over the last two months—and he must have known that Mr. Murphy was a very effective jury advocate.

Mr. Cross, like the good advocate he was—after a general survey of the whole case—dealt with the documents, and he made out a strong case in a masterly summary.

I shall content myself with this short extract from that part of his speech which deals with the typewritten documents:

> I call to your attention Exhibit 11. Exhibit 11 is a summary or excerpt from 16 underlying State documents. In other words, you had to have 16 documents, or information copies of 16 different cablegrams, to have written the four pages that made up Baltimore Exhibit 11. No. 2 on this list did not go to Mr. Sayre's office. Now, if No. 2 did not go to Mr. Sayre's office and wasn't available to Mr. Hiss, how in the world could he have typed the full four pages of Exhibit 11? Whoever did it had to have all of the underlying documents. And where did you find all the underlying documents? From the schedule you will find every one of 11 went to Far Eastern Division.
>
> I will take another one, Exhibit 42. 42 is only two paragraphs. The second did not go to Sayre's office, did not go to Hiss; he did not have it. Whoever had that could type Exhibit 42. 42, both of them, went to Far Eastern Division.

Then after dealing with Exhibit 13—the short memorandum of Jones—Mr. Cross continues as follows:

> And there are still others about the typewritten documents showing that at least five of them never went to Mr. Sayre's office, which would mean, if you count up the underlying documents, I think about 20 out of some 72.
>
> Now the significant thing about this schedule is that an information copy of all these documents that form the basis of these Baltimore typewritten documents either went to Trade Agreements, where Wadleigh was stealing papers, or FE, where we know the Baltimore Exhibit 10 was stolen, and all these others you can trace back to Far Eastern and only Far Eastern and one other office, Dr. Pasvolsky's. He had an office in the Trade Agreements suite. Wadleigh testified, I am sure to Mr. Murphy's great surprise, that when he was given documents to look over by Dr. Pasvolsky, even before he started to work for him, he stole them and gave them to Chambers. Some of those documents, including one of the handwritten documents, is dated after March 9, 1938. Wad-

> leigh left this country on March 9, 1938. Did he leave a successor?

In the course of his speech Mr. Cross dealt, and dealt most effectively, with the material at his disposal, some of which I have indicated previously.

On the morning of the 20th January 1950 it was Mr. Murphy's turn to address the jury.

Anyone who had to serve on an American jury might count himself fortunate if Mr. Murphy were one of the advocates, for he could at least be sure of this—that whilst Mr. Murphy was speaking there would not be a dull moment.

He possesses penetrating wit, and puts across his wise sayings in a breezy—almost slapdash—manner which would endear him to the average juror.

Let me recall this extract:

> How about Pressman and Witt and Abt, and Henry Collins, all of these people who were friends? Why weren't they here? You don't suppose it is because perhaps I had a file on some, do you? You don't suppose that they were afraid to sit there [indicating witness chair]? And these were his friends, the maids told us, at the house discussing office affairs on Sunday. They couldn't see enough of each other during the daytime, the week time, but had to come on Sundays to discuss office matters.
>
> And now he wants us to give him a medal because he didn't claim his constitutional privilege when he testified before Congress. He went to the Grand Jury and answered the questions. He did not claim his privilege. He was a citizen, but he waived it.
>
> Can you imagine his job sort of hanging that way, twenty thou, and he says, "I won't answer because the Constitution says I don't have to"? Twenty thou. He sent a telegram and said, "I want to answer." It would look silly getting down there and saying, "Yes, I sent it, but the Constitution says I don't have to answer." Why, he would not only have lost his job, but just think of the position he was in. He had to admit or deny—admit or deny—fish or cut bait. If he ad-

mitted—bang. Everything crumbles at once, the job to boot. So you deny, you accuse, accuse the other guy, yell cop. That is standard CP practice, isn't it? Accuse the other guy, accuse me, accuse the judge, everybody.

He had to forswear his association with Chambers; he had to deny it, because the American public got the picture—what was he doing with this guy? He couldn't do that. He could not do it and hold on to the job. He could not do it and hold on to these friends who have come and have stood by him. He just could not do it.

If he got a rug, as I said, and he did not get it from Chambers because of what Chambers says, if he got it in 1936 when he was living in P Street, shouldn't he have brought it and have the expert look at it and say, "Sure, that is not the rug I sold at all. Of course not"?

Isn't that what you would have done? Of course.

And then that P Street shelter for wandering sub-tenants. Now there's something. A P Street shelter just for sub-tenants—and I have been paying rent all these years. This is the landlord I am looking for. Waiting for a van.

And then that 28th Street lease. There is the legal mind for you at work, the legal mind at work. Some moocher comes and says that he would like to move into your place, can't find an apartment.

"Oh, I have got just the place for you; it is full of furniture."

"Gee, that's swell. How much?"

"Just cost. Just what I pay."

"Fine."

"Do I have to pay in advance?"

"No, let it ride."

"How about the gas and electricity?"

"No. I will even throw in a phone."

"Gee, you're swell, mister."

"Don't mention it. I will give you a Ford—I will give you an old Ford with a sassy trunk—give you an old Ford with a sassy trunk. Don't worry about the rent. Just move in. Just move in."

Then Mr. Murphy recalled that on the 5th August 1948 Hiss had said to the House Committee, "The name Whittaker Chambers means nothing to me."

He continued as follows:

> Now, just how was that mind working when he said that? Did he mean that he didn't know the name? Did it mean that he didn't know the man that the name was attached to? Did he mean that he had no present recollection of the name? He had heard the name in the Grand Jury in March of 1948; he had heard the name from two F.B.I. agents in 1947; he heard from a lawyer friend of his that some guy by that name was calling him a Commie; he heard all that, but "The name," he told Congress, "Whittaker Chambers, meant nothing to me."
>
> Assuming he heard it only in February of 1948 from a lawyer, how long do you think it would take him to find out who and where is Whittaker Chambers? A man on the masthead of a leading magazine getting thirty thousand. Would it take him long with his friends? He found the name of the man who wrote to Mr. Dulles. Mr. Dulles did not tell him. Mr. Kohlberg. He found out that name. Now, he has friends, intelligent friends. He didn't have to find out. But he told Congress that the name meant nothing to him; he would like to see him, like to see this guy that says that he was a member of an apparatus together with eight or nine other fellows.

Mr. Murphy next expressed the view which he expected the jury to take of the confrontation. He told a story of a talk between a giraffe and a hippopotamus.

> There was a talk between the giraffe and the hippopotamus, and the giraffe says to the hippopotamus, "I don't remember you at all."
>
> The hippopotamus says, "You must remember me. We were in the jungle together, the two of us; we were friends."
>
> He says, "No, I don't remember you."
>
> But he says, "You must. We lived together. We ate together."

"No."

So the giraffe says, "Let me see your teeth."

So he looks and he says, "Oh, George Crosley, I know you."

George Crosley, my aunt.

Then Mr. Murphy dealt with the disposal of the typewriter to the Catletts:

Now, what probably happened was that the Catletts did in fact get the typewriter. When? When Chambers quit, when Chambers broke with the Party they realized, "Well, we haven't got the—we got that rug stored away. The only thing remaining to get us into trouble other than his word is the typewriter. If they find those instruments we are sunk." So what do they do? If they sold the typewriter they might be traced. If they brought it over to the bridge going to Roslyn and dropped it in the Potomac, somebody might see them. Guilty knowledge. So they give it to their trusted maid's children, knowing full well that they didn't type, that it would be put to abuse and gradually disintegrate, gradually.

Then an effective piece of ridicule of the theory that Chambers, either by himself or his agent, got access to the typewriter:

Well, you start off with the fact that the Catletts had the typewriter, and here is a picture of their hall. You see how these two things follow. The Catletts had it. Here is the hall where they used to keep it. Here is the picture of the back entrance. You see all that space back there, people come in and out there all the time. Then there is the den, then there are the dancers.

Now, what probably happened, Mr. Cross testified, is that somebody, not Chambers—he is too smart, but one of his conspirators, one of his confederates—those are good names, "conspirators," "confederates"—he went up to the Volta Place house and asked innocent Clidi Catlett, "I am the repair man. Where is the machine?" I can just see it now. It's terrific. You can have this guy coming with a Woodstock hat on, "Woodstock Repair," with a jumper "Woodstock," ringing the bell—no, it isn't a bell, you have to pull that one, I think—and saying to Mrs. Catlett, "I am the repair man to fix the typewriter."

Then Clidi says, "Well, which one do you want? The Remington, the Royal, the L. C. Smith? Which one?"

"No. We want the Woodstock."

"Oh, that's over in my boy's house, over at P Street."

And then the next scene, it is the middle of one of these dances. And you see Chambers sneaking in at night, mingling with the dancers, and then typing, typing the stuff, holding the State Department document in one hand——

Oh, Mr. Cross, you got better than that.

Thus in his witty and breezy way Mr. Murphy put his finger on the weak points in his opponent's case. He was plainly trying to laugh the Defence out of court.

Towards the very end of his speech he turns to the documents, promising that he won't take more than two minutes on the distribution of the documents.

Here he seems to me to have been no longer in his element. It is an odd contrast between these two advocates—whereas Mr. Cross was at his best when analysing the documents, Mr. Murphy was at his best when commenting on the evidence.

Mr. Murphy started by developing a theory of his own. He attempted—in two paragraphs only—to find some typing errors common to both the typed secret documents and to some letters which had undoubtedly been typed by Mrs. Hiss on that same typewriter.

Had this happened in England, I can hear the judge saying: "But, Mr. Murphy, have you laid any foundation for this suggestion in anything you have said to the expert witnesses who have dealt with this matter?" and when Mr. Murphy had replied, as he would have replied, in the negative, the judge would have continued: "Then surely it cannot be right that you should advance a new theory when the proceedings have reached such a stage that Mr. Cross no longer has an opportunity of answering this suggestion."

I should certainly not wish to make too heavy weather over this two-minute interlude in a trial which had lasted over two months, but it may have had serious consequences; for when at long last the jury retired, they sent back a message to say that they wanted not only the typewritten documents which had admittedly been typed on the Hisses' typewriter, but also the letters written by Mrs. Hiss which had also been typed on that typewriter. As I see it, the only possible reason why the jury should have wanted these letters was to enable them to pursue the suggestion which had been thrown out by Mr. Murphy. I have already referred, in considering the documents, to the evidence of Mr. Feehan, the Government's expert who was called both at the first and at the second trials. If there had been any ground for the suggestion that it was possible to infer from the typing not merely the idiosyncrasies of the machine but also the idiosyncrasies of the typist, is it not quite certain that he would have said so? For this would really have ended the whole controversy and would have established that Mrs. Hiss was the person who typed out the documents—in which case Alger Hiss must have been guilty.

The judge in his charge, as will be seen when I deal with this matter in the next chapter, made no reference to this suggestion. I feel quite certain that Mr. Murphy did not realise that he was being unfair in throwing out this idea, but I am bound to say that in my opinion it was a suggestion which should not have been made for the first time at that stage of the case. It is impossible to say whether or not the jury allowed it to influence them in coming to a decision.

Mr. Murphy's speech contained only the briefest possible reference to the typewritten documents. He said this:

> Now, ladies and gentlemen, if you want to forget the typewritten documents, dismiss them from your minds. That leaves you clear of the Catletts. You don't have to worry then where was the typewriter on a certain date. Skip that. Just confine your attention to the handwritten documents. There is no question there about this mysterious typing. There is no question of Wadleigh even. You can just forget that because none of them are dated on January 14. That is the mysterious day that Mr. Sayre took the afternoon off, so you can't assume that Wadleigh stole them on that day. One is

> even dated—No. 4—when he was on the high seas. Just take those documents—and they are in the handwriting of Mr. Hiss; we have that concession; it took a long time coming, but we got it.

I have looked to see what justification there was for the statement: "We have that concession; it took a long time coming, but we got it." The facts were these: When Hiss first of all examined the four handwritten documents, he was very doubtful whether one of them was in fact in his handwriting. He consulted a handwriting expert, who showed him an enlargement of the document; and on seeing this he became satisfied that the doubt which he had expressed to the Grand Jury was not in fact justified. Accordingly, at the first trial it was admitted that all the four handwritten documents were in the handwriting of Hiss. All these facts were brought out by Mr. Murphy in his cross-examination of Hiss at the second trial.

I feel bound to say that under these circumstances I think it was not accurate to say that the concession took a long time coming. It was admitted not only throughout the course of the second trial, but also throughout the first trial, that this document was in the handwriting of Hiss.

There follows a passage dealing with the handwritten documents. I find this odd—for I should have thought that Mr. Murphy's case was far weaker on these documents than on the typewritten ones; but I notice that he does not attempt to meet the criticisms of Mr. Cross about the typewritten documents, and indeed—instead of attempting to meet this criticism—he counters with a reference to the handwritten documents.

Mr. Murphy concluded his speech with these words:

> And now, ladies and gentlemen, consider again those proofs. Take them with you to the jury room, those photographs; take the machine, the instruments. What do they prove? Ladies and gentlemen, it proves treason, and that is the traitor. And come back with the courage of your convictions and tell this world that our faith in the American jury system is well founded.

I do not think it any part of my duty to express any criticism of Mr. Murphy's speech. I have already, in Chapter XX, given my view of the standard at which Counsel for the Prosecution should aim. Whether or not Mr. Murphy's speech, notwithstanding all its wit and charm, complied with this canon must remain a matter of individual opinion. That speech was the last word the jury heard about the evidence, for the judge did not undertake any final review. In my view, a final and dispassionate review of the evidence by the judge at the conclusion of the case is a useful safeguard, for Counsel inevitably tend to see one side of the case to the exclusion of the other.

CHAPTER XXXIII
THE CHARGE OF THE COURT

The judge started his charge on the afternoon of the 20th January 1950.

After thanking the jury for the attention they had given to the case and outlining the nature of the charge, he proceeded as follows:

> Now, the burden is upon the Government to prove beyond a reasonable doubt that the defendant willfully and knowingly testified falsely when he testified that neither he nor Mrs. Hiss in his presence furnished and delivered to Chambers secret and confidential documents and copies thereof which he had abstracted from the State Department in or about the months of February and March 1938, as charged in Count I, and the burden is upon the Government to prove beyond a reasonable doubt that at the time he testified before the Grand Jury the defendant knew and believed he had seen Chambers after January 1, 1937. The defendant does not have to prove how or from whom Mr. Chambers obtained the documents and handwritten exhibits, for the burden is upon the Government to prove beyond a reasonable doubt that

Mr. Hiss or his wife in his presence did deliver and furnish them to Mr. Chambers in or about February and March 1938.

Now, reasonable doubt does not mean a possible doubt or a fanciful doubt. It means a doubt which is reasonable in view of the evidence or the lack of evidence. It is a doubt which a reasonable person has after carefully weighing all the testimony. By my use of the word "weigh" I do not mean the greater number of witnesses nor the larger volume of testimony is to be your criterion. You should be governed by the convincing force of the evidence—to state it very simply—by its quality rather than its quantity.

A reasonable doubt does not mean a doubt arbitrarily and capriciously asserted by a juror because of his or her reluctance to perform an unpleasant task. It does not mean a doubt arising from the natural sympathy which we all have for others. It is not necessary for the Government to prove the guilt of the defendant beyond all possible doubt. For if that were the rule, very few people would ever be convicted. It is practically impossible for a person to be absolutely sure and convinced of any controverted fact which, by its nature, is not susceptible of mathematical certainty. In consequence, the law says that a doubt should be a reasonable doubt—not a possible doubt.

Now, there has been testimony as to the previous good character of the defendant. You should consider such evidence of good character, together with all the other facts and all the other evidence, in determining the guilt or the innocence of the defendant. Evidence of good character may, in itself, create a reasonable doubt where, without such evidence, no reasonable doubt would exist. But if from all the evidence you are satisfied beyond a reasonable doubt that the defendant is guilty, a showing that the defendant previously enjoyed a reputation of good character does not justify or excuse the offense, and you should not acquit a defendant merely because you may believe that he has been a person of good repute. It may be that those with whom he had come in contact previously have been misled and that he did not reveal to them his real character of acts.

The testimony of a character witness is not to be regarded by you as expressing the witness's personal opinion of the defendant's character, nor is it to be taken by you as the witness's opinion as to the guilt or innocence of the defendant. The guilt or innocence of the defendant is for you—and you alone—to determine.

Now, if, after a careful and full consideration of all the testimony and the exhibits, you are convinced of the defendant's guilt, and such conclusion is one in which you yourself would be willing to rely upon and to act upon in the more important matters of your own private life, then it may be said that you have no reasonable doubt.

The issues in the case are simple, and I believe that you have a clear idea of what you are to decide. I shall not attempt to refer to the testimony and the evidence except in some instances where it may be necessary to advise you as to the particular law applicable, for unless I repeated it at great length I might seem to be unduly stressing evidence which you believed was not so important and omitting portions which you found influenced you.

You have—each of you—I think, given careful attention to the testimony as it came from the witnesses themselves. You have had a full opportunity to observe the witnesses and you have heard the testimony discussed in great detail by able Counsel who have prepared and presented their cases well. The exhibits consisting of the various documents and papers will be available to you if you wish to examine them.

The court decides questions of law only. The jury decides all questions of fact. You are the exclusive judges of the relative importance and credibility of the witnesses.

He pointed out how important it is to see whether any witness has an interest in the case—for in such a case a witness may be tempted to deviate from the truth to sustain that interest—both Hiss and Chambers and their respective wives, the judge pointed out, had such an interest.

Then after a reference to the evidence of the doctors—"these opinions are purely advisory"—he referred to the distinction between direct and circumstantial evidence in the following passage:

> In considering the evidence you may, and naturally will, draw the reasonable inferences and conclusions from the evidence, whether this evidence be a direct statement of the fact or circumstances. For you may not have direct proof of the fact, but you may have circumstances from which you are able to draw reasonable conclusions and deductions.
>
> Circumstantial evidence is evidence that tends to prove or disprove a disputed fact by proof of other facts which have a legitimate tendency to lead the mind to a logical conclusion as to the existence or nonexistence of the disputed fact.
>
> Circumstantial evidence is entitled to as much consideration as you find it deserves, depending upon the inferences you think it necessary and reasonable to draw from the circumstances. The law makes no distinction between direct evidence of a fact and evidence of circumstances from which the existence of the fact may be reasonably deduced. Whether a fact is proved by circumstantial evidence or by direct proof is immaterial, for in either event it must be proved beyond a reasonable doubt.

Then he reminded the jury again of the nature of the charge against Hiss—and he emphasised the necessity for corroboration.

> Now, the law provides that no person may be convicted of the crime of perjury unless the alleged falsity of the statements made by a defendant under oath be established by the testimony of two independent witnesses or by one witness and corroborating facts and circumstances. In the absence of such proof, the defendant must be acquitted.
>
> The Supreme Court has held, and I quote, "Two elements must enter into a determination that corroborative evidence is sufficient. (1) That the evidence, if true, substantiates the testimony of a single witness who has sworn to the falsity of the alleged perjurious statements; and (2) that the corroborative evidence is trustworthy. To resolve this latter question is to determine the credibility of the corroborative testimony—a function which belongs exclusively to the jury."

As there is but one witness who has sworn to the falsity of the alleged perjurious statement in the first count in this case, it follows that to find the defendant guilty on Count I, you must believe beyond a reasonable doubt both:

A. Mr. Chambers' testimony as to the passing of the documents in or about February and March 1938; and
B. That there is other trustworthy evidence which substantiates that particular part of Mr. Chambers' testimony.

To find the defendant guilty on Count II, you must believe beyond a reasonable doubt:

A. Mr. Chambers' testimony that he met Mr. Hiss after January 1, 1937; and
B. That there is trustworthy corroboration of his testimony as to this meeting or meetings by either
(1) Other evidence as to this particular meeting or meetings;

or

(2) Mrs. Chambers' testimony regarding that particular meeting of Mr. Hiss and Mr. Chambers after January 1, 1937.

If you are convinced beyond a reasonable doubt by Mr. Chambers' testimony and by corroborative evidence that Mr. Hiss did deliver to Mr. Chambers the State Department documents and papers in or about February and March 1938, you may find the defendant guilty on Count I, even though you have a reasonable doubt on some other portions of Mr. Chambers' testimony. Similarly, if you are convinced beyond a reasonable doubt by Mr. Chambers' testimony and either by other evidence that corroborates that part of his testimony or by Mrs. Chambers' testimony that the defendant saw Mr. Chambers after January 1, 1937, you may find the defendant guilty on Count II, even though you may have a reasonable doubt on some other portions of Mr. and Mrs. Chambers' testimony.

The corroborative evidence referred to as necessary must be evidence which you find corroborates that portion of Mr.

> Chambers' testimony which relates to the alleged furnishing and delivery of the State Department documents by Mr. Hiss to Mr. Chambers and/or that portion of Mr. Chambers' testimony that relates to his having met Mr. Hiss after January 1, 1937, and you must believe beyond a reasonable doubt that the corroborative testimony is inconsistent with the innocence of the defendant. Mere corroboration of other parts of Mr. Chambers' testimony would not be sufficient. Corroboration may be supplied either in the evidence presented by the Government (which includes the exhibits) or in the evidence presented by the defendant (which includes the exhibits).
>
> Now, the Government says that the affair was carried on with great secrecy so as to escape possible detection, and that no one else was present when the alleged acts took place. The Government, however, urges that facts and circumstances have been proved which, it says, fully substantiate the testimony of Mr. Chambers. This is an issue to be determined by you.
>
> If, as to either count, you do not believe Mr. Chambers or if you do believe Mr. Chambers but do not find such corroborating evidence, you must return a verdict of not guilty on that count.

The learned judge concluded his charge as follows:

> Now, ladies and gentlemen, if you find that the evidence respecting the defendant is as consistent with innocence as with guilt, the defendant should be acquitted. If you find that the law has not been violated, you should not hesitate for any reason to render a verdict of acquittal. But, on the other hand, if you find that the law has been violated as charged, you should not hesitate because of sympathy or for any other reason to render a verdict of guilty, as a clear warning to all that a crime such as charged here may not be committed with impunity. The American public is entitled to be assured of this.

At 5 P.M. the jury retired. They returned shortly afterwards to say that they wanted to have the evidence of Mrs. Hiss, of

Wadleigh and of the Catletts, and the evidence of Chambers relating to the trip to Peterboro. They wanted also the typewritten copies of secret documents, but not, it would seem, the handwritten documents, for they asked for the Exhibits 5–47, and the handwritten documents were Exhibits 1–4.

Thereupon, the reporter started reading the evidence of Priscilla Hiss. The forelady stopped him and said it would be sufficient if "he comes to the part that we really want"—so it was arranged that the jury should retire again to formulate what it was they really wanted.

At 5:30 the judge announced that he had another note from the jury, which was as follows:

> Testimony of Mrs. Hiss giving date of disposal of typewriter to the Catletts. Also date Catlett boy claimed to have received typewriter from the Hisses.
>
> Testimony of disposal of typewriter by the Catletts.
>
> All typewritten material matter written on the Woodstock typewriter, including Mrs. Hiss's personal correspondence and F.B.I. sample.
>
> Above includes all Baltimore exhibits.

Now, it is not clear whether the jury thought that the "above" included the handwritten documents. They were not specifically mentioned.

Mr. Murphy expressed his bewilderment—which I entirely share—as follows:

> I think the reading of the transcript is not a simple problem at all. For instance, as I understood one of their questions—the disposition by the Catletts of the typewriter. I haven't the vaguest idea what that means. Then it says "the Catlett boy." There just happened to be two.
>
> *The Court:* I am afraid I can't answer your question.

It was arranged that the jury should have their dinner whilst the two Counsel got together the relevant portions of the evidence.

At 8:25 the jury returned and there was read to them the portions of the evidence which had been agreed upon by Counsel as being appropriate.

This reading occupied an hour, and the jury were then given permission to retire for the night. They were instructed to meet the following morning at 10 A.M.

At 10:40 the next morning the jury entered the courtroom with another message, as follows:

> Your Honor, without reading the entire charge, will you please define the following: reasonable doubt, circumstantial evidence, acceptable corroborative evidence and their relation to each other.

The judge met this request by reading to the jury again those passages from his charge dealing with these topics.

Finally, shortly before three o'clock on the afternoon of the 21st January 1950, the jury returned. They had agreed upon their verdict. Hiss was pronounced guilty on both counts.

On the 25th January 1950, Hiss came up for sentence. He was allowed to make a statement, and this is the statement he made:

> I would like to thank Your Honor for this opportunity again to deny the charges that have been made against me. I want only to add that I am confident that in the future the full facts of how Whittaker Chambers was able to carry out forgery by typewriter will be disclosed.

He was sentenced to five years on each count—the sentences to run concurrently.

No one can, I think, reasonably criticise the charge which the judge delivered under a system in which it is not the general practice for a judge to make a survey of the evidence.

The phrase, "You must be satisfied beyond a reasonable doubt," is a phrase hallowed by long usage. It is quite impossible to define what constitutes a reasonable doubt, and perhaps it would be better to avoid a phrase which has no precise meaning.

Quite recently the Court of Criminal Appeal in England has suggested that the phrase, "beyond a reasonable doubt," should be no longer used, and that the judge in the future should content himself with telling the jury that they must be "satisfied of the prisoner's guilt" without any qualifying phrase.

The odd assortment of information that the jury required does make me suspect that they were not finding the issues as simple as they were to the judge—and this is hardly to be wondered at.

Why on earth, for example, did they ask to be reminded of Chambers' testimony relating to the Peterboro trip—a matter on the outermost fringe of the case—and the Catletts' testimony relating to the disposal of the typewriter?

Much confusion might have been avoided if the judge had reviewed the evidence and assisted the jury by pointing out which part of the evidence bore directly upon the accusation and which part was merely incidental.

But that would perhaps hardly be consistent with a system in which "the Counsel try the case," and I admit that the institution of such a system might lead to abuse. On the other hand, the risk of the jury not appreciating the essential issues in a long and difficult case is a very real risk.

For example, the jury had been told by the judge that they must look for the necessary corroboration of the story told by Chambers to that portion of the evidence which related either to the furnishing of secret documents, or to the fact that meetings had taken place between Hiss and Chambers after the 1st January 1937. They were told that mere corroboration of other parts of Chambers' evidence would not be sufficient. As an abstract proposition, this is of course correct. But surely the difficulty which confronted the jury lay in the application of the principle. Presumably all the evidence called in the case for the Prosecution related to one or the other topic in some degree; for, if not, I cannot understand why the evidence was admitted at all. These two topics cover the entire case against Hiss.

Did the evidence, for example, of Mr. Dulles, of Mrs. Hede Massing or of Mrs. Edith Murray relate to these topics? Were the jury entitled to rely on the evidence about the occupation of the apartment, or the gift of the car, or the handing over of secret documents belonging to the Nye Committee as being corroborative of these parts of the evidence? Would it have been permissible to the jury to find the necessary corroborative evidence from the story of the confrontation?

I do not believe that any jury can derive much help from these general propositions, and I confess to feeling a very real difficulty myself. Certain evidence is admissible; other evidence is inadmissible. Is there still another distinction? Is there evidence which, though admissible, is not sufficient? I can well understand that that may be true in regard to that evidence which was merely designed to negative the evidence of Hiss. For example, if the defence were an alibi, evidence to destroy the alibi would not directly corroborate the case for the Prosecution—if, indeed, such corroboration were necessary. Such evidence is not a spear to sharpen the case for the Prosecution; it is evidence which, if accepted, removes the shield put up by the Defence.

But much of the evidence I have referred to was given in support of the Prosecution's case and was not given to destroy the defendant's answer. I have already expressed the view that in our courts in this country such evidence would have been inadmissible unless, if believed, it would have been corroborative.

I mention this matter not with the view of criticising the charge of the judge, but to support my contention that unless the judge is prepared to review the evidence, he cannot give the jury any real help in performing their responsible duty. Under the system prevailing in this country the judge would have been not merely entitled, but required, to make such a survey of the evidence.

CHAPTER XXXIV

RETROSPECT

My self-appointed task is over. The time has come for me to say farewell to all these characters—be they saints or sinners—with whom I have lived, though only on paper, over these last few months.

Alger Hiss was found guilty after a careful and prolonged trial; and the patience which the judge showed throughout the many weeks it lasted proved that he had nothing to learn from Job. I am one of those who believe that a trial by jury is, of all systems invented by the genius of man, the least likely to lead to injustice; and I see no reason to doubt that in this case the jury gave most anxious care and attention to their task. They had, of course, the immense advantage of seeing and hearing the witnesses—an advantage which I have not shared. Moreover, the appeal against their decision was dismissed by the Court of Appeals. So I suppose that I ought to feel completely satisfied that justice has been done; yet I should not be honest if I said that my doubts had been allayed, and I hope I shall be forgiven if I summarise—even at the cost of some repetition—why I feel these doubts.

Since the trial Whittaker Chambers has published his book *Witness*, which has not only not allayed my doubts but has increased them. It throws much light on the character of its author which was never revealed to the jury. They never knew that during the hearing before the Grand Jury he tried to commit suicide; they never knew that as one of the steps he took to leave the Communist Party he determined to obtain a "life preserver" in the form of incriminating documents. This book, indeed, provides material for psychiatrists and psychologists—material which was not available to Dr. Binger and Dr. Murray. I have at least this advantage over the jury, that I have been able to read *Witness*.

I would not have it supposed that I attach little importance to the decision of the jury, but my readiness to accept their verdict as concluding the matter is qualified by these considerations. First, because it seems—and no one is to blame for this—that there had grown up at the time of the trial a climate of opinion in America which was inimical to a calm and dispassionate hearing of the case. I do not doubt that public opinion had been profoundly shocked by learning, as a result of the investigation of the House Committee, of the extent to which Communist influence had infiltrated into the various Government departments. In exposing these facts, the House Committee performed a useful service, but it was an unfortunate prelude to a trial on a serious criminal charge, for the public are prone to look for a scapegoat. I do not suggest that any member of the jury consciously allowed himself to be influenced by these considerations, but there is always a risk of unconscious influence if the jury hear about the facts of a case before they have to try it.

Secondly, I believe there was one serious blemish in the trial itself; namely, that a wholly new case, based on the proposition that the peculiarities in the typewriting could be used to identify not merely the machine but also the typist, should have been raised for the first time in the concluding speech for the Government. If any such case had been made by the Government expert—and he had not made any such case—he could have been challenged and tested by cross-examination. It was admitted that the typed incriminating documents had been typed on the Hiss typewriter, and it follows that the only possible object the jury could have had in asking for both the standard letters and the typed documents was to enable them to follow out their own investigations into this suggestion, and to find out for themselves by a comparison of the standard letters and the documents whether the identity of the typist as well as of the typewriter could be revealed. A jury are entitled to draw their own conclusions. Experts are merely there to help them; but it seems to me unwise for a jury to attempt to reach a conclusion on such a technical matter without the slightest guidance from those best able to speak with authority. No one can, of course, assert positively that the jury were influenced in their decision by this consideration, for the proceedings in the jury room are fortunately hidden from the public view; but it seems clear to me that they might have been so influenced. If only the system prevailing had required the judge to survey the evidence, this would, I feel sure, have been cleared up. He would have reminded the jury of what the expert had said and of what he had not said. But the judge did not survey the evidence. However, the Appeals Court dismissed the appeal. Their decision is reported in 185 *Federal Reporter* at page 822. The learned judges make no reference to this point. I could wish they had done so.

Thirdly, I do not think that, without some summing up of the facts, a jury can be fairly expected to pronounce on a difficult question which has been debated before them for many weary weeks. A survey of the evidence by the judge, just because he is completely impartial and has a trained mind, is surely an essential step to assist the jury in their deliberations.

These considerations, coupled with the new facts which have been stated in *Witness*, must be both my excuse and my justification for looking further into the case notwithstanding the jury's decision. Of course I recognise the difficulties in the way of those who would assert positively that Hiss was innocent. For instance, I can well understand the attitude of mind of those who say that they believe that the association between Chambers and Hiss was much closer than the latter would admit. Hiss had said, for example, that he had never visited Chambers at his house at Baltimore. Edith Murray's evidence, if it was correct—and the jury were in a position to judge—proved that this statement was untrue. Some whom I have met were convinced of Hiss's guilt by his hesitance in admitting the identity of Whittaker Chambers with the man he had previously known as George Crosley. In their opinion, this whole incident was an elaborate piece of play-acting on Hiss's part and demonstrated that he was lying to conceal some guilty conduct. Others, who were in an equally good position to judge, have expressed to me the opposite view.

The evidence of the confrontation, which had taken place during the House Committee hearing, was of course read to the jury, but they did not have the advantage of seeing the event with their own eyes. If they drew from a reading of it a conclusion adverse to Hiss, there was certainly, to my mind, material to justify such a conclusion. Hiss had known that he was accused of being a Communist. On the advice of his Secretary of State he had gone to the F.B.I. and offered himself for interrogation in the year 1946. He had, he said, first heard the name "Whittaker Chambers" mentioned in the year 1947 and had heard it again as a piece of cocktail gossip early in 1948. Is it not inevitable that he must have searched the tablets of his memory to seek out any possible explanation of this allegation? Must he not have gone through in conversation with his wife every single incident in his past life which could throw any light on this accusation? Must he not have recalled the odd figure of George Crosley, whom he did in fact refer to on his second appearance before the House Committee? Would he not have made some enquiries as to the identity of this Whittaker Chambers? Would he, if he had been really responsive and determined to stick to the plain unvarnished truth, have recognised Chambers without difficulty?

Other people have been impressed by the many unexplained kindnesses that Hiss showed to Chambers. If Chambers had really been such a casual acquaintance, would he have allowed him the use of his apartment and the furniture in it? Would he have put himself in the position of being liable for Chambers' gas, electricity and telephone bills—Chambers himself being, at most, only required to repay the cost of the apartment to Hiss?

Still others will drew a conclusion adverse to Hiss from the strange story of the car. Why should Hiss have given away his old Ford car? More particularly, why should he have given it away at a time when it was clear that Chambers had defaulted on his obligation to pay the rent and had proved himself, according to Hiss, to be a "deadbeat"? How came he to get in touch with the Cherner Motor Company?

There was also the incident of the withdrawal of $400 from the Hiss banking account, which was not mentioned until the first trial, when it could indeed have come to the knowledge of Chambers through the F.B.I. But it is an undoubted fact that this money was withdrawn only a few days before Chambers paid a deposit of $486 on the purchase of a new car. Hiss's rival explanation—that he withdrew the money because he needed it to buy furniture for his new and larger house in Volta Place—is by no means convincing, more particularly as at the time of withdrawal he was not certain of getting the house.

There was, too, the odd incident of the giving and receiving of the rug, first mentioned, be it remembered, by Hiss himself; a matter to which some people may attach more importance than I do myself.

Added together and multiplied by the fact, if fact it be, that both Hiss and his wife had made untrue statements under oath, what do all these things amount to? They amount to this, and nothing more than this: that the association between Hiss and Chambers was much closer and much more enduring than Hiss admitted. They bear directly upon the credibility of Hiss. They make it easy to draw the inference that he had, in fact, Left-wing, or perhaps Communist, sympathies and affiliations, and perhaps that he was a member of a Communist study group, as Chambers had stated to Mr. Berle. But they do not prove, and, indeed, do not begin to prove, that Hiss handed over secret documents to Chambers. All this evidence, except that of the loan of $400, was given long before there was any suggestion of the handing over of documents. The fact that there had been a close association, and perhaps a close friendship, between Chambers and Hiss without there having been any espionage or any handing over of documents is entirely consistent with the statements which Chambers made to Mr. Berle in 1939 and to Mr. Ray Murphy in 1945 and 1946, and with the evidence which he gave before the House Committee in 1948. At none of these times, nor before the Grand Jury up to the disclosure of the Baltimore documents, was there the faintest suggestion that Hiss had been guilty of espionage, and, indeed, any such suggestion was expressly negatived on many occasions by Chambers himself when on his oath.

According to the evidence of Chambers, the group of which Hiss was supposed to be a member was undertaking far more important and devastating duties than mere espionage. Its role was "to mess up policy" and to try to influence that policy on to lines which were helpful to Russia. If this was so, I should have thought it would have been very foolish for the Communists to impose upon the members of a group already charged with such important work the additional task of furnishing confidential information, which could in the somewhat lax conditions prevailing in 1937 have been procured by any petty thief.

It may, of course, have been that the group was in reality little more than an intellectual study group; Chambers admitted that he had supplied the necessary material for this sort of study. But what of its other members? There was Lee Pressman, in whose case there was certainly material to lead a jury to the conclusion that he either was or had been a Communist. Yet, so far as I know, no one has ever suggested that he was guilty of espionage or that he handed over documents; in his book *Witness*, Chambers makes it plain that he makes no such charge. Nathan Witt, according to Chambers' evidence before the House Committee, was another member; and, indeed, he had become its leader on the death of Ware. Here, again, no one suggested that he was guilty of espionage, and the same, certainly so far as handing over documents to Chambers was concerned, could be said of all the members of the group, except for Alger Hiss. It does not seem, therefore, that it was the function of the group, as a group, to furnish information. For this reason it would not have been in the least surprising if Hiss, assuming him to have been a member of the group, had restricted his activities and, like the other members, had not himself engaged in espionage.

Even if the group had been no more than an "intellectual study group," I can readily understand that Hiss in 1948 would have been reluctant to admit that he had ever been a member of such a group even as far back as the years 1935–38. I can understand, too, that under these circumstances he might have felt himself obliged to bring a libel action. I cannot, however, understand how a man as intelligent as Hiss undoubtedly was would not have thought out a line of defence behind which he could have stood if the fact that he had turned over secret documents was liable to be revealed. The risk of revelation, once Chambers had deserted, must have been obvious. The documents turned over within a few weeks of this desertion had included documents written in the handwriting of Hiss and others typed on his typewriter. Surely there was one obvious line of defence which an intelligent and unscrupulous man would have adopted. So far as the documents written in his own handwriting were concerned, Hiss was bound to say that they had been stolen from him by Chambers. As for those typed on his own typewriter, he must say that they were typed not by Mrs. Hiss but either by Chambers or by some person whom Chambers employed for that purpose. The closer the association between Hiss and Chambers, the greater the number of visits which Chambers paid to the house which Hiss was occupying, the greater would have been the facilities for using his typewriter and taking his documents.

Hiss's attitude might well have been something like this: "I met him when I was working for the Nye Committee. He described himself as a free-lance journalist. I never had the slightest idea that he was a Communist. He was obviously very intelligent, and it was equally obvious that he was passing through hard times. I felt confident that after a struggle he would make good, and I went out of my way to befriend him. He came frequently to our house; indeed, he made it his headquarters. He often used our typewriter, sometimes when we were there and sometimes when we were not there. We sometimes went to his house. I can only explain the fact that he has these documents by saying that he must on one of his visits have stolen from me the documents in my own handwriting, and he must have taken advantage of the opportunity afforded him to use my typewriter to type out documents which he had somehow obtained from the State Department."

Yet, when we come to consider the evidence which Hiss gave,

we find that the line he took was exactly the opposite of this. He was concerned to reduce to a very minimum the occasions when he met Chambers, by this very fact making it more difficult to explain the obvious acts of generosity and kindness which he undoubtedly showed Chambers from time to time.

There is one other piece of evidence to be considered before we come to the documents, and that is the evidence about Donald Hiss. He, too, was said by Chambers to have been a Communist. The only evidence in support of this was Chambers' story before the House Committee that Donald Hiss had paid him his Communist dues—a matter which was not mentioned at the trial. If ever a man was cleared of the aspersions cast upon him, that man was Donald Hiss. This, in turn, casts doubt and discredit on the story Chambers has told. Let us assume—and the case against Hiss cannot be put higher than this—that there was ground for equal hesitation in accepting the evidence of Hiss as there undoubtedly was in accepting that of Chambers. But all this is on the fringe of the case, and as we penetrate deeper and come to the documents the difficulties increase.

What of the Nye Committee documents? If in fact these were not secret at all, but were made available to Chambers by Hiss in the course of his duty just as they would have been made available to any other journalist, what becomes of this part of Chambers' story? If they were not secret, then, as I see it, Chambers must have been guilty—so far as these documents were concerned—of manufacturing a false case against Alger Hiss. The whole story of the conversation at which Hiss offered to bring out these papers, to which Chambers replied that he must first get the consent of Peters, falls to the ground; and with it falls the story of the photography of these documents in the P Street house. The handwritten documents raise most interesting questions. What is the explanation of the two chalks used in two of them? Why was one of them in substance written out twice, once more or less illegibly, and the second time more legibly? Then, the photographed documents: can we be sure of the source of the originals? Is it established that Hiss had access to all of them, even if he was ready enough to hand them over?

I have not in this brief survey mentioned the typed documents; and without these what sort of case would there have been? When the Grand Jury were deliberating in December 1948, at a time when they had nothing proving that the typed documents had been typed on the Hiss typewriter, but when presumably they had all the other evidence, they were unable to find a true bill. The matter is tersely and accurately stated in *Seeds of Treason:* "On Friday the 10th December 1948 the foreman of the Grand Jury stated that the jurors could find no indictment, but on the following Monday the letter typed by Mrs. Hiss to the headmaster of her son's school was found." In other words, until it was possible to identify the typewritten documents as having been typed on the Hiss typewriter, the Grand Jury were unable to find that there was a prima facie case which called for an answer. All the evidence of the association between Chambers and Hiss, all the evidence which Chambers gave about the handwritten documents, and about the photographed documents, did not, in the opinion of the Grand Jury, even justify a trial. For my part, I should be very far from saying that they were wrong in this view.

The real case against Hiss rested, and in my opinion must rest, upon the typewritten documents. They were typed on the Hiss typewriter; but who typed them? Did Chambers have an opportunity, either by himself or his agent, of getting access to that typewriter? If he had had such an opportunity, would he have taken it? Was he the sort of man who would have been willing to build up a case by means of "forgery by typewriter"? It is on this point that the view which should be taken about the Nye Committee documents and the handwritten documents becomes so important. Is it the fact that Chambers was trying to build up a case against Hiss by falsely alleging that Hiss had delivered to him secret documents belonging to the Nye Committee? If so, what guarantee have we that he was not also trying to build up a false case on these later documents? It is on this point, too, that the knowledge of Chambers of the incriminating nature of a typewriter—as evidenced by the care he took to get rid of his own—becomes significant. And it is on this point that the knowledge we now possess about his desire to build up a life preserver—a knowledge which the jury did not possess—may throw new light on this most difficult case.

It is considerations such as these—which would have been stated by the trial judge if he had thought fit to review the facts—and others arising from facts which have been brought to light since the trial, which give rise to the doubts I have expressed.

I must take my leave of any reader who has had the patience and interest to follow me thus far. I have tried to put him in a position to supply his own answers to some of the questions that emerge from a consideration of this case.

Was Alger Hiss a "dedicated and disciplined" Communist when he first came to meet Chambers? Was Chambers then passing under the name of "George Crosley," or was he simply "Carl"? Was it the fact that Chambers used to collect Communist Party dues from either Alger or Donald Hiss? What was the real explanation of the many kindnesses shown by Alger Hiss to Chambers?

Why was it that until November 1948 Chambers repeatedly testified on oath that he had no knowledge of espionage? Was it with the object of shielding Hiss? If so, why did Chambers assert in 1946 that Alger Hiss was engaged in work "far more important and cunning" than mere espionage? Was it a fact that Chambers contemplated "self-execution" before producing the incriminating documents and actually attempted to end his life shortly after being summoned before the Grand Jury? What was the explanation of this conduct?

Were the Nye Committee documents secret, or was Chambers building up a false case against Hiss in regard to these documents? Did Hiss prepare the handwritten documents for the purpose of giving them to Chambers, or were they stolen from him after having served a legitimate purpose? Why were three out of the four written in different-coloured pencils? Was it established that Hiss had had access to all the original documents from which the photographs were made?

Finally, and most important of all, whose hand was it that operated the typewriter belonging to Mrs. Hiss to produce the incriminating typewritten documents?

If the reader can supply confident answers to these and similar questions, which I have found so baffling, he will—at least to his own satisfaction—have solved the mystery which underlies *The Strange Case of Alger Hiss.*

APPENDIX I

Notes made by Mr. Adolf Berle of his conversation with Whittaker Chambers in September 1939

LONDON Underground Espionage Agent

(1) *Dr. Philip Rosenbliett*—(Formerly of 41st B'way, NE).
Dr. Greenberg—MD (West 70th NY)
Brother-in-law
American leader of British Underground C.
Head in America Mack Moren (alias Philipovitch—allegedly Yugoslav)—real name—?

Rosenbliett—in U.S.
connected with Dr. Isador Miller—Chemist's Club—41st St. Chemist, Explosive Arsenal, Picatinny, N.J., war "front" behind Mack Moren existed—in Miller's employ
Knew Pressman—his alias was "Cole Philips"—
Introduced him to Mack Moren, buying arms for Spanish (Loyalist) Gov't.—
Pressman—as counsel—helped Moren—made a flight to Mexico with him; forced down at Brownsville, Tex., in late '36 or early '37—probably fall of '36.

Pressman

Underground organized by the late Harold Ware; Pressman was in his group—(1932–3??) Pressman then in the A.A.A.—

Nathan Witt—Secretary of the NLRB—head of the underground group after Harold Ware—

John Abt—followed Witt in that group—Tax Div'n—Dep't of Justice & now in CIO (M. Ware's widow—Jessica Smith Ed. Soviet Russia).

Mr. Abt—Sister: Marion Bacharach—Secretary—Communist from Minnesota.

(Jessica Smith: With Reuters in 1926—friend of Louis Fischer.)

Meeting place: John Abt's house—15th St.

Charles Krivitsky—alias Charles Kramer—(CIO) worked in La Follette Committee—Physicist.

Vincent Reno—Now at Aberdeen Proving Grounds—Computer—Math. Assist. to Col Zornig (Aerial bombsight Detectors) Formerly CP organizer under alias "Lance Clark."

Philip Reno—in Social Security (??)—was head of Underground Trade Union Group Political leader

Elinor Nelson, treasurer of Fed. Employees' union—(Fed. Workers' Union, CIO—headed by Jake Baker)

Reno connected with Baltimore Party

organizer—Benjamin (Bundey) Friedman alias Field—then California—then Russia—now organizer for Baltimore & Washington of Above-Ground Party—Underground connections—

STATE

Post—Editorship, *Foreign Service Journal.* Was in Alexandria Unit of CP—in "Underground Apparatus"—

Duggan—Laurence—(Member CP??)

(Wadleigh?) Wadley—Trade Agreement Section

Lovell—Trade Agreement Section

Communist Shop Group

Elinor Nelson—Laurence Duggan—Julien Wadleigh—

West European Div'n—*Field*—still in—
(Levine says he is out went into I.E.O.
Then in committee for Repatriation
His leader was Hedda Gumpertz)
Laughlin Currie: Was a "Fellow Traveler"—helped various Communists—never went the whole way.

S.E.C.
Philip Reno—used to be

TREASURY
Schlomer *Adler* (Sol Adler?)
Counsel's Office
Sends weekly reports to CP (Gen. Counsel's Office)
Frank Coe—now teacher at McGill.
There are two: brother—one of them in CP's "Foreign Bureau"—Bob Coe

Known from Peters—formerly in Bela Kun
Govt. Agricultural Commissariat—called Gandosz (?) Then to Russia—then here, in Business Office of Communist paper "Uj Elori"—then, after 1929—head of CP Underground, lived in Hamilton Apts., Woodside, L.I.—under alias "Silver"—& lectured in Communist camps—Friend: "Blake" of "Freiheit"—real name—*Wiener*—American: Polish Jew—
Peters was responsible for Washington Sector
Went to Moscow—where is he now?—
Wife—a Comintern courier—
West Coast—Head: "The Old Man"—Volkov is his real name—daughter a Comintern courier. He knows the West Coast underground—Residence: San Francisco or Oakland—

Alexander Trachtenberg—Politburo—
member of the Execu. Committee
Head of GPU in U.S.
Works with Peters—

Plans for two Super-battleships—
secured in 1937—who gave—
Karp—brother-in-law of Molotov—working with Scott Ferris, got this released—
Now: Naval Architect working on it, why??
Field was original contact
He introduced Duggan to Gumpertz (Hedda)
Duggan's relationship was casual—
Shall excuse?—Where is Hedda Gumpertz?—
Duggan & Field supposed to have been both members of party.—
Donald Hiss
(Philippine Adviser)
Member of CP with Pressman & Witt—
Labor Dept.—Asst. to Frances Perkins—
Party wanted him there—to send him as arbitrator in Bridges trial—
Brought along by brother—
Alger Hiss
Asst. to Sayre—CP—1937
Member of the Underground Com.—Active
Baltimore boys—
Wife—Priscilla Hiss—Socialist—
Early days of New Deal

NOTE—When Loy Henderson interviewed Mrs. Rubens his report immediately went back to Moscow. Who sent it? Such came from Washington.

APPENDIX II

Memorandum of Conversation between Mr. Ray Murphy and Whittaker Chambers, 20th March 1945

The person talking was the liaison man for the Communist Party of the United States with most of the persons listed below and he spoke from personal knowledge, not hearsay. At the time he described the official line of the Communist Party was anti-Administration, pretty violent, and the antithesis of the Popular Front days of post-1935. It is true that this second phase blended in with the first period during which these persons continued co-operation.

It seems that in 1934, with the establishment of the Agricultural Adjustment Administration and the introduction of much reform legislation in Washington, the Communist Party decided its influence could be felt more strongly by enlisting the active support of underground workers not openly identified with the Party and never previously affiliated with the Party, but whose background and training would make them possible prospects as affiliates under the guise of advancing reform legislation. The Hungarian, party name J. Peters, was selected by the Central Committee to supervise the work from New York. His Washington representative and contact man was the informant, and he personally met and discussed many times various problems with the persons listed below except those specifically named as coming under another person's jurisdiction. The persons listed below are said to have disclosed much confidential matter and to have arranged among themselves a program committing this Government to a policy in keeping with the desires of the Communist Party.

The opportunity presented itself for the formation of an underground group with the appointment to a leading position in the Agricultural Adjustment Administration in 1934 of one Harold Ware. Ware had worked for years in agricultural collectivization projects in Russia. He was a son of Ella Reeves Bloor, veteran American Communist, by one of her numerous marriages. On being assigned to this agency, Ware found a group of very promising, ambitious young men with advanced social and political ideas. Among them were Lee Pressman, Alger Hiss, Henry Collins and Charles Kramer (Krivitzky). They all joined the Communist Party and became leaders of cells. No cell had over ten members. This was the nucleus of the Communist underground organization in Washington. The purpose was for each member to advance as high as possible in the Government to shape legislation favorable to the program of the Communist Party. The top leaders of the underground were:

1. Harold Ware
2. Lee Pressman
3. Alger Hiss

In the order of their importance.

There were various underground headquarters in Washington at the time. Among these were a violin studio near Dupont Circle run by Helen Ware; another place was a school on the outskirts of Washington run by Alice Mendham.

The informant dealt with these people from 1934 to the end of 1937, when he broke with the Party and attempted to persuade various of these contacts to break also. He remembers several conversations with Alger Hiss in the early part of 1938 during which Hiss was adamant against the plan of breaking with the Party. He described Hiss as a person with a charming personality, absolutely sincere in his convictions and motivated by the idea that he was on the right track.

The informant traced the jobs of these men until the end of 1937, and in each job they worked together with each other and with the Party. Later adherents to the Party included Donald Hiss, Henry Collins and a man named Post in the State Department.

In a special category were Noel Field and Laurence Duggan of the State Department. Field was described as a member at large of the Party, Duggan was not. Neither was connected with the underground, and in fact the underground had orders to refrain from contacting them. The special liaison of Field and Duggan was one Hedda Gumpertz. She is now in the personnel department of the Todd Shipbuilding Corporation and is married to Paul Massing, a former member of the German Communist Party, described by General Krivitzky in his book. Massing is a penologist for the State of Pennsylvania and they have a farm near Quakertown, Penna. He is also known as Karl Billinger. Hedda Gumpertz is a Viennese Jewish girl. When Field went to the League of Nations in 1936, he left Duggan in her special care. Gumpertz was a Communist International agent. It is understood that Field and Duggan disclosed any information she wanted to know.

Harry White of the Treasury was described as a member at large but rather timid. He put on as assistants in the Treasury Glasser, a member of the underground group, and an Adler or Odler, another Party member. The two Coe brothers, also Party members, were also put on by White.

Nathan Kaplan, head of the National Research Project, was a Party member, as was the other head and his sister Rose Weinstein.

Lee Pressman was not only a Party member, he was directed by the Party to accept the offer of John L. Lewis in 1936 to become General Counsel of the C.I.O. Pressman is said to have run arms to Spain during the Civil War via Mexico, and to have worked with General Mark More in that project. More was involved in the Rubens-Robinson passport case in 1938.

Nathan Witt of the Labor Board was a Party member and also underground.

When Harold Ware was killed in an auto accident near Baltimore about 1936, John Abt succeeded him as leader of the underground in Washington. Abt not only succeeded him in the job, he married Ware's widow, Jessica Smith. Abt today is associated as counsel of the C.I.O.-P.A.C. with Sidney Hillman, and was a delegate to the recent Trade Union Conference in London.

Eleanor Nelson ran a low-grade but important Communist group in the Government. More of a trade-union group, but its members had access to Government files which would be made available to the Party. Hiss was a member of this group.

APPENDIX III

Memorandum of Conversation between Mr. Ray Murphy and Whittaker Chambers, 28th August 1946

The Communist underground in Washington is believed to have been set up some time in 1933 after the inauguration of President Roosevelt. My informant does not know how or when it was set up, but he believes that Harold Ware had a prominent part in creating the underground and in enlisting key members. Ware, of course, would have acted pursuant to orders from the Central Committee of the Communist Party of the United States.

My informant entered into the Washington picture in the summer of 1935 and left it and the Party at the end of December 1937. The group was already in being and functioning actively. His superior was the Hungarian known as J. Peters, the national head of the Communist underground movement. My informant acted as a courier between Washington and New York. He participated in oral discussions in Washington with the group which Peters himself conducted. They met only the top layer—in other words, leaders of cells of the Communist underground in Government circles.

My informant did not know the Coe who taught at McGill

University, but he understood that he was a Communist. The other Coe he definitely knew to be a Communist. Harry White was reported to be a member of one of the cells, not a leader, and his brother-in-law, a dentist in New York, is said to be a fanatical Communist. Alger Hiss was never to make converts. His job was to mess up policy. The Post of the State Department was a cell member. He thought he was of Nat Perlow's group. Post was formerly on the W.P.A., where he measured skulls. He was definitely of minor importance in the movement compared with Hiss.

The heads of the various underground groups in Washington who met with Peters were the Hisses, Kramer (Krivitzky), Henry Collins, who was either Secretary or Treasurer of the group, John Abt, Lee Pressman, Nat Perlow and Nat Witt. These men met regularly at special meetings. With the exception of Donald Hiss, who did not have an organization, they headed parallel organizations. But they did not know the personnel of the different organizations.

Hal Ware was the top man of these organizations. Upon his death in 1936 a fight broke out for leadership, but Nat Witt won out. Some time after 1937 Witt is said to have been succeeded by Abt.

(There were other underground Communist groups operating in Washington, but this was the elite policy-making, top-level group.) This group did not exchange secret documents from the Government Departments, but did give sealed reports on the membership of the groups and on policy. It was not a spy ring, but one far more important and cunning because its members helped to shape policy in their Departments. Henry Collins, as Secretary or Treasurer, delivered most of the sealed reports to my informant. At that time Henry Collins was believed to be working in the Forestry Division of Agriculture.

Peters was in the Agricultural Department of Hungary under Bela Kun. He was in the Austrian Army in World War I. He is a little dark fellow, small feet and wavy black hair.

At the meetings in Washington with this group Peters would give pep talks on Communist theory. He would then talk to each leader separately. Peters often discussed the morale with my informant. He praised the Hiss boys to my informant very highly, but was doubtful of Pressman. He had a high opinion of Witt, a slightly less high opinion of Abt, thought Kramer was a nice boy but shallow and had very little use for Perlow. He liked Henry Collins.

My informant asked Alger Hiss personally to break with the Party in early 1938, but Hiss refused with tears in his eyes and said he would remain loyal to the Party.

After his break with the Party, Grace Hutchins telephoned the mother of my informant on Long Island one night and said that if he did not return to the Party by the following Thursday it was a question of his death.

APPENDIX IV

Statement to Federal Bureau of Investigation, signed by Alger Hiss December 4, 1948

Baltimore, Maryland
December 4, 1948

I, Mr. ALGER HISS, residence, 22 East 8th Street, New York City, in the presence of my attorney, Mr. WILLIAM L. MARBURY, give the following voluntary signed statement to DANIEL F. X. CALLAHAN and FRANK G. JOHNSTONE, who have identified themselves to me as Special Agents of the Federal Bureau of Investigation. I have been advised that I need make no statement and that anything I say may be used against me.

At the request of my attorneys, Mr. WHITTAKER CHAMBERS, defendant in a libel suit filed by me in the United States District Court for Maryland at Baltimore, was called for an examination before trial. This examination took place in Mr. MARBURY's office, 1000 Maryland Trust Building, Baltimore, Maryland, on November 4, 5, 16 and 17, 1948, but a portion of the time stated was consumed in taking depositions from Mrs. WHITTAKER CHAMBERS.

On the afternoon of November 17, 1948, in the course of

the pre-trial examination, Mr. CHAMBERS introduced 65 letter-sized pages of typewritten material and four small sheets of paper bearing handwritten material. For simplification, hereafter in this statement the 65 pages will be referred to as the large documents and the four smaller pages as the small documents.

In introducing these documents, Mr. CHAMBERS stated that they had been received by him from me for transmittal to a Russian named Colonel BYKOV. Photostatic copies of the documents introduced by Mr. CHAMBERS at the pre-trial examination were first exhibited to me by Mr. MARBURY in New York City on November 18, 1948. The agents have exhibited to me similar photostatic copies of these documents, which I am satisfied are photostatic copies of the same documents introduced by Mr. CHAMBERS under the above circumstances. I have read portions of the court reporter's transcription of the deposition of Mr. CHAMBERS and I know from the portion of that transcription which I have read that on November 5, 1948, Mr. CHAMBERS was asked whether he had ever obtained any documents from me for transmittal to the Communist Party and he replied that he had not.

With reference to the large documents, I would say from a cursory examination of them that they appear to be authentic copies of United States State Department documents or summaries of such documents. From the date standpoint, these documents appear to be restricted to a period extending from about January to March 1938. At that time I was Assistant to the Assistant Secretary of State, the Honorable FRANCIS B. SAYRE. Documents similar to these normally passed over my desk for perusal prior to being referred to Mr. SAYRE. I do not have any independent recollection of having seen any of these documents or the documents summarized while I was in the employ of the State Department. By and large, these do not appear to be documents of a very highly confidential nature, and would not have been treated in the State Department with any special precautions at that time, according to security regulations in effect then.

With reference to the smaller documents, three of the four pages appear to be in my handwriting. The fourth page, consisting of five handwritten lines, may or may not be in my handwriting, but it does not look to me as if it were.

I have learned from talking with Mr. MARBURY and from reading the above-mentioned deposition that Mr. CHAMBERS claimed these documents and others like them were obtained by me from the State Department, and that I took them to my home, where typewritten copies of the larger documents were made on a typewriter in my home by either my wife or me. CHAMBERS claimed that I then returned the documents to the State Department files. The agents have told me that Mr. CHAMBERS claims that on some occasions I turned over the actual State Department documents to him, upon which he would have photographic copies made in a manner unknown to me, and then would return the original documents to me for replacement in the files of the State Department.

I deny that any of the above claims of Mr. CHAMBERS is true. I also deny that I ever gave the originals of the small documents to Mr. CHAMBERS at any time for any purpose whatsoever.

From Mr. MARBURY and the deposition, I have also learned that CHAMBERS claims he introduced me to a Russian named PETER, whom he claims later to have discovered was Colonel BYKOV. CHAMBERS claims that this meeting took place on the mezzanine floor of a movie theater in Brooklyn, New York. CHAMBERS claims that after the meeting, the three of us took a long walk and that during the conversation while walking, Colonel BYKOV asked me if I could obtain documents for him from the files of the State Department. CHAMBERS claims that I agreed to co-operate in this regard with this Colonel BYKOV and that as a result of this oral agreement I later produced the documents mentioned above. I deny that any of these claims of CHAMBERS is true. I have never met and had never heard of any Russian named PETER or Colonel BYKOV until I was told of the testimony given by Mr. CHAMBERS.

During the period from about June 1, 1936, to about January 1938, I resided with my family at 1245 30th Street, N.W., and subsequent thereto, until sometime in 1943, at 3415 Volta Place, N.W., both Washington, D.C. During the period from 1936 to some time after 1938, we had a typewriter in our home in Washington. This was an old-fashioned machine, possibly an Underwood, but I am not at all certain regarding the make. Mrs. HISS, who is not a typist, used this machine somewhat as an amateur typist, but I never recall having used it. Possibly samples of Mrs. HISS's typing on this machine are in existence, but I have not located any to date, but will endeavor to do so. Mrs. HISS disposed of this typewriter to either a secondhand typewriter concern or a secondhand dealer in Washington, D.C., some time subsequent to 1938, exact date or place unknown. The whereabouts of this typewriter is presently unknown to me. Prior to this typewriter coming into the possession of my immediate family, it was the property of Mr. THOMAS FANSLER, Mrs. HISS's father, who was in the insurance business in Philadelphia. Mr. FANSLER lived the later years of his life on Walnut Street in Philadelphia, but is now deceased, having died in the early 1940's.

Until I met Mr. CHAMBERS face to face at a hearing of a subcommittee of the House Committee on Un-American Activities on August 17, 1948, in the Hotel Commodore, New York City, I did not know whether I had ever previously met CHAMBERS, although I thought that newspaper pictures of him looked somewhat familiar. When I first appeared before the House Committee on Un-American Activities on August 5, 1948, I stated that to the best of my knowledge I had never met CHAMBERS. At that time it had not occurred to me that he might be GEORGE CROSLEY. On August 16, 1948, before a subcommittee of the House Committee on Un-American Activities in Washington, D.C., I stated that CHAMBERS might be a person previously known to me as GEORGE CROSLEY. Upon confrontation on August 17, I realized that CHAMBERS is identical with a man I had previously known as GEORGE CROSLEY. I first met CHAMBERS as GEORGE CROSLEY when I was employed as Legal Assistant to the United States Senate Munitions Committee, commonly known as the Nye Committee, about December 1934, or January 1935. CHAMBERS came to me in my office in the Senate Office Building in Washington, D.C., and stated that he was a free-lance magazine writer and desired information for a series of articles on the munitions investigation. At that time I was on loan to the United States Senate Munitions Committee by the Agricultural Adjustment Administration of the

United States Department of Agriculture, where I was regularly employed as Assistant General Counsel. At that time CHAMBERS gave me the impression that he was making periodic trips to Washington from New York City, where, I assumed, he lived.

Between the turn of the year 1934–35 and the spring or summer 1936, CHAMBERS contacted me perhaps six or eight times, always for the purpose of obtaining information for his magazine articles or discussing the problems of the munitions investigation. CHAMBERS was merely one of the number of newspapermen, writers and students who came to see the employees of the Munitions Committee about the Committee's activities. I deny that I ever saw or heard from CHAMBERS from the spring or summer of 1936 until we confronted one another at the above-mentioned hearing in the Commodore Hotel in New York City.

During the period when CHAMBERS periodically contacted me in Washington, he occasionally borrowed small sums of money from me, totaling twenty to thirty dollars, four or five dollars at a time. He appeared to be hard-pressed financially. Also during this period, under an oral agreement, I sublet my apartment at 2831 28th Street, N.W., Washington, D.C., to Mr. and Mrs. CHAMBERS and child. Prior to subletting this apartment to CHAMBERS, at sixty dollars a month, I and my family moved into a three-story house at 2905 P Street, N.W., Washington, D.C. Before taking occupancy of the above-mentioned apartment, CHAMBERS and his family spent two or three days on the third floor of my home on P Street. My recollection is that Mr. CHAMBERS informed me that some of his furniture or other possessions had not arrived on time; that his family and he could not, therefore, move into the 28th Street apartment immediately.

We put them up as a favor to sub-tenants. As far as I know, CHAMBERS and his family lived in the apartment on 28th Street until the expiration of my lease on July 1, 1935. During subtenancy of my apartment on 28th Street by CHAMBERS, I continued to pay the rent and CHAMBERS has never reimbursed me, nor has he repaid the small loans. He did on one occasion give me a rug which he said he had received from some patron of his, and while they were staying at my house on P Street, his wife painted a portrait of my young stepson, TIMOTHY HOBSON, who was then eight years old. I have no clear recollection of the date of my last contact with CHAMBERS, which probably occurred in the spring or summer of 1936, while I was employed as an attorney by the Department of Justice in Washington, D.C. However, I do recall the contact quite well and on this occasion I told Mr. CHAMBERS that I did not think he would ever repay the loans he had made, and that I thought we should discontinue any further contacts. I also want to state that CHAMBERS never paid me any funds for any purpose. During the period mentioned above when CHAMBERS was contacting me, most of the contacts were made by him at my office or for lunch, with the possible exceptions that he may have contacted me on several occasions at my residences.

In connection with the sublease of the apartment, I occasionally lent Mr. CHAMBERS the use of my 1929 model Ford roadster. This Ford was dark blue in color, had a rumble seat and a small trunk in the rear, and bore District of Columbia plates. Some time in the summer of 1935, I acquired a 1935 Plymouth, two-door sedan, a demonstrator model. Some time after acquiring the Plymouth, I told Mr. CHAMBERS he could have the Ford roadster, which I had been told had a trade-in value of twenty-five dollars when I bought the Plymouth. If Mr. CHAMBERS used the Ford in the fall of 1935 or the winter of 1935–36, it must have been only occasionally because I recall it sitting on the streets of Georgetown during a number of months of that winter. Some time before I left P Street, about May or June 1936, CHAMBERS took permanent possession of the car under circumstances I do not now exactly recall. At that time or earlier I had turned over to him the certificate of title. I did not have the Ford after that date and have never seen it since. I have no recollection of the occasion on which I signed the certificate of title. The certificate of title for the Ford bears what appeared to be my signature witnessed under date of July 23, 1936, by MARVIN SMITH, a notary public, who was also employed in the same office where I was in the Department of Justice. I can only assume that the certificate was brought to me in my office in the Department of Justice by someone who said that I had disposed of the car without completing the legal technicalities and that I signed under those circumstances and asked MARVIN SMITH to witness my signature.

As far as I can remember, the above represents a history of all my contacts and dealings with Mr. CHAMBERS to date which appear to me to be pertinent.

I have made an effort personally, through counsel and private investigators, to locate other persons who knew CHAMBERS as GEORGE CROSLEY during the period from the turn of the year 1934–35 to the spring or summer of 1936, but without success. I have discovered one person who claims that CHAMBERS at one time submitted a manuscript to him for publication under the name GEORGE CROSLEY, but that was during a much earlier period, approximately in 1926. Both Mr. and Mrs. CHAMBERS state that during this time they were living in Baltimore under the name of LLOYD CANTWELL, as I have learned from the deposition. This search, of course, excepts Mrs. Hiss and TIMOTHY HOBSON, my stepson, who was only eight years old during the above-mentioned period. This search included inquiry among known fellow employees of the United States Senate Munitions Committee, and persons that either my wife or I introduced CHAMBERS or his wife to under the name of CROSLEY. This search to confirm my statement that CHAMBERS was going under the name of GEORGE CROSLEY during the above-mentioned period will continue and, if successful, the Government will be advised.

I deny that I am now or ever have been a member of the Communist Party or that I have ever attended any Communist Party meetings. Likewise, I deny that I have ever been a member of a Communist Party espionage apparatus or underground group in Washington, D.C., or anywhere else, at any time.

I never saw Mr. CHAMBERS at any time in the State Department. I know of no opportunity had by Mr. CHAMBERS, either in my office in the State Department or in my residence or any other place, to obtain any documents pertaining to State Department business, during the period 1937–38 or any other time. I do not know whether CHAMBERS personally obtained these documents from the State Department or whether he had some confederate who co-operated with him in obtaining these documents.

I assert that Mr. CHAMBERS' entire story, with respect to the matters covered above that relate to me, is a complete fabrication except as otherwise indicated in this statement by me.

I do not know what motive Mr. CHAMBERS could have for making these accusations against me, but I think that a thorough examination of Mr. CHAMBERS's life and personal background might throw some light on this problem.

The foregoing represents an accurate account of statements I have made today to Mr. JOHNSTONE and Mr. CALLAHAN. It was dictated in my presence and that of my counsel, Mr. MARBURY, and I assisted at various places in the phrasing of that dictation. I have read the entire statement and have signed it below this paragraph and have initialed each page at the bottom thereof.

(S) ALGER HISS.

APPENDIX V

Statement to Federal Bureau of Investigation, signed by Priscilla Hiss December 7, 1948

New York, New York
December 7, 1948

I, Mrs. Priscilla Hiss, residing at 22 East 8th Street, New York City, give the following voluntary statement to Special Agents Thomas G. Spencer and Francis D. O'Brien, who have identified themselves to me to be Special Agents of the Federal Bureau of Investigation. I am making this statement in the presence of my attorney, Mr. Edward C. McLean. I know that any statement that I make may be used against me in a court of law.

Some time in 1935, the exact date I cannot now recall, I was introduced to an individual by the name of George Crosley, whom I now believe to be Whittaker Chambers. I did not know that Crosley's name was Whittaker Chambers at any time while I knew him. At the time of this introduction I was residing at 2831 28th Street, N.W., Washington, D.C. For a short period of time Chambers and his wife lived at our house in a spare room which we had at 2905 P Street while waiting to move into the premises at 2831 28th Street, N.W., which premises were sublet to Mr. Chambers by my husband, Mr. Hiss. As far as I know, no lease was drawn for the subletting of the apartment. I also met Mr. Chambers on several occasions when he called at my home to visit with my husband. I recall that Mr. Hiss had a Ford automobile, namely a 1929 model, and that he gave this Ford car to Mr. Chambers. I have not seen Mr. Chambers, as far as I can recall, since some time in 1936.

I have been advised of the allegations that Mr. Chambers has made against my husband, namely that Mr. Hiss removed documents from the Government offices where he was employed and turned these documents over to Mr. Chambers in order that they might be photographed. Mr. Hiss never turned over any documents to Mr. Chambers in my presence or, in so far as I know, at any other time.

During the time my husband was employed by the Government he occasionally brought work home from the office. However, I never personally examined any of this material and have no knowledge of its contents.

I have been asked to recall all of the facts concerning a typewriter which was in my possession. Some time in 1932 or 1933, as far as I can recall, my father, Mr. Thomas L. Fansler, who was in the insurance business in Philadelphia (he was connected with the Northwestern Mutual Life Insurance Company, for which company he acted as a general agent), had in his possession a typewriter which he gave to me. I do not recall whether I had this typewriter while I was residing in New York City. I do not recall the make of this typewriter. I do not recall now how I disposed of it. I myself am not a proficient typist, but I have typed several things on this typewriter which my father gave to me. I did prepare a manuscript for a book which was later published by the Carnegie Corporation, but as far as I can recall I did not type this manuscript in its entirety. I typed some of it and prepared the rest in longhand.

I wish to state that I have never heard my husband, Alger Hiss, or Mr. Chambers discuss any material which had been obtained from the Government or documents which Mr. Hiss might have had in his possession in his official capacity. I also wish to state that I have never been acquainted with an individual by the name of Colonel Bykov, who I understand Mr. Chambers has stated was introduced by him to my husband. I wish to state that I have never copied or typed any U.S. Government documents for the purpose of giving them to Mr. Chambers.

I wish to state that I have read this statement, consisting of one and one half pages, and it is true to the best of my knowledge. I have initialed each page.

(S) Priscilla Hiss.

APPENDIX VI

The document written in the handwriting of Harry Dexter White which was contained in the envelope produced by Whittaker Chambers at Baltimore on the 17th November 1948

January 10, 1938: Taylor tried to press the Secretary (indirectly through Feis to Hull to Secretary) to hurriedly accept an offer from Hungary of settlement of her $2,000,000 debt to United States Government. The payment offered was trivial. Secretary refused to be hurried and said did not want to establish a pattern on these international debt settlements without considering the whole problem. The fact that the Hungarian amount involved was trifling was no reason to accept this offer as it raised matters of principle, precedent, policy, etc.

(What is behind Taylor's, and possibly Feis', desire to press M into a debt-settlement arrangement of that character at this time? Why didn't Taylor try to convince Secretary directly instead of surreptitiously via Feis?)

January 9, 1938: United States Naval Captain Ingersol will remain in London until English want to communicate anything to us with respect to Japan boycott or exchange controls. He is to act solely as an agent of communication and not discuss matters. English are not now interested in economic boycotts against Japan. Some incident may develop which will lead them to be desirous of our co-operation. We are likely to act alone only if unusually bad incident occurs such as another *Panay* incident.

Japan, according to Colonel Strong, has increased greatly its storage facilities for oil. Tanks built underground with two layers of thick cement and air space between as protection against bombing.

Reported yesterday through private Japanese banking connection (unknown but supposed to be important) that J will not declare war on China for some time at least.

Secretary reading *Red Star over China* and is quite interested.

Japan's dollar balances in United States are not declining much. They are about $50,000,000.

Purchases of Japanese goods by . . . are decreasing sharply while our exports to those countries are increasing.

State Department believes British moves toward Italy and Germany will reduce substantially European fear of war in the near future.

If Japan repeats another incident like the *Panay* incident, Treasury machinery is all ready to embargo Japanese imports into United States and freeze her dollar balances. This was done at the President's orders. It remains unknown outside of Treasury.

We have just agreed to purchase 50,000,000 more ounces of silver from China. China will have left (almost all in London) about 100,000,000 ounces of silver. Her dollar balances are almost all gone.

Bullitt just called to Secretary (copy not available) comments by Herriot, Blum, Reynaud to him. Herriot says if he were Premier he would quickly strengthen ties with U.S.S.R. and reassure Czechoslovakia that France will at once come to her military aid if Germany enters Czechoslovakia. He also stated that if U.S.S.R. goes to aid of Czechoslovakia she would cut through Roumania's resistance like butter and would also go through quickly Latvia, Esthonia against their wishes. Herriot doesn't think there is any chance, however, of his becoming Premier.

Reynaud believed the solution of French economic situation

is to permit a sharp drop in the franc. Also to form a national cabinet that would include all elements. Blum claims he doesn't want to be Premier at this time.

Marchandeau tried feebly to get England and United States to agree to support the franc. (Not the slightest chance.) The prospects of continued depreciation of franc are very strong.

I have heard nothing yet as to Captain Ingersol's mission in England beyond my earlier explanation. So far as the Treasury is concerned he is supposed to be there in case of another incident with Japan. In that event he would serve as secret liaison man between England and the United States unknown to anybody as to the nature of his mission. Chamberlain turned us down at the time of the *Panay* incident when we asked him whether he would co-operate with us in placing exchange restriction against Japanese operations in case we decided to do so. But another Knatchbull incident may bring them around.

State Department was eager to accept Hungary's debt offer and sold idea to Secretary Marshall and the President. But Congress doesn't want to begin debt negotiations with Hungary. The Van Zeeland report was not taken seriously here.

(Via Cochran) Bachman of the Swiss National Bank said (February 15, 1938) that the Japanese have recently put out a feeler to some of his banks for a loan for industrial development in Manchukuo. "However, his bankers had not sufficient interest in such a proposition even to submit it to the National Bank for consideration and possible approval."

"Schacht impressed me—and some of my friends also—as finding some hope in the Van Zeeland report as a basis for a possible approach between German and the British and the French.

"Schacht said he positively did not know what had taken place at the meeting between Hitler and Schuschnigg."

INDEX

Abt, John, 61, 65, 122–24, 151–53, 155, 235, 237, 311, 316, 346, 352, 354–55
Acheson, Dean G., 64
Adler, [Sol?], 247, 348, 351
Agricultural Adjustment Administration, 61–62, 121, 349–50
Anderson, Walter H., 209, 291
Appell, Donald T., 208

Babcock, F. Lawrence, 198
Bentley, Elizabeth, 243–46
Berle, Adolf A., Jr., 26–27, 45, 56–57, 77, 120, 123–24, 128–37, 146, 184, 222, 234, 247, 254, 280, 288, 339, 345–48
"Bill," 228
Binger, Dr. Carl A. L., 218–19, 221–24, 314, 336
Boucot, Joseph R., 52, 109–11, 191, 215
Breen, David, 49–50, 52, 82, 109, 192. *See also* Chambers, Whittaker
Bridges case, 131, 236, 239, 348
Bryn Mawr, 84, 208
Brown, Mrs. Norma B., 110–11, 216
Bullitt, William C., 212
Bullitt, William M., 218
Bykov, Colonel Boris, 52–55, 76, 98, 101, 134, 237–38, 249–50, 284, 358–59, 367
Byrnes, James F., 64, 155, 218, 255–56

Callahan, Daniel F. X., 208, 357, 364
Cantwell, Lloyd, 50, 82, 118, 192, 220, 363. *See also* Chambers, Whittaker
"Carl," 44, 50, 62, 74, 177, 189–93, 235, 248, 344. *See also* Chambers, Whittaker

Carnegie Endowment of International Peace, 63–66, 185, 218, 252–55, 259–61
Carpenter, David, 248
Case, Edward, 108
Catlett, Burnetta, 276–77
Catlett, Clidi, 87–89, 103, 214–15, 272, 274, 319–21, 331, 333
Catlett, Perry, 272–76, 319, 321, 333
Catlett, Raymond, 273–76, 319, 321, 331, 333
Chambers, Esther, 29, 35, 38, 44, 48, 51–52, 54, 55, 70–71, 81–84, 86–88, 92–93, 100, 109–10, 116–18, 182, 183, 190–93, 208, 215, 220, 329, 361–62
Chambers, Mrs. Jay (mother of Whittaker Chambers), 42–43, 83–84, 100
Chambers, Whittaker
  Aliases, 50, 189–93. *See also* Breen; Cantwell, Lloyd; "Carl"; Crosley, George; Dwyer
  Allegations against Hiss, 15–18, 20–21, 25–29, 50–54, 62–63, 134, 181–84, 258
  Alleged association with Hiss, 34–35, 50–56, 62, 69–79, 82–84, 91–118, 120–21, 151–54, 156, 175–79, 214–15, 222, 227–30, 237, 280–81, 325–26, 329, 338–39, 343, 359–64
  Attempted suicide, 45–46, 58, 183, 223, 282, 336, 344
  Baltimore examination, 29, 57–58, 76, 181–83
  Before the House Committee, 26–28, 151–61, 175–79. *See also* House Committee
  Break with Communist Party, 54–55, 78, 98, 100, 130, 134, 135–37, 151, 185–86, 244, 279–80, 299
  Brother's suicide, 44, 49, 222
  Character and early life, 42–48, 81–82, 217, 222
  Communist activities, 44–45, 49–54, 175–79, 216, 227–28, 248–49, 272
  Denials of espionage, 28, 57, 123–24, 130, 134–35, 151, 154, 247, 248, 340
  Early statements, 26–27, 120, 123–24, 127–37, 234–35, 247, 280, 288, 345–55
  Identification by Hiss, 28, 34, 155, 157. *See also* Confrontation
  Production of documents, 15–18, 20–21, 29–31, 36–37, 45, 58, 147, 182–84, 207–14, 247–48, 283, 301, 358
  Psychopathic personality, 46, 116, 218–19, 221–24. *See also* Binger, Dr. Carl; Murray, Dr. Henry
  Religious views, 45, 55, 56, 230, 280. *See also* Berle, Adolf; Cherner Motor Company; Communist Group; Crosley, George; Four-hundred-dollar loan; Hiss, Alger; Libel action; Life preserver; Nye Committee; Pumpkin papers; Rug; Subletting of the 28th Street apartment; *Time*; Trips and visits; *Witness*

Cherner Motor Company, 95–96, 104–5, 209–10, 313, 339
Choate, Joseph H., Ambassador, 6
Churchill, Winston S., 120
Claessens, August, 219
Cleveland, Richard F., 183, 184
Coe brothers, 247, 347, 351, 353–54
Coleman, Harry C., 216
Collier, Teunis F., 216
Collins, Henry, 65, 75, 122–24, 132, 151–52, 153, 175, 178, 214, 234, 237, 239, 311–12, 316, 350–51, 354–55
Communist group, the, 20–21, 27–28, 34–35, 75–76, 119–25, 130–34, 136–37, 151–54, 175–79, 184, 250, 267–69, 311–12, 316, 339–40, 345–55
Confrontation, 28–29, 155, 157–74, 318–19, 338
Corroborative evidence, 16–17, 36–37, 39, 114, 328–30, 332–34
Cowley, Malcolm, 65, 216, 224
Crosley, George, 28, 34, 50, 55, 62, 64, 69–72, 74, 87, 92, 108, 157–74, 189–93, 228–29. *See also* Chambers, Whittaker
Cross, Claude B., 98, 105, 113, 129, 178, 191–92, 224, 230, 253–54, 311–16, 320

Daily Worker, 44
Daladier, Edouard, 212*n.*
Dales, Ida, 44
Darlington, Charles, 213, 303–5
Davis, John W., 66, 212–13, 218, 260, 261
Davis, Lucy Elliott, 112–13, 216
De Lashmutt. *See* Lashmutt
Dickey, John Sloane, 62, 213
Dickover, Erle, 238
Du Bois, Cornelius, 198
Duggan, Laurence, 125, 346, 348, 351
Dulles, John Foster, 63, 65–66, 218, 221, 251–63, 318, 333
Dumbarton Oaks Conference, 63, 217
Duvall, Frank E., 212
Dwyer, 50, 82, 192. *See also* Chambers, Whittaker

Eagleton, Dr. Clyde, 217
Easter, Dr., 276–77
Eichelberger, Clark M., 218
Eisler, Gerhart, 266–67
Evidence (English and American practice), 36–39

Fansler, Mr. Thomas (father of Mrs. Hiss), 84, 272, 275, 360, 366
Fansler, Thomas (brother of Mrs. Hiss), 36, 84, 86, 115, 215, 216
Fansler, Mrs. Thomas (sister-in-law of Mrs. Hiss), 85
Federal Bureau of Investigation, 64, 65, 89, 97, 98, 113–14, 118, 181, 207–11, 214, 216, 220, 247, 257, 267, 274, 277, 338–39
Feehan, Ramos, 210–11, 229, 308, 321
Ferguson, John, 239
Field, Noel, 125, 267–69, 347–48, 351
Flanagan, Mrs., 99
Fountain, Plum. *See* Tesone, Olivia

Four-hundred-dollar loan, 35, 55, 83, 97–100, 105, 114, 221, 279, 313, 339
Frank, Jerome N., 61, 122, 214

Gaston, Herbert, 246
Gauss, Clarence E., 295–96
Generation on Trial (Alistair Cooke), 5
Gilliat, Mr., 99
Glasser, Harold, 247, 351
Goddard, Henry W. (judge at the second trial), 104, 204, 314, 323, 325–34
Grand Jury, 18, 30–33, 57, 65, 121, 124, 145, 256–57, 262, 316, 318, 322, 343
Green, Joseph C., 213, 225–29, 230
Grieb, Henry Norman, 219
Gumpertz, Hedda, 346–48, 351. *See also* Massing, Hede
Gumpertz, Julian, 267

Hall, John L., 214
Handwritten documents, 15–17, 21, 29, 36, 58, 282, 283–99, 310, 313, 321–22, 342–44
Harvard Law Review, 59, 61, 121, 258
Hawkins, Harry, 212, 302–6
Hebb, Walter M., 219
Hébert, F. Edward, 74, 153
Helfrich, Karl, 217
Henderson, Loy, 286–88, 348
Henry, Henri P., 219
Hepburn, Admiral Arthur J., 217
Hillegeist, W. M., 207, 210
Hiss, Alger
  Accusation against, 15–18, 20–21, 25–29, 50–54, 62–63, 134, 175–78, 181–84, 258–59, 325–29
  Alleged meetings with Bykov, 134, 237–38
  Alleged meeting with Hede Massing, 265–70
  Association with Chambers, 33–35, 50–56, 62, 69–79, 82–84, 91–118, 121, 151–54, 156–57, 214–15, 222, 227–30, 237, 325–26, 329, 338–39, 343, 360–64. *See also* Chambers, Whittaker; Crosley, George; Four-hundred-dollar loan; Nye Committee; Payment of dues; Rug, the; Subletting of the 28th Street apartment
  Association with alleged Communists, 119–25, 155, 258, 262–63, 267–70, 348. *See also* Communist group
  Attitude of Carnegie Endowment towards, 260–61. *See also* Carnegie Endowment
  Before the House Committee, 142, 155–56, 159–72. *See also* House Committee
  Bird-watching, 93, 156
  Career, 59–64, 154–55
  Character, 65–67, 133, 222, 350–51
  Character witnesses, 211–14, 217, 218
  Communications with Mr. Dulles, 63, 65, 251–63
  Conflict between his story and Chambers', 73–79
  Denial of charges, 20–21, 22, 28, 31–32, 72, 359–64
  Early statements of Chambers, 348, 350–51, 352, 354–55

Examination by F.B.I., 64, 65, 155, 208, 338, 357–64. *See also* Federal Bureau of Investigation
Final statement in court, 281, 310, 332
First alleged act of treachery, 51, 225–31, 282. *See also* Nye Committee
First heard the name Whittaker Chambers, 65, 155, 318, 338
Lie-detector test, 143–44, 157
Memorandum on neutrality, 72, 217–18
Recognition of Chambers, 28, 34, 155, 157, 159–72, 338
Sentence, 18, 22, 332
Typewriter, evidence on, 272–76
See also Cherner Motor Company; Confrontation; Grand Jury; House Committee; Indictment; Libel action
Hiss, Donald, 20–21, 27–28, 37, 53, 61, 75, 77, 123, 130–33, 151, 154, 177, 212*n.*, 233–41, 312, 342, 344, 348, 351, 354
Hiss, Mrs. Donald, 152, 234
Hiss, Priscilla, 20–21, 35, 38, 47, 49–56, 60, 73, 77–79, 82–87, 93, 97, 101–2, 109–18, 131–32, 152, 176–77, 185–86, 190–93, 207–8, 219, 220, 275–76, 326, 339, 348, 361, 365–67
Typing of documents, 31, 36, 54, 73, 77, 132, 210, 272 73, 281, 298, 307, 310, 320–21, 331, 341, 343–44, 360, 365–67
Hobson, Thayer, 60, 85
Hobson, Timothy, 60, 85, 88, 114, 116, 215, 219, 275, 362, 363
Holmes, Oliver Wendell, Jr., 60, 238
Hornbeck, Stanley, 63, 72, 212
House Committee on Un-American Activities, 18, 26–29, 30, 34, 46, 57–58, 74–75, 78, 94, 97, 111, 119, 121–24, 129–31, 135–36, 139–78, 184, 194, 222, 235–37, 243–47, 252, 258–60, 301, 336, 338, 340, 342, 360
Hull, Cordell, 62, 225, 286, 295
Hyde, Charles Cheyney, 72, 217

Indictment, 32–34
Inslerman, Felix, 53, 211
International Juridical Association, 61, 64

Jeffries, Mrs., 70
Jessup, Philip C., 72, 211–12, 217
Jessup, Mrs., 212
Johnson, Herschel, 293–94
Jones, Mr. (State Department), 310, 315
Jury system, 199–206

Kaplan, Irving, 54
Kaufman, Samuel H. (judge at the first trial), 195–97
Kellog Smith, Mrs., 216–17
Kelly, John, 43. *See also* Chambers, Whittaker
Kohlberg, Mr. (publisher of *Plain Talk*), 252, 254–58, 318
Kramer, Charles (Krivitsky), 61, 65, 76, 122–24, 151, 235, 237, 311, 346, 350, 354–55

Ladd, Mr. (of the F.B.I.), 64
Lashmutt, Lynn O. De, 207
Last Sergeant, The (Sergeant A. M. Sullivan), 204–5
Levine, Isaac Don, 56, 128–31, 137, 254
Levine, Nathan, 182–83, 208
Libel action, 18, 21, 29–30, 45, 135, 181–87, 218
Lieber, Maxim, 52, 109–11
"Life preserver," 45, 56, 137, 231, 278, 279–81, 299, 313, 336
Lincoln, Eunice A., 210, 284, 298
Lockey, Ira, 276–77
Lyons, Mr. and Mrs. Eugene, 268

McCool, John S., 220
McDowell, John, 152, 160–61, 171
McLean, Edward C., 196–98, 209, 267, 269–70, 277
Marbury, William, 135, 181–83, 187, 218, 260, 261, 357–59, 364
Marlow, Vernon, 276–77
Martin, Mary, 287–88
Massing, Hede, 37–38, 125, 197, 211, 218, 265–70, 333, 347–48, 351
May, Geoffrey, 214
Mensh, Samuel A., 209–10
Miller, Mr., 65
Moore, R. Walton, 291, 295
Morgenthau, Henry, Jr., 147–48, 369
Mundt, Karl E., 152–56
Murphy, Ray, 27, 56–57, 77–78, 120, 133–36, 146, 222, 234–35, 247, 280, 339, 349–52
Murphy, Thomas F., 32–33, 41, 66, 82, 97–98, 104, 105, 108, 111, 114, 121, 124, 178, 198, 215, 218, 221, 227, 229–30, 234, 237–41, 257, 261–62, 278, 286, 308, 312–23, 331, 336
Murray, Dr. Henry A., 219, 221–24, 314, 336
Murray, Edith, 38, 84, 117–18, 220–21, 333, 337–38

National Research Project, 54–55
Nelson, Eleanor, 133, 346, 352
Newcomb, Miss, 210, 284
New York *Herald Tribune*, 212*n*.
New York *Times*, 72, 217, 286–87
Nicholson, Dr. Margaret, 219
Nixon, Richard M., 94, 146–47, 159–69, 171–72, 175–78
Nye Committee, 37, 51, 61–62, 69–70, 72, 74, 75, 93, 157, 163–66, 189, 225–31, 235, 282, 310, 312, 333, 341–44, 360

O'Brien, Francis, 209
Odler. *See* Adler

Pasvolsky, Dr., 315
Payment of dues, 20–21, 28, 75, 123, 344
Perlo, Victor, 122–24, 151, 158, 175–79, 235, 237, 239, 312
Perlow, Nat, 235, 354–55
"Peter." *See* Bykov, Colonel Boris
Peters, J., 50, 51, 74–76, 96, 105, 121, 123, 133, 153–54, 176,

178, 228, 235, 342, 347, 349, 353–54
Peterborough, N.H., trip to, 111–16, 208, 215, 223
Peurifoy, John, 257, 258
Photographed documents, 16, 56, 184, 280–81, 301–6, 342–44
Ploscowe, Morris, 269
Polier, Shad, 61, 64
Pope, Martha, 214
Post, Richard, 65, 235, 346, 351, 354
Pressman, Lee, 61, 64, 65, 75, 77, 120–24, 130–32, 142, 151, 153, 155, 214, 235, 237, 246, 256, 258, 262, 311, 316, 340, 344–46, 348, 350, 351, 354–55
Pumpkin papers (photographed documents), 30, 48, 58, 184, 207–8, 220–22, 301

Queensberry, Marquess of, 21

Rabinavicius, Henrikas, 218, 265–70
Rankin, John E., 153
Rankin, Julia, 82, 192
Raushenbush, Stephen, 226
Reed, Stanley, 62
Reilly, Gerald, 238
Roosevelt, Franklin D., 63, 120, 128, 353
Rosen, William, 38, 95–96, 104–5, 210, 313
Roulhac, George N., 219, 274–76
Rubens-Robinson case, 286–89, 348, 351
Rug, the, 35, 52, 71, 76, 87, 94, 100–4, 157, 168–69, 178, 208, 215, 313, 317, 319, 339
Sagona, Joseph, 208–9
San Francisco Conference, 63
Sayre, Francis B., 62–63, 65, 72, 125, 209, 210, 212–14, 216, 224, 238, 266, 284–306, 309, 315, 321, 348
Schapiro, Meyer, 51, 101–4, 208
Seeds of Treason (Toledano and Lasky), 5, 343
Shaw, G. Howland, 212
Shotwell, James T., 218
Silverman, George, 54, 101, 104, 208
Silvermaster, Nathan, 243–44, 246
Smith, Mrs. Kellog, 216–17
Smith, Marvin, 95–96, 105, 362–63
Stafford, Florence T., 207
Stearns, Edith Bond, 208
Stettinius, Edward, 63
Stripling, Robert, 94, 151–55, 157, 160, 169–70, 173, 175–76, 184
Struggle for Europe, The (Chester Wilmot), 120
Subletting of the 28th Street apartment, 51, 70–71, 92–94, 157, 162–74, 317, 338, 361–62, 371–72
Swope, Gerard, Jr., 213

Tally, Gladys F., 99, 221
Tesone, Olivia (Plum Fountain), 191, 216
Time, 48, 84, 128, 137, 159
Touloukain, Edward H., 208
Trips and visits, 51–52, 70–71, 107–18, 215

Truman, Harry S, 63
Typewriter, the Woodstock, 16–17, 29–31, 72, 87, 186, 210–11, 214, 271–82, 307–10, 319–21, 333, 341, 343, 359–60, 365–67
Typewritten documents, 15–18, 21, 29–31, 36, 58, 210–11, 248–49, 281–82, 297, 307–10, 313–16, 320–21, 336–37, 343–44

Ullmann, W. L., 142, 244, 246

Wadleigh, Henry Julian, 76, 134–35, 210–11, 213, 243, 248–50, 306, 309, 315–16, 321, 331, 346, 350
Walsh, John J., 208
Ward, Mr. (of the F.B.I.), 267
Ware, Harold, 50, 74, 75, 77, 120–23, 133, 151–53, 214, 257, 340, 346–54
Washington *Post*, 99
Webb, Frederick E., 211
White, Harry Dexter, 56, 111–12, 114–15, 132, 134, 142, 147–48, 152–54, 182, 243–48, 280, 299, 309, 351, 354, 369–71
Wilde, Oscar, 21
Wilson, Edwin Carleton, 289–91
Witness (Whittaker Chambers), 41–42, 46, 56, 58, 77, 82, 92, 96, 97, 98, 110, 125, 128, 133, 144, 178–79, 182–83, 214, 218, 223, 247, 250, 282, 313, 336, 337, 340
Witt, Nathan (Wittowsky), 61, 65, 122–24, 130–31, 151–53, 216, 235, 237, 279, 311, 316, 340, 346, 348, 351, 354–55

Yalta Conference, 63, 120, 155–56